"One belongs to New York instantly, one belongs to it as much in five minutes as in five years..."

~ Thomas Wolfe

"You look back and see how hard you worked and how poor you were, and how desperately anxious you were to succeed, and all you can remember is how happy you were."

~ Jack London

"You are young, broke and beautiful."

~ Broke-Ass Stuart

broke-ass
stuart's

guide to
living cheaply in
NEW YORK CITY

Falls Media

Published by Falls Media
276 Fifth Ave, Suite 301
New York, NY 10001

First Printing, November 2008
10 9 8 7 6 5 4 3 2
Copyright Stuart Schuffman, 2008
All Rights Reserved

ISBN- 13 978-0-9788178-0-0

Design and Comic by Mike Force
Cover Design by Kenny Liu
Maps by Angela Hathaway

Table of Contents

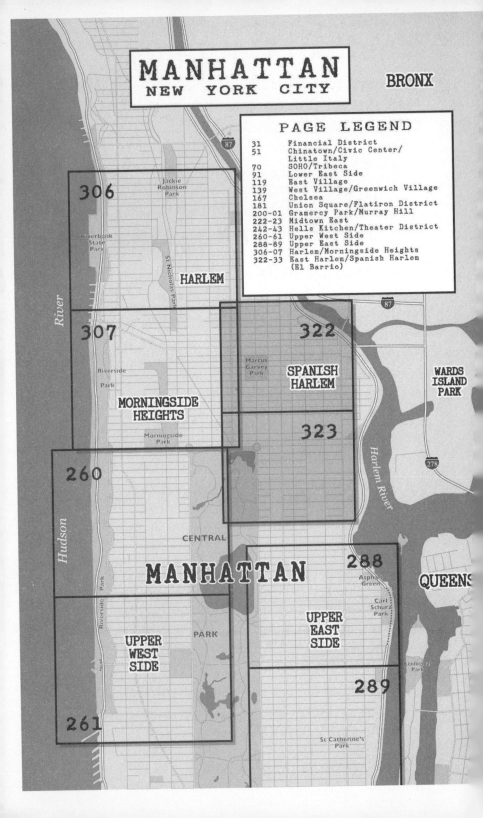

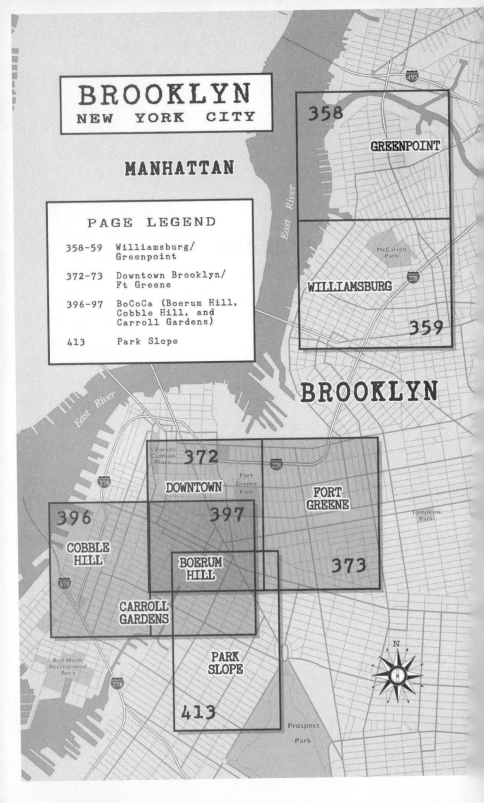

This is my best attempt at being Tom Waits. Photo by Nicki Ishmael

Introduction

I'm sitting now in my Bushwick apartment coming to terms with the realization that my time here in this strange and brutal city is coming to an end. I maintain that, no matter how much you love New York, this city fucking hates you. Don't take it personally; this bitch is just badder than you are. Her game is tighter, her mind is quicker, her swagger is more believable. She's not the one who got away, she's the one you never had a chance of getting, and that's what makes just being near her so exhilarating. There's a quote from Thomas Wolfe that goes something like, "One belongs to New York instantly; one belongs to it as much in five minutes as in five years." And I think old Mr. Wolfe was onto something. New York will never be yours; you will always be hers. She's got you pussy-whipped and you fucking know it.

But me, I'm leaving. Two and half weeks and I'll be gone. I'm filling my days (and notebooks) wandering through these streets, getting to know them as well as one gets to know a friend with benefits who lives in another town. I'm learning and admiring the creases, cracks, and character of these thoroughfares, but I'll never know what it's like to be with them forever. This has just been an affair and I'm heading home to California, to my wife–San Francisco; the one who takes the love I give to her and repays it in spades.

But I'm gonna miss New York. It's quite possibly the best city in the world. I'm gonna miss the electric fervor of summertime rooftops, and the girls who wear next to nothing on the humid, fetid subway. I'm gonna miss the snow that sneaks in while I'm dreaming and piles itself up on the cars while they sleep in the street. I'll miss the little badge of pride that goes along with saying that I live in Brooklyn, not in Manhattan. I'll miss all the beautiful people who have nothing to say, and all the ugly ones who say too much. Anything you could ever want is here, as long as you're willing to work for it and know where to look. Magic happens on a daily basis; the hard part is finding time to take it all in.

Thank you New York, you've been a sweet and charming mistress who deals out pleasure and pain equally the way a blackjack dealer can just as easily give you 21 or make you bust. I'll be back, probably sooner than you'd like, but this is it for us, kiddo. This affair is over. I want to ask you to never change, to stay just the way you are, so that when I do come back you'll be just as you are now. But you and I both know that can't happen. At least I'll have my book, which will let me pin down exactly who you were to me for the past ten months. Just do me one favor after I leave: tell all the developers they can suck my dick.

This book isn't simply just a guide to living cheaply in New York; it's more. It's a celebration of the fact that you don't have to be rich to enjoy this city. You don't have to have designer clothes and expensive things to love this place and make it your home. What makes life interesting is not the things that you own, but the shit that you do. This book is also about searching for glimpses of old New York, the way it was before the douchebags completely took it over. So if that's what you were looking for when you picked up this book, well pal, you've come to the right place.

Who the Fuck is Broke-Ass Stuart?

I was working in a candy store in San Francisco when all this madness started. One day, an older kid from my neighborhood in San Diego came into the store with his fiancée (they're married now). It had been years since I'd seen him, so it was really nice to hear what was going on in his life. After we chatted for a bit, and they bought some candy (I slang candy like a motherfucker), the fiancée handed me her card and told me that I should give them a shout next time I was in San Diego. After they left, I looked at her card. It said she was a travel writer. I thought to myself, "Travel writer? I wanna be a travel writer," and it was then that I decided to be one.

If you know where to look, San Francisco is a town full of cheap places to eat and drink, so when it occurred to me to write *Broke-Ass Stuart's Guide to Living Cheaply in San Francisco*, I had already built up a nice array of fine establishments (meaning dive bars and greasy spoon diners) from which I could draw inspiration. I was pretty fucking broke at the time (still am), and so was everyone else I knew. I figured I would put something together to help out all the other young, struggling folks in the City. The original *Broke-Ass Stuart's* was a 33-page zine, with the only photo being the cover shot, taken in the basement of my girlfriend at the time's apartment building in the Tendernob. The first run of only 50 copies quickly sold out, so in the next run I printed 100. It was with these 100 copies that I started hitting up bookstores around the City and somehow talking them into not only carrying them, but, also, in some cases putting them up near the checkout counter. I sold an amazing 1,000 or so copies of this first zine and won the "Best Local Zine" in the *SF Bay Guardian*'s Best of the Bay issue. Truthfully, my reaction to this minor success was, "Holy shit! I can't believe people really dig this stuff."

By the time *Broke-Ass Stuart's Guide to Living Cheaply v.2* came out in July 2005, this shit had gotten a lot of hype, so I threw a big release party with bands, DJs, free food and a whole bunch of other crap. *Broke-Ass v.2* is when everything really took off; I sold 300 copies of it in the first week (remember, this is a zine with no PR and I was doing all the distribution by foot and mass transit). Lots of good things came about because of it; I was on TV a few times, on the radio, got "Best of the Bay" again, people recognized me at bars, I had some groupies, and ultimately, I got to write for Lonely Planet (I did the Ireland chapter for the *Western Europe* and *Europe on a Shoestring* books). I was finally, officially, a travel writer; I even had business cards that said so.

After Ireland, I decided that doing everything myself was too much work, and that if I was gonna continue to do the whole *Broke-Ass Stuart* thing, I should have a publisher so I could just write the books and let them handle the rest. I blew every guy in Hollywood before I realized that the publishing industry was based in New York. Then (this part is actually real) I found Falls Media on Craigslist, and conned them into putting out my books … suckers.

Broke-Ass Stuart's Guide to Living Cheaply in San Francisco came out as an actual book in November 2007, and I celebrated once again by throwing a party with bands, DJs, free food, clowns, and even fucking laser projections. This time 700 people showed up and there was a line around the block … holy shit was that crazy.

So here we are. Now holding *Broke-Ass Stuart's Guide to Living Cheaply in New York*. I poured over a year of my life into writing and researching this book, and I'm glad that it has found its way to you. I don't want to say that it's fate because I don't believe in that shit, but you and I have both made the decisions that have landed this book in your hands at this particular point in history. For that, I just want to say, I love you motherfucker. I hope you enjoy reading this book as much as I enjoyed researching and writing it.

–Broke-Ass Stuart

Manhattan

S windled from the Native Americans, settled by the Dutch,
captured by the British, liberated by the Revolution, populated by immigrants, industrialized by robber barons, built
by the unions, beatified by the Beats, immortalized by rock n' roll,
personified by hip-hop, and now gentrified by the rich, Manhattan is
the place most of the world thinks of when they hear the words *New
York.* Too bad most of New York can't afford to live in Manhattan
anymore. The battle for that island is done and the douchebags have
won. And while being young, broke, and beautiful in New York City
now means most likely living in Brooklyn, Queens, the Bronx, or
Staten Island, Manhattan is still the sun that all of our little worlds
revolve around. What follows is a guide to help you take Manhattan
before it takes you.

The Financial District

Hordes of people pour through concrete and glass canyons created by mountainous skyscrapers; decisions affecting the world's economy are made on an hourly basis within these towering edifices. This is where fortunes are won and lost, companies bought and sold, people made and broken. The Financial District is where the rich become truly wealthy and the rest of us punters are stuck either filing papers inside cubicles or sweeping the steps of the empire. But that's only if you're here to play their game. Others come to snap photos of statues and institutions, while still more come to wander museums and ogle history.

Down here at the tip of Manhattan is where New Amsterdam was founded in 1625 by Willem Verhulst's Dutch West India Company, and where Peter Minuit purportedly purchased the island from the Lenape Indians for 60 guilders ($35–40 today) and/or a handful of beads. This, of course, set a precedent for New York, and poor people have been pushed out in the name of "progress" ever since. The Dutch were onto something with regards to location though, and their settlement, which was renamed for the Duke of York and Albany after the Brits conquered it in 1664, has been a major commercial center ever since.

Does this make me a terrorist?

Today the Financial District is exactly what the name suggests–it's the heart of American commerce, it's where the money happens. Wall Street is here, as is the New York Stock Exchange, the Federal Reserve Bank and a giant bronze bull whose balls get rubbed for good luck. It was also the home of the World Trade Center, before it was hatefully attacked and destroyed on September 11th, 2001. But the Financial District has also become a center for culture and entertainment with access to sights like Ellis Island and the Statue of Liberty, stellar museums, the lovely Battery Park, and the super-touristy South Street Seaport. For all intents and purposes, it really is as expensive as it sounds, but luckily for you (and me, too), you've picked up the right book and can now manage this costly terrain a lot easier than the Dutch did (they didn't even put up a fight when the British came). As for what constitutes **the Financial District**, the lines are strange and convoluted, but it's basically from Barclay St. in the north to the southern tip of the island, and from the East River west to the Hudson. **Battery Park along the Hudson** is lumped in here, too.

Food

Baluchi's Masala

60 Pearl St. @ Broad St.

When I walked out the door of this joint, I noticed that I didn't reek like curry, which means that the good people of Baluchi's Masala have accomplished a bloody amazing feat. I commend them for that. And I also commend them for making me very full. Granted it cost $8 for a combo bowl of rice, chicken tikka masala and saag paneer, but the serving was heaping and I wasn't able to finish it, which means there were leftovers. Continuing with this pseudo mathematical equation, leftovers = two meals, which in turn = $8 well spent. Who said I'm no good at mathematics? Oh yeah, that was every math teacher I ever had.

Café 52 (in the UFT building)

52 Broadway btw Morris St. & Exchange Alley

Café 52 is a tiny little place in the United Federation of Teachers building that has more lottery scratcher options than food options. That being said, you can get a pre-made sandwich and a soup for $4.25. That's a damn good deal. Because I dream of winning the lottery and leaving all you lousy suckers behind, I bought a scratcher instead of food. When I didn't win, the insane woman behind the counter tried to belittle me into buying another ticket. Then when I tried to explain to her that I had spent my last dollar, she pretended not to speak English. I think I kinda hate her.

P.S. You don't have to sign in with the security guard, you can just tell them that you're going to the café.

P.P.S. If the woman behind the counter seems insane, pinch her *really* hard for me. She deserves it.

Café Doppio

55 Broad St. btw Beaver St. & Exchange Pl.

Sandwiched between corporate giants like Starbucks and some other bland and tasteless crap, Café Doppio sits on Beaver St. to the right of the main entrance of 55 Broad St. Its cheap sandwiches and soup are on some gourmet shit and everything here is under $6. If you like soup then this is gonna be your spot because it has tons of options, and since it's only open until 3pm, they serve super-cheap breakfast until they close. The décor is cutesy, which is about all that I feel like saying about it. How many superlatives can a man use in one paragraph?

Café Fonduta
32 Water St. btw Broad St. & Coenties Slip

This busy lunchtime spot is quite unassuming from the outside. In fact, when I first walked by it just looked like a random building with the windows all fogged up (reminding me of all those nights in high school spent in the back of my mom's minivan with lovely coeds). But upon stepping inside, I was confronted not with pubescent heavy petting to the music of Al Green, but instead with sizable Chicken Parmesan sandwiches for $5.60 and delicious freshly made salads and pasta. While it wasn't nearly as exciting, at least with a chick-parm sandwich I didn't end up going home with blue-balls.

Financier Patisserie
1 World Financial Center/Liberty St. @ West St.

This is in the middle of some rich people shit. I don't even know why I'm including it other than that you can get a cheese platter for $7.75, which, paired with a cheap bottle of wine and a stroll in Battery Park, might get you laid.

The Grotto Pizzeria
69 New St. btw Beaver St. & Exchange Pl.

If you were to rank a place by its frills, this place would be like a -5, but honestly, is that why you're coming here? No. The reason one goes to the Grotto is because it's a cheap spot to get one's fix of all the unhealthy shit one swore off for one's New Year's resolution. Well that and the fact that you either work nearby or you're doing research for a guidebook about living cheaply in New York. I will tell you that I did see a roach in here, but fuck it, who cares? I've worked in enough restaurants to tell you that pretty much every restaurant you've ever eaten in has roaches. So if you do see one here, don't trip, just finish your food and leave quietly. Either that or eat the roach. It might taste good on your pizza.

My Daddy's Pizza
77 Pearl St. @ Coenties Slip

The Financial District doesn't have the most amazing pizza, so this spot is probably the best around. A slice is $2.20 and the name sounds like it should be a gay bar. Doesn't it?

New Golden Chopsticks
77 Pearl St. @ Coenties Slip

This cheap Chinese food place may or may not make your belly hurt, but that's irrelevant right now, isn't it? The main reason I'm putting it in here is because it's on what I've dubbed "Broke-Ass Row" (My Daddy's Pizza, New Golden Chopsticks, Reuben's Empanadas, and Terrace Fish & Chips). The lunch special is $5.95 or you can do the lunch buffet for $5.29 a pound. It's really not that remarkable of a place but it's cheap and there's an outdoor public space in front of it with free WiFi (which does you no good during the winter).

Roxy Coffee Shop
20 John St. btw Nassau St. & Broadway

Roxy is a greasy spoon diner with an emphasis on greasy (just touch the fries and you'll know what I mean). But shit, it's 24 hours and cheap as hell; a burger and fries is just $5. In fact, the most expensive thing here is $7.25, and it's a steak sandwich. While Roxy's menu is printed up, all the prices are actually handwritten which, combined with quick service and a bunch of regulars who all know each other, lends to a fairly welcoming place. So if you want some solid, cheap and greasy food, sit down at the lunch counter or one of the booths and eat some grub while you stare at a flat-screen that tells the weather and plays videos of people doing weird things.

Sophie's Restaurant
73 New St. btw Beaver St. & Exchange Pl.

At first glance $9 might seem slightly pricey for a plate of food, but when said plates are huge and delicious, it becomes a bit more reasonable. So to answer your next question, yes, you will probably end up taking the food home to eat at a later date. That's what "huge" means. There are daily specials at this popular Cuban restaurant, and they are all classic Cuban fare (did I just really say Cuban

twice in a sentence? What the fuck, Stuart?). I like how the brightly painted yellow and orange walls are decorated with old Pan-Am "go to Cuba" posters. They obviously date from before Castro was the head honcho down there. If you wanna get yourself a free meal, I suggest dropping by Sophie's the day Castro dies and scream *"Viva Cuba!"* It might just work. And if he's already dead by the time you read this, try it anyways.

Tandoor Palace aka Spice Route
88 Fulton btw Gold & William Sts.

Most "normal" travel writers would say something like, "Lunch at Tandoor Palace is busier than a Calcutta thoroughfare in the middle of the Festival of Ganesh." Right? Haven't you totally read cheesy, ridiculous shit like that before? This is nothing like the Festival of Ganesh, nor is it like Calcutta; this is a motherfucking tasty-ass Indian restaurant with modest decorations and a lot of Indian businessmen. Luckily for you (and me), I can say whatever the fuck I want. So I'mma put it to you like this; 90 percent of the menu is $6.95 and under, and all entrées come with either naan or rice. This is love at first sight.

Terrace Fish & Chips
77 Pearl St. @ Coenties Slip

Remember a few entries ago (New Golden Chopsticks) when I dubbed this area "Broke-Ass Row"? Well this is kinda the anchor for that shit. Here you can get a heaping portion of fish and chips for $6.99. What makes this especially sweet is that if you went to any of the pubs around the corner and ordered the same thing, it would be like $15. Fuck $15! The rest of the menu is pretty damn reasonable as well. Clam strips & fries is $7.25 and a fish sandwich is $4.99 (insert obligatory quote from *Ladies' Man*). If you're tired of eating all the fried foods I lead you to, you can order grilled fish here, too. Just be warned that it's twice as expensive, to which I once again say, "Fuck $15!"

This is what someone waiting for a train looks like. Photo by Krista Vendetti

Ulysses

95 Pearl St. btw Coenties Alley & Hanover Sq.

If you're like me and can eat a lot of oysters and drink a lot of champagne, then Ulysses should be where you spend every one of your Sunday afternoons. During Sunday brunch, $20 will get you a brunch entrée, all you can eat oysters, and all you can drink champagne. Sure if you're on a tight budget, it's a bit pricey, but you need to occasionally reward yourself for surviving as many years as you have. Come on, you're worth it, snookums; let's just hope you're not the one who gets the bad oyster that day (with this many free oysters, it's gonna be someone).

Bars

Fresh Salt
146 Beekman St. btw Front & South Sts.

The décor at Fresh Salt can best be described as "upscale mariner chic". Really, it's like red neon "Cocktail" signs, cool old maps, and comfy lounge seating in the back. But the truly remarkable thing about this bar is how warm the vibe is. The regulars are all super welcoming, the bartenders are sweet and helpful, and half the patrons bring cute snuggly dogs with them. Sure the Buds are $4, but look where you are, everything is expensive over here. Plus, if my soggy notes are correct, most drinks are $3 during happy hour. That's not too bad, right? I was here in the winter, but during the warmer months, they have outside seating and there's food year round.

Jeremy's Ale House
228 Front St. btw Beekman St. and Peck Slip.

How much is a quart? The answer is 32 ounces (thanks, Google), but I'd like to officially tell the British "Fuck you" for sticking us with a shitty system of measurement. That being said, Jeremy's sells quarts of Busch beer for $5 a pop. That's good shit (the deal, not the beer). If a quarter gallon of beer for five bucks isn't enticing enough for you, maybe the lure of the décor will be. At Jeremy's (that cheeky bastard) bras dangle from the ceiling while various people's decorations (pen drawings) decorate the ceiling's tiles. And there's a whole wall devoted to firemen who lost their lives in 9/11. Bras and beer must make for good business because a fair amount of tourists come in here. I was there one time during the cold-ass off season, when the door opened and literally 20 French people walked in. They just kept coming like they were exiting a clown car. But there are lots of locals, too. I overheard one of them saying, "Yeah, it took the Marine Corps three years to get me out of a Japanese prison." Maybe "colorful" is a good word for Jeremy's. Colorful and cheap. Besides the cheap beer, all food is under $10 (except the scallops) and most of it, like the bbq chicken sandwich, for example, is around $5.95, which generally

I was sorely disappointed to realize they were talking about beer, not fellatio.

includes fries. Don't sleep on this equation: cheap quarts of beer + cheap food + drunk, possibly attractive foreigners + bras on the ceiling = a high probability of sloppy drunk sex wherein someone is talking dirty in a different language ... HOT! (Practice this: *Voy a poner me pito en tu culo!*) But of all this, my favorite thing might be that the graffiti in the bathroom said "Local 52". Since when do unions tag shit up? Is there a graph writers' union I didn't know about?

Fun fact: Reagan was the only president to ever be head of a union (even if it was the Screen Actor's Guild). He also made serious efforts to break up organized labor during his presidency. What a fucking asshole.

John St. Bar & Grill
17 John St. btw Broadway & Nassau St.

In terms of Financial District bars, this is probably one of the better of the lot. Each day sees great happy hour specials, like a bucket of beer and a basket of wings for $12 on Mondays, $10 all you can drink Thursdays, and $8 pitcher Fridays. And if for some reason you miss happy hour, pints of Bud, Bud Light, Rolling Rock and John St. Ale are $3 all the time. The way John St. Bar generally works is that it's busy during happy hour, and then as the week progresses, these happy hours end up bleeding into longer, blurry nights. Then again, for the real drunks that go here, I've just described your entire week. If you want some description of the joint, I'll just throw some phrases out there for you: the floor is checkered (like your past), lots of beer mirrors, dart boards, pool table, big TVs ... blah blah blah ... sports bar. One thing I will say though is that if these chicken wings were on craigslist, they would describe themselves as "thick" or "healthy".

Nassau Bar

118 Nassau @ Ann St.

Overall, this place really isn't very good and the drinks aren't all that cheap. From 5–6pm, drinks are $3. Yup that's it. That's the whole deal. Otherwise beers start at $5. The only reason I'm putting this in here is that the girls here wear bikinis and that seems to be a strange trend I've been noticing here in New York. It's definitely a dive bar in the sense that it's lit by red bulbs and X-mas lights and the jukebox plays all classic rock, but only the shitty songs. To be honest, the only reason to come here is to perv out, and I get laid enough not to need to do that. If, as I've always said, going to a strip club is like watching the Food Network (all looking, no tasting), then going to a bikini bar is like watching the Food Network on a really small TV with horrible reception.

Note to God: if you exist, please don't make me eat my words by having me be one of the guys that frequents this place in 20 years. Thanks.

Whitehorse Tavern

25 Bridge St. @ Broad St.

No, this isn't the cool Whitehorse Tavern where Dylan Thomas drank himself to death (that comes later in the book). This is the Whitehorse Tavern where Financial District people go after work to drink $3 Budweiser drafts (always this price) and talk about sports and money and which prostitution service they use when they go to Vegas. Other than being busy at happy hour (all beers are $3 including Guinness), it can be pretty dead, but rumor has it that it picks up a little on the weekends. They also have affordable bar food that is worse for your arteries than your wallet. Throw in a very long bar, some red vinyl/leather-ish booths, and a nonplussed bartender, and you have ... a dive bar! If you're wondering why there are two Whitehorse Taverns in the city, it's because the tricky guys here spelled White Horse as one word.

Shopping

Century 21

22 Cortlandt St. btw Broadway & Church St.

Imagine if there was a store that sold you a piece of the "American Dream" (consumable goods with name brands on them) at a discounted price. There is, and that place is called Century 21. Who cares if they're last season's or even last year's styles? No one will know the difference, right? I mean, that one chick in your office still gets away with wearing one of those fucking J-Lo ponchos, and how many years ago was that shit hot? Like six? The architecture of this insane department store, which is housed in the former East River Savings Bank building, is supremely Art Deco with minor hints of the WPA, but I doubt the crowds here bother to notice it. All they seem to care about is making sure they get that Ralph Lauren shirt that's selling for 50 percent off. To be honest, Century 21 is one of those sores signifying the sickness of our culture. Don't get me wrong; I love a deal just as much as anyone (I write books on the shit), but people wile' the fuck out when they think they can get a discounted piece of the unattainable lifestyle being forced down our throats. What, you don't believe me? Then why is the motto here "Fashion Worth Fighting For"? Still don't believe me? Come here a few days before Christmas.

Dijon Boutique

80 Maiden Lane @ Gold St.;

also at 30 New St. @ Beaver St.

Dijon takes clothing brands you only marginally care about like Jessica Simpson and knocks a chunk off the price. Personally, I hate brands and try to avoid them as much as possible. Why would you want to be branded? But I guess cheap clothes are cheap clothes. Between here, Century 21, and Syms, you should be totally taken care of in terms of things to wear. As for the confidence to pull them off, you're on your own for that (I recommend booze).

P.S. Unless you're a woman or wear women's clothing, you might as well skip this place.

Ralph's Discount City

80 Nassau St. btw John & Fulton Sts.

This is the type of place that sells Brut cologne and Stetson perfume for women. Any spot with a name like this though has a place in my heart (and apparently my book). Ralph's occupies a musty, humid, basement and sells discount *everything* like: super glue, hair products, soap, condoms (not sure if I want discount condoms), vitamins, Windex, notepads, etc. It's kinda like Duane Reade's immigrant cousin.

Syms

42 Trinity Pl. btw Rector St. & Exchange Alley; *also* at 400 Park Ave @ E 54th St.

If Century 21 had a main competitor, it would probably be Syms. It's basically the same idea as Century 21 but less classy (yeah, that's possible), and it's also less crowded. Quite simply, it's a good place to buy cheap clothes. I didn't know there was a ticker tape parade celebrating the New York Giants' Super Bowl win on the day I had planned to research the Financial District. This was a mistake. I ended heading into Syms to take refuge from the madness outside. When I didn't buy a NY Giants hat, the bag check lady got all mad and said, "I shouldn't have even checked your bag." Since when is a bag check a favor to me? I thought it was to keep poor fucks like me from shoplifting.

TKTS

199 Water St. @ Fulton St.

Want discount theater tickets? Go here instead of the one in Times Square; the line is a lot shorter.

Sites & Entertainment

In the summer, there are free concerts every Friday night at the South Street Seaport.

There are free movies once a week at the Elevated Acre on Water Street.

Battery Park

That park at the very bottom of Manhattan. It's kinda hard to miss.

Grab a bottle of Two Buck Chuck (a $2 bottle of Charles Shaw from Trader Joe's) and make Battery Park the location of your next cheap date. After drinking the bottle and drunkenly peeing on any number of statues, you can stroll along the promenade on the banks of the Hudson and take in fantastic views of the Statue of Liberty, Ellis Island, and yeah, um, Jersey.

Irish Hunger Memorial

250 Vesey St. & North End Ave.

Wandering around the Financial District one day, I saw a random clump of shrubbery and stones and said to myself, "Wow, it totally looks like someone took a really small chunk of rural Ireland and left it in Manhattan." Considering I hitchhiked through West Cork for a while when writing for Lonely Planet, I was pretty confident that I knew what rural Ireland looked like. When I approached and saw that it was actually the Irish Hunger Memorial, I said to myself, "Ha! I knew it was something Irish!" and then wondered inwardly why I was talking smugly to myself. For those of you who don't know shit (now I'm speaking smugly to you), Ireland had a great famine from roughly 1845-1852, in which millions died and millions more emigrated to the US, Canada or Australia. This free memorial commemorates the plight of the Irish during this period.

Iron Fence at Bowling Green
Bowling Green
Built in the 1770s, this fence is one of oldest man-made artifacts in New York. There used to be crowns on the tops of each post, but they were chopped off and used for ammunition during the Revolutionary War.

Museum of Jewish Heritage
38 Battery Pl. btw 1st Pl. & Little West St.
While traveling in Argentina, I met a kid from Pennsylvania who thought he was funny when he called New York, "Jew York". That was until I told him I was Jewish, which was funny for me, because I got to see him backpedal and sputter some kind of apology. But the kid was right: There's a shit load of Jews in New York, which is why there are multiple Jew-seums (see, it works in so many ways) in the city. The Museum of Jewish Heritage sets itself apart from its brethren by focusing on 19th and 20th century Jewry, specifically using artifacts and testimony to study Jewish life before, during, and after the Holocaust. It's a wonderful and relatively new museum worth checking out; plus it's free.

National Museum of the American Indian
1 Bowling Green @ Broadway
The NMAI is housed in the Alexander Hamilton U.S. Customs House, a beautiful Beaux Arts building completed in 1907, and originally used as (you guessed it) a customs house. Even if you're a racist asshole who hates Native Americans, you can at least come admire the lovely architecture of this building. Hopefully you're not though and you'd like to learn about the culture and heritage of this country's original inhabitants. Luckily for those of you who would like to assuage your white guilt without paying a hefty entrance fee, the NMAI is totally free. Assuage away!

Place where toilet paper was invented
41 Ann St. @ Nassau St.
There's actually just a random business here now, but seriously, this place saved my ass.

Fuck this place.

Staten Island Ferry
South Ferry Plaza

Easily one of the best things to do in New York, the Staten Island Ferry is 100 percent free to ride. Why pay $15 to go to the Statue of Liberty when you can pay ZERO bucks and get almost as close? Besides offering amazing views of Lady Liberty and Lower Manhattan, the SI Ferry also sells 16 oz. cans of Bud for $3. Talk about a great date: nothing brings out sexy like $3 tall boys, a boat ride, and a 151 foot green woman.

World Trade Center Site

I highly doubt I have it in me to put together the right words for this; we all know what happened here. As of now it's a big construction site; let's see what it looks like when all the building is done.

FINANCIAL DISTRICT

Grub-a-dub-dub

1. Baluchi's Masala
2. Café 52-In UFT building
3. Café Doppio
4. Café Fonduta
5. Financier Patisserie
6. The Grotto Pizzeria
7. My Daddy's Pizza
8. New Golden Chopsticks
9. Roxy Coffee Shop
10. Sophie's Restaurant
11. A Spice Route
12. Terrace Fish & Chips
13. Ulysses

DRINKS DRINKS DRINKS

14. Fresh Salt
15. Jeremy's Ale House
16. John St. Bar & Grill
17. Nassau Bar
18. Whitehorse Tavern

Shopping

19. Century 21
20. Dijon Boutique
21. Ralph's Discount City
22. Syms
23. TKTS

Stuffis to See and Do

24. Battery Park
25. Ground Zero, Former Site of World Trade Center
26. Irish Hunger Memorial
27. Iron Fence at Bowling Green
28. Museum Of Jewish Heritage
29. National Museum of the American Indian
30. Place Where Toilet Paper Was Invented
31. Staten Island Ferry

Free Food Bitches!!

32. Ryan Maguire's Ale House

Herbivore Friendly

33. Little Lad's Basket

Street Meat

34. Dominic's Italian Sausage
35. Veronica's Kitchen

Rich people making ungodly amounts of money and will never buy this book.

Ghost of dead Dutch colonists

Teeny sliver of sunlight through skyscrapers

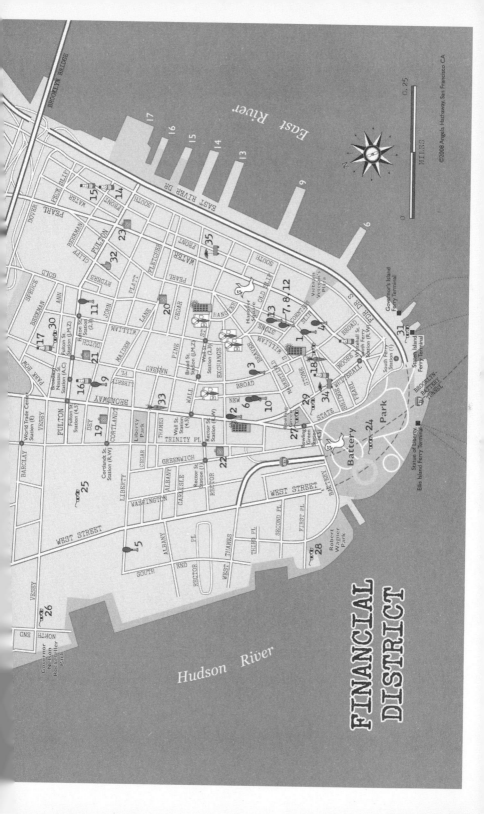

Civic Center, Chinatown & Little Italy

Once called the Five Points, the area currently consisting of the Civic Center and Chinatown was considered the worst neighborhood in the US, and possibly the world, in the mid-19th century. It was a filthy mess of rundown tenements and squalid streets, where gangs ran shit and honest laborers could barely make enough to survive. Today things are a bit different: Civic Center is a mixture of skyscrapers and government buildings (including City Hall), while Chinatown is, well, Chinatown. Strange smells emanate from shadowy shops while vendors all along Canal Street hock fake designer bags made overseas by child labor. But in terms of cheap places to eat, there are few better neighborhoods in the entire five boroughs.

Little Italy, on the other hand, is a parody of its former self. What was once a large neighborhood of working class Italian immigrants has been reduced to about two and a half blocks of expensive Italian restaurants, a couple of cigar stores and the John Jovino Gun Shop (the oldest firearms retailer in the city), all pandering for tourist dollars. The shrinking of Little Italy is due both to people moving the fuck out of the old neighborhood, and a Chinatown that has been expanding ever since the Immigration and Nationality Act of 1965 made it easier for Asians to immigrate to the USA. Because of this constant broadening of Chinatown's borders, it can be difficult to figure out where one neighborhood ends and the next begins (that's why I lumped these three areas together).

Speaking very roughly, the borders of **Chinatown** are the Bowery/St. James Pl. east to the East River, and Grand St. south to the Brooklyn Bridge. Chinatown's main thoroughfare is Canal St. **Civic Center** lies between Canal St. at its northern border and Barclay St. to the south and from Church St. west to the Bowery/St. James Pl. You can find the ever-shrinking **Little Italy** between Houston St. to the north and Canal St., to the south, and, from east to west, from Centre St. to the Bowery. But like I said before, these boundaries are constantly in flux.

Food

Chinatown Ice Cream Factory
65 Bayard St. btw Elizabeth & Mott Sts.

At $3.50 a pop, the scoops may seem a little overpriced, but then once you have your first taste, you'll be hooked like the junkies in those "Don't do drugs" commercials. Look man, I slanged ice cream for a year and a half in high school and I gotta tell you, the range of flavors they have here is totally unique. They have shit like lychee (my spell checker hasn't even heard of it), taro, black sesame, wasabi, avocado, and even durian flavored ice cream. If you don't know what durian is, it looks like this and smells like diarrhea and dirty feet. Yeah, they even have the diarrhea and dirty feet ice cream, but if I were you, I'd go for the mango. Eating it is about as good a feeling as being in junior high and getting love letters.

Cup and Saucer
89 Canal St. @ Eldridge St.

The weirdest part about finding a genuine old-school, greasy spoon diner in the middle of Chinatown is that the primary language spoken here is English. Outside it's all "Ni hao ma", while inside it's mostly "Ay, how you doin'?" with a little bit of "Como estas?" But I guess that makes sense considering it's been here for more than 65 years. Besides being a cultural anomaly, Cup and Saucer also acts as a place where a lot of the kids from the nearby high school play hooky. But hey, the food comes quickly and everything is cheap; even a hot pastrami sandwich is just $7.50. The only things that are relatively pricey are the omelets (strange, I know).

drawing by Mike Force

Da Nico Restaurant

164 Mulberry St. btw Grand & Broome Sts.

Despite a few differences, like patios and décor, most of the Italian restaurants are the same in Little Italy. They're all very touristy, but if you're hungry and not tripping on carbs and calories and shit, you can get a decent sized plate of pasta for as little as $6.50 during lunch. After 3pm, when lunch ends, the prices double or triple and suddenly rubes like us are priced out. Really, what sets Da Nico apart from the other spots is that it has a dope garden patio in the summertime and a really cheesy Italian caricature out front. My guess is that it serves to hammer home the point that most of Little Italy is a joke.

Fried Dumpling

106 Mosco St. btw Mulberry & Mott Sts.;
also at 99 Allen St. btw Broome & Delancey Sts.

The only English words the ladies at Fried Dumpling know are, "How many?" And that's enough, because the answer is usually five. Yes, friends, you get five of the best dumplings you've ever had for $1. And apparently instead of change, they give you dumplings. I bought a 75-cent Coke and instead of giving me back a quarter, she just gave me another dumpling. Sweet, right? What's funny is if you come and say you want $20 worth of dumplings, the ladies kinda bug out, curse at you in Chinese, and then go into hyper drive. My fantasy is to bring in that Japanese eating champion kid, (Kobayashi or something like that) throw down $50 and let him face off against the dumpling ladies. It would probably be the best 50 bucks ever spent.

Lunch Box Buffet

195 Centre St. @ Hester St.

Oh Chinatown—feeder of empty bellies, giver of bellyaches. What have you wrought upon us now? A five-combo plate of food for $4.50? Is it nobler to tempt the gods in this way or to simply starve?

Answer: it's far better to tempt the gods. The food here, despite being a little poop-inducing, is pretty fucking decent, and considering the $4.50 also includes soup, you're not gonna find a better deal this side of Hades ... or Haiti for that matter.

Pakistan Tea House
176 Church St btw Duane & Reade Sts.

The name here makes it seem like it's gonna be a fancy place with elaborate service and old British ladies reminiscing about "growing up in the colonies" but, surprise! It's not. It's actually just a busy spot where you can get a meal consisting of one meat dish, two veggie dishes, and rice or naan, for $6.49. You can tell by all the articles in the window that, in the late 90s, it was a bit of a "cheap eats" darling for the local food critics (even though they have the same *New York Times* review posted twice). Plus it's open from 10am–4am, making it almost always possible for you to stuff your face with cheap and scrumptious Pakistani food. I don't know if they actually serve tea though.

Pho Bang Restaurant
157 Mott St @ Grand St

Eating vermicelli noodles is so much better than not eating vermicelli noodles.

In SF, I used to eat cheap Vietnamese food like twice a week, but since it seems like there aren't nearly as many Vietnamese people here as in SF, I've been seriously jonesing for some. This place fits the bill. 90 percent of the menu is under $7.50, and they serve pho, as well as that amazing vermicelli noodle shit that I love. The pictures on the walls are of pretty girls in front of various Vietnamese scenes as if they were taken from a brochure called "Come to beautiful Vietnam and go home with a lovely bride". The place is popular and they give free tea, which is awesome considering it was 20 degrees outside last time I went. I hate 20 degrees.

Prosperity Dumplings
46 Eldridge St. btw Hester & Canal Sts.

Yet another glorious "five dumplings for $1" place. They even sell them frozen to take home with you and give you a bulk rate price of

100 dumplings for $15. I personally wouldn't do it because I know that I'd come home drunk some night and try to see how many I could eat. Don't pretend the thought hasn't crossed your mind.

Saigon Banh Mi

138 Mott btw Grand and Hester Sts.

Where else can you get a foot tall jade Buddha and a big Vietnamese sandwich? While the jewelry sold here is fairly reasonable for jewelry, I guess, the sandwiches are really what you should come for. The most expensive thing on the menu is $5.50 and that's a shrimp papaya salad. It's got them scrimps son! Otherwise a pork sandwich is $3.75. Word.

Super Taste Noodle

26 Eldridge St. @ Canal St.

You know you've got a gem when you walk up to a place and see a bunch of "Cheap Eats" plaques and articles in the window. Super Taste Noodle is just such a place. You can watch the staff standing in the back, hand-pulling long strands of noodles from a big thing of dough, while you sit and slurp up a big, hot, steaming bowl of $4–$6 goodness. There's a good variety of ingredients to choose from, too, everything from something mundane like dumplings, to more exotic dishes like beef feet, oxtail, and pork bone. I wish I were eating here right now instead of taking periodic breaks from my computer to eat turkey cold cuts.

Sheng Wan

27 Eldridge St. @ Canal St.

Josh Bernstein, who does cheap eats stuff for publications like *Time Out NY*, took me here one day when he hipped me to all the ill spots in Chinatown. Similar to Super Taste Noodle across the street, Sheng Wang is a really cheap noodle soup place where they are surprised if you tip. While the food is bomb on its own, it's really all about mixing in the chili sauce. I love my shit spicy, and I love getting a full meal for $4.

Vegetarian Dim Sum House

24 Pell St. btw Mott & Bowery Sts.

In most Chinese restaurants, "vegetarian" means just adding more broccoli and using less pork fat, but not here—this is the real deal.

Never thought you'd actually find a real veggie/vegan restaurant in Chinatown did you? Now that I've given the good news, here's the bad news: as far as dim sum goes, this place is definitely not the cheapest (although everything on the dim sum menu is under $4). Don't give me that look; this is the lifestyle you've chosen. You should be used to this shit by now.

Wo-Hop

17 Mott St. @ Mosco St.

This basement level Chinese diner has been around since the 1930s and is a Chinatown classic. Headshots of people who never made it big cover the walls, while waiters shuffle back and forth trying to make sure you eat up, pay up and get the fuck out. It doesn't matter what the prices are, the portions here are so big that if Weight Watchers had an AMBER alert, that shit would be set off. Luckily the prices are cheap, and for $7 I got a plate of food that made me say, "There is no way in hell I can eat all that." I ended up giving my leftovers to a homeless guy. Even their T-shirts are cheap; you can get your very own for only $6.

P.S. Word to the wise: spicy mustard = all spicy, no mustard.

Bars

Botanica Bar

47 E. Houston btw Mott & Mulberry Sts.

Botanica Bar is a deceivingly big place. You walk through the front door and head to the back only to realize there is a whole other room there filled with tons of loungy couches. Yes, oodles of them. But thankfully this is not a lounge. There's a difference. You follow? This is not a high-end place where Nordic snowmen made the furniture and the clientele consists of anorexic 17-year-old models drinking $15 Cosmos. No, it's quite the opposite. The loungy couches are part Salvation Army, part bar booths, part vintage retro, and the drinks range from $3 PBRs to various potent specials. Sure there might be the occasional anorexic 17-year-old model, but they have to drink what the rest of us drink. Truthfully, if I were you, I'd be more worried about gypsies anyway. There's enough "watch your belongings" signs here to make anyone think they were in a small Central European village. But enough about your prejudices, let's get back to the loungy couches, goddammit! These couches and the low lighting make it seem like the bar is nothing but a collection of cozy dark corners perfect for smooching (if you're lucky enough to meet a cutie or smart enough to bring a date). And don't let all the religious paraphernalia make you feel guilty about it either; it's mainly just to justify calling the place Botanica ... and to scare off the gypsies.

Milano's Bar

51 E Houston St. @ Mott St.

I must have been off that night because my normal candor was ill received. I insulted a Kiwi bartender by telling her that she spoke like she was Irish and then another girl thought I was crazy when I made sure she hadn't lost her purse. But fuck it; the night ended with J– choking a cabbie and his girlfriend kissing me (the rest of that strange story may come up later). Budweisers here are $3, which is beautiful in a city where people stupidly pay $10 for a beer in some places. The establishment itself is skinny and has tons of pics of patrons on one wall while beer signs and photos of Bogart, Sinatra and Joe Louis round out the hip, old, dive bar motif. Other ancient seeming knick-knacks, like a scimitar and a sailor hat hanging behind the bar, only add to this feeling. And sitting amongst the derelict old drunks you'd expect to find here are cute girls and boys who love good dive bars. Basically, Milano's is about 100 times better than the last bar you drank at.

South's Bar
273 Church St. @ Franklin St.

South's serves $4 bottles of Bud. Why has this become the standard price in NY? That sucks. Anyway, this is pretty much the spot for after-work drinking for restaurant people. So, if you saw a hunky guy behind the bar at Bubby's and you wanna see him drunk(er), come here when the restaurant closes. His name is Mac.

The Spring Lounge
48 Spring St. @ Mulberry St.

Amongst the photos of Frank Sinatra, various Native Americans, Muhammad Ali, and Jake Lamotta that dot the walls of this great, old school bar, are a couple real dead sharks ... I think. I say, "I think" because, well, this was the second to last bar on a research trip; I was pretty drunk. I know the sharks were there, I just don't know if they were fake; just like I know they served cheap PBR, but I don't know how much they cost ($2 or $3?). I managed to write the dollar sign and neglected to put a number next to it. According to my notes they have free bagels on Sundays and free hot dogs on Wednesdays. Thankfully my drunk ass writes this shit down or else this would be a really sorry entry. Let's see what else the notes say: the spot is big and sits on the corner and has big windows so you can see all the people soberer than you walking by and flip them the bird because you forget that they can see you too. Wooden floors, low lit and always a good crowd. Bar opens at 8am if you want an eye opener ... apparently my grammar gets even worse when I drink.

Sweet Paradise
14 Orchard St. btw Canal & Hester Sts.

Every time I'm here I'm too wasted, which isn't necessarily a bad thing. All I have to say is that they have beer for $2 all the time; it's called Genesee Cream Ale and it's not very good. But did I mention that it's $2? This place is exactly like being in Williamsburg, except that when you step out of the bar you're in Chinatown. They sell boxes of movie theatre candy like Hot Tamales, Runts, and Sour Patch Kids, and according to a sign, they sell Red Bull and Dr. Pepper too. I don't know the candy prices though because, like I said, I'm always too drunk when I'm here. I think there is always a DJ, and I think there is always a chandelier, but I can't promise you either. I can promise you fogged-up windows though and people wearing those stupid looking granny glasses.

Winnie's
104 Bayard btw Baxter & Mulberry Sts.

With $5 Budweisers, this place goes against one of the basic tenets of Broke-Assdom, that the cheapest beer in a place should cost no more than $4. But in extreme circumstances, like Winnie's, such tenets can be overlooked. Mike, Maleeha and I walked in here after a long night of research, and an old drunk Chinese guy (who we found out was the owner) was wrestling another old drunk Chinese guy off his barstool. Besides old, grappling, drunk Chinese guys, the bar was filled with young, cool-looking kids (not being standoffish), other random unclassifiable drinkers and karaoke-ers. In fact karaoke is one of the main reasons people come to Winnie's. It's $1 per song and when no one is singing there are these weird little original-Nintendo-looking birds dancing around the screen (which is a big 50-inch TV from the '90s). And the karaoke screen not only has words, but also has low-budget late-'80s/early '90s music videos made *not by the bands,* but instead specifically for the underground karaoke world. Their quality is a half step below late night HBO soft-core porn. And the songs/videos are all on laserdisc, too! This place is so amazing. The booths are big and can hold seven or more people, and, somewhere at the end of our stay, a guy came in with a giant blue Muppet. When all of these things happen in one night, and nobody bats an eye, it says one thing: Winnie's is where God lives.

Shopping

Chinese Street Cobbler
Intersection of Mulberry & Bayard Sts.

This dude just sits at the corner and fixes shoes. He speaks zero English, so I'm not sure how negotiations go down (I've yet to get my shoes cobbled by him), but it can't be too expensive; the guy has no overhead. If you get him to fix your shoes, let me know how it goes.

Deluxe Food Market
79 Elizabeth btw Grand & Hester Sts.

It's like they took all the food markets you've seen wandering around Chinatown, condensed them and put them in a single place. Deluxe Food Market really has everything: ridiculously cheap hot food, ridiculously cheap seafood to take home, a bakery with desserts, raw meats, fresh produce and tons of shit I would have to be drunk to eat, like pork bung (is that what I think it is?). My only question is this: why does it seem like old Chinese people are always yelling at me?

East Broadway Mall
88 E. Broadway under the Manhattan bridge

Close your eyes and imagine all the weird shops (not markets) that you pass on the streets of Chinatown (I guess it's hard to close your eyes if you're reading this). Now imagine if they were all tightly lumped together into a single three-story building. Pretty wild right? Well the East Broadway Mall is exactly like what you imagined but much crazier. There are herb shops, stationery stores, clothing outlets, perfumeries, video game hawkers and even salons. Plus everything is negotiable; you're almost expected to haggle. And all the vendors talk to me like I speak Chinese. In fact I'd bet you hear more English in China. As for eats, there's a nice dim-sum place upstairs called Palace 88, but I always opt for the cheap-ass restaurant downstairs where everything is like $2.75. The menu is only in Chinese, though, so you gotta basically point to something that someone else is eating and say you want it. I got a plate of peanut noodles and a bowl of wonton soup for $3! Even a bottle of water was only $0.80. And what's great about Chinatown is that you're supposed to slurp your food and eat fast. I finally found a place where I belong!

Kysmo Bike Shop

35 Orchard St. @ Hester St.

Wanna bike around New York, but you're really lazy? Rent an electric bike here for $10 a day.

Fake Bags on Canal Street

Everywhere

I really hate our country's culture of consumption and the way it places the value of Things so highly. All a Louis Vuitton bag says about a person is that they were dumb enough pay $1400 for a fucking bag. All a *fake* Louis Vuitton bag says about a person is how badly they want to look like they were dumb enough to pay $1400 for a fucking bag. That being said, if you really want to be part of the club, you can get amazingly realistic-looking fake designer bags on Canal Street. The way it works is kinda the way drug deals happen in *The Wire*, meaning there are multiple people and relay points involved before you get your silly bag. I just want you to know that most of those bags are created by children in sweatshop conditions. But hey, little hands make little stitches, right?

P.S. Do you think Prada makes body bags? And if so, do you think people would buy knock-offs?

Unimax

269 Canal St. btw Broadway & Lafayette St. (2nd floor)

A kid I worked with named Tanner first told me about Unimax because we both have stretched ears. Essentially, Unimax is a manufacturer and wholesaler of all things involving body modification. You can get plugs, studs, hoops, barbells, tattoo guns, ink etc., all at wholesale prices. It actually has the biggest body jewelry selection in New York and is where many of the city's tattoo and piercing spots get their shit. But honestly, Unimax is more than just a tattoo and piercing wholesaler; it's a celebration of body art in all its forms. They sell all kinds of books on the history of tattooing and piercing, as well as books on random shit like circus freaks (hopefully they'll carry this book, too). I ended up getting into a long conversation with Wes Wood, the owner of Unimax and Saved Tattoos, and he philosophized to me for 20 minutes or so about the history of tattooing, and how he thinks that people have the urge to be tattooed first and that they make up the reasoning for it later. We also talked about tattooing as a folk art. I liked him a lot. So yeah, if you're a tattooed or pierced freak, this might be your new favorite place in the city.

Sights & Entertainment

African Burial Ground

Duane St. @ African Burial Ground Way (Elk St.)

During construction of a federal building in 1991, the remains of more than 400 Africans, who had been buried in the 17th and 18th centuries, were discovered. The site, now a National Historic Landmark, has a memorial on it that's free to explore. It's pretty cool to check out and you can see some of the mounds where the bodies are buried.

Brooklyn Bridge

Do you really need an address?

Brooklyn Bridge was a TV show that I really liked as a kid. It was kinda like an urban Jewish version of *The Wonder Years.* One of my cousins (who I don't know if I've met) played Jack Kerouac on one episode. I've been told the show was named after a real bridge somewhere, but I've never heard of it.

Chinatown Fair Video Arcade

8 Mott St. @ Worth St.

I haven't seen an arcade this populated since 1997 when the arcade in my neighborhood started giving out four free tokens to kids, hoping that they'd end up spending money, too. Fuck, I actually haven't

See the kid on the right? Never bet money that you can beat him at video games. I owe him $20 and my firstborn child.

seen any arcade at all in almost that long. If you're down for getting punked at Street Fighter vs. X-Men by some 16-year-old Asian kid, then this is your spot. The best part about this place is that there used to be a chicken here that was trained to play tic-tac-toe. And you know what? The chicken never lost. Seriously.

Columbus Park (The Five Points)
Mosco St. btw Mulberry & Worth Sts.

This lovely locale was once called the Five Points because the area was centered on the intersection of Anthony (now Worth), Orange (now Baxter), and Cross (now Mosco). In the mid 19th century, the Five Points was the most notorious slum in the world; it was so fucked up that rich people would take police-protected tours so they could view the squalor themselves. When I first moved to New York, I was fascinated by the area and bought a book on it called *The Five Points*, which was super boring. I wanted the book to be more like the movie *Gangs of New York*, with motherfuckers cutting each other up, and less about describing what kind of cups the people drank out of. I guess I should have just gotten the book *Gangs of New York*. There's a plaque commemorating the Five Points neighborhood nearby in Foley Square.

Mahayana Temple Buddhist Association
133 Canal St. btw Chrystie & Forsyth Sts.

If sitting in silence, lighting incense and meditating is what you call relaxing, but your roommate blasts Cannibal Corpse and is allergic to nag champa, this might be your spot. While the Mahayana Temple

Buddhist Association isn't completely silent (because of squawking tourists), it is totally free. You can learn about the mythology of Buddhism by reading the story placards on the wall, and if you feel like it, you can drop a buck in one of the many donation boxes scattered around and pick up a fortune. Mine said:

> *Probability of Success: Excellent*
> *When you feel exhausted, do go to retire.*
> *When you are hungry, eat what you desire.*
> *You will sure acquire all what you require.*
> *For you have the fire that others admire.*

Thank Buddha, I fucking hope so! I wonder if any say, "Probability of Success: eh, not so good". I'd like to be the guy who writes those fortunes.

Ramps under the Brooklyn Bridge
On the north side of the bridge

You know what's funnier than seeing a kid fall off his skateboard and break his arm? Nothing. What? Don't give me that shit; I've got enough road-rash scars on my left arm and shoulder from skating to

If I were an orthopedic surgeon, I'd pay someone to hang out here all day and give out my card to every kid who fell.

Where's the rest of this guy's fucking teeth?

earn the right to laugh at those kids. It's not like I'm laughing if they bust their heads open. Anyway, if you wanna see a shit ton of kids doing tricks on bikes and skateboards, come here on a nice day.

Attn: Kids. Take it from your uncle Stuart and wear a helmet. It's super fucked up to watch your buddy eat it, knock his head and start seizing up and snorting and shit. Head trauma is so fucked up and only ha ha funny way after the fact.

LITTLE ITALY, CHINATOWN
and CIVIC CENTER

Grub-a-dub-dub
1. Chinatown Ice Cream Factory
2. Cup and Saucer
3. Da Nico Restaurant
4. Eastern Noodle House
5. Fried Dumpling
6. Lunch Box Buffet
7. Pakistan Tea House
8. Phobang Restaurant
9. Prosperity Dumplings
10. Saigon Banh Mi
11. Sheng Wang
12. Super Taste Noodle
13. Wo-Hop

DRINKS DRINKS DRINKS
14. Botanica Bar
15. Milano's Bar
16. South's
17. Sweet Paradise
18. Winnie's

Shopping
19. Chinese Street Cobbler
20. Deluxe Food Market
21. East Broadway Mall
22. Fake Bags on Canal Street
23. Kysmo Bike Shop
24. Unimax

Stuffis to See and Do
25. African Burial Ground
26. Brooklyn Bridge
27. Chinatown Fair Video Arcade
28. Mahayana Temple Buddhist Association
29. Ramps Under Brooklyn Bridge - Brooklyn Banks

Free Food Bitches!!
30. The Spring Lounge

Herbivore Friendly
31. House of Vegetarian
32. Vegetarian Dim Sum House
33. Wild Ginger

Unidentifiable smells

Dead animals hanging in windows

Fake designer bags

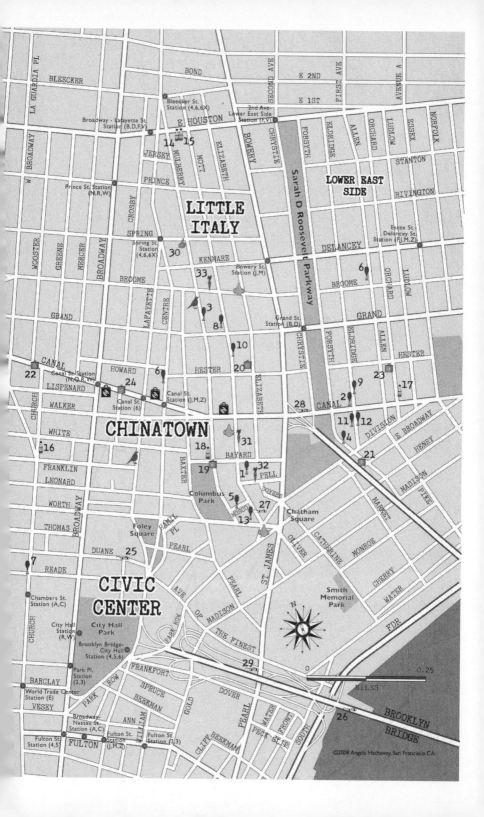

Tribeca & Soho

S oho was once an industrial area referred to as the Cast Iron District because of its unique architecture. As the economy and means of production changed throughout the United States in the late 1960s, artists began to move into the district's former warehouses and factories and convert the virtually worthless real estate into artist lofts and galleries. It was during this time that people started calling the neighborhood Soho (short for "South of Houston"). Things have changed since then. Today Soho is the ultimate destination for good, little capitalists willing to go into debt to purchase overpriced designer clothing. I hate that shit, but I'm not gonna tell you what to do with your money. I'm just gonna give you some good alternatives so hopefully you won't have to donate blood in order to pay your rent after spending your whole paycheck on fucking Gucci sunglasses. This neighborhood is also packed to the gills with modeling agencies, so if you see abnormally tall and skinny girls with giant heads, don't be alarmed–they're supposed to look like that. **Soho** is bounded by the Hudson River to the west, Lafayette St. to the east, Canal St. to the south and, obviously, Houston St. to the north.

Tribeca, whose name is an abbreviation for "Triangle Below Canal Street", has a history similar to that of Soho. It was once a center for warehouses and manufacturing and is now a collection of lofts, historic buildings and rich people. While it doesn't have the same cache of high-end retail stores that Soho does, Tribeca makes up for it by having some of the best restaurants in New York. Unfortunately they are also some of the most expensive, so don't expect to see them in this book. **Tribeca** is bounded by the Hudson River to the west, Church St. to the east, Canal St. to the north and Chambers St. to the south.

Food

Café Duke
Broadway btw Prince & Spring Sts.

Café Duke is just like any other buffet-style, pay by the pound, lunch place, except much less skuzzy feeling. This is probably because the food doesn't seem like it's been sitting around since David Dinkins' administration, and also because the variety here is impressively wide. They've got folks making sushi, pasta, salads, and paninis, plus they have candy bars, juices and other shit. Most everything is around $7 a pound, and the sandwiches are all in the $6 range. They also have ramen soup for about $6 ... and it's not that kind you ate in the dorms.

Calexico
Food cart at Wooster & Prince Sts.

Us California folk take our Mexican food pretty seriously; it's comfort food for us and long periods of time without it makes us both wistful and ornery. In normal circumstances, if you tried to charge me $7 for a carne asada burrito, I'd laugh at you and curse your mother. But seeing as New York's Mexican food choices are generally horrific, the burritos from Calexico are a viable option. The guys who run it are all from the San Diego area, and the food is actually pretty good. I wouldn't ever pay that much for it in California, but sometimes in life, you gotta take what you're given, and in this case it's a pretty good $7 burrito.

Ceci Cela
55 Spring St. @ Lafayette St.

This cute, small, rustic looking French bakery is where many New York restaurants get their pastries. Why not just cut out the middle-man and go to the source? They even employ real French people.

La Conquita

236 Lafayette St. @ Spring St.

La Conquita might be one of the last hole-in-the-wall spots left in Soho and I wholeheartedly commend it for this. The only decorations are a Keith Haring print from the Humane Society, a mirror and a couple of small Dominican Republic flags. Speaking of Dominicans, there aren't a whole lot of them on the West Coast (except for at this one café at 24th & Mission in SF), so the first time I heard a brotha speaking in Dominican Spanish it totally caught me off guard. But enough of my cultural insensitivity, I'm here to tell you that La Conquita is THE spot for cheap plantains, beans, rice and meat. For $7 you get a plate of food so big that I guarantee* you will have leftovers. Que pasa mami?

La Esquina

114 Kenmare St. @ Lafayette St.

While not being amazingly priced, La Esquina is also not cripplingly expensive. And the tacos are super good, like almost California good. The really classic looking, pie-slice-shaped building has probably been around since the '30s, and there's a club downstairs that doesn't let people like you and me in there, so don't bother. If you can get a seat, it's a nice place to sit and watch people go by, and in the summer they put tables and chairs outside … I think. Make sure to try the *elote* (grilled corn) because it's amazing. Then again, *elote* is always amazing.

Lahore Deli

132 Crosby St. btw Houston & Jersey Sts.

Goddamn, this is my type of shit! A tiny, hole-in-the-wall Pakistani place that smells so good you want to hump one of the few stools they have in the place (this behavior is not favorably looked upon). It's super cheap, too: a full meal of chicken and rice is $5 and most everything else is way cheaper. It's easy to miss though if you're just walking by, so pay attention. The tag line here is "Feel the taste of the East," which is what I was trying to do when they kicked me out for humping the stools.

Publisher's note: This guarantee is not binding and anything that Broke-Ass Stuart says should be considered suspect. All problems with the text should be taken up with him personally. Try buying him a beer and giving him a foot rub. He hates that shit.

Ñ

33 Crosby St. btw Broome & Grand Sts.

While this sexy little place isn't priced in the "super broke-ass" category, it's a good spot to go on a date and seem like you're someplace swanky without dropping a lot of dough. One side of the restaurant is a brick wall, while the other has lots of weird polka dots on it, and there is a single super-sultry VIP booth (though I don't know how one reserves it). The food is tapas style and almost all the plates are $7. Look, I know it's not the cheapest thing in this book, but I'd also like to help you get laid, and taking someone to a nice place in Soho and spending less than $50 for two people is fucking dope.

Pepe Rosso

149 Sullivan St. btw Houston & Prince Sts.

This rustic looking, well-priced Italian place is tiny; there are only three tables and maybe ten seats; and the food is hearty and good. Pepe Rosso is owned by the same people as Pepe Verde in the West Village. And you know what? They even have real Italians working inside, oooh la la. Paninis are all either $6.95 and $7.95 and most of the pastas are under $10. Plus, if you stop in for lunch, the special is $8.95 and comes with either soup or salad.

Ruben's Empanadas

505 Broome St. @ W Broadway; *also* at 64 Fulton St.; 122 1st Ave.; and 149 Church St.

Ruben makes real Argentinean empanadas, roughly the size of a human heart (which is a grim reminder that I'm gonna have a heart attack if I keep up this lifestyle). When I was in Argentina I practically lived off empanadas. They are the perfect food; they're like hot pockets without making you feel like you have dysentery. The big difference is that in Argentina, empanadas are one peso, which roughly equals $0.33 American. Old Rube here sells them for $3.75. But hey, Soho and Buenos Aires have very different economies.

The Soda Shop
125 Chambers St. btw W. Broadway & Church Sts.

While not being an authentic old school soda place, (it's only been in this location for two years) it's a cool spot because they do real soda fountain drinks like New York egg creams, floats, old broadways, cracker jacks, and shakes. The food really isn't that cheap although most of it is under $10. The place is decorated with tons of old soda bottles and tin signs, plus there's a stained glass that says "Ice Cream" and a big candy counter. Did you know that Tribeca is not a very good place to find cheap food?

Square Diner
33 Leonard @ Varick St.

Serving Tribeca since 1971, this diner is a solid place to get a good square meal (what does that mean anyway?). The menu here is big and filled with standard diner food, and while, yes, there are cheaper diners in NY, none of them are in Tribeca. A burger is $5.00 but doesn't come with fries. If you're around for lunch though, the daily lunch specials are generally good. They're like $9.50 and include a big sandwich, soup and a soda/coffee/tea. Not too bad considering it's enough that you can take half the sandwich for later. I got pastrami. I'm trying to eat as much of it as possible before I leave NY. The Square Diner might be the only place in this neighborhood that has a lot of cool working-class regulars, my type of folks.

Bars

Antarctica
287 Hudson St. @ Spring St.

Antarctica is a sizeable place with a pool table and a big, ornately carved bar with postcards, foreign money and photos behind it. One wall is completely covered with a giant black and white photo of guys with mustaches from the 1880s or maybe the Gay '90s (I just wanted to say "the Gay '90s"). These are mustaches good enough to make every Williamsburg hipster tip his hat in deference. While the Buds are $4 here, it's almost worth it because it's one of the only truly good bars in this neighborhood. (Plus all the mixed drinks come in pint glasses.) The clientele is cool, as are the bartenders and the place is steady on most nights and packed on the weekends. More than anything though, I like the fact that, because of its embossed metal ceiling and long, wood plank floors, it looks like an old saloon. And it's one of those places where if it's your name on the board that night, you drink for free.

Biddy Early's
43 Murray St. btw Church St. & W. Broadway

An Irish Pub with real Irish employees is not a terribly hard thing to find in New York, but one with $3 beers and a menu where most things are under $10 is. Biddy Early's has all of these things, and un-fortunately, also has a beer pong table, which as we all know, attracts douche bags like I attract crazy chicks. The walls here are covered with autographed football (soccer) jerseys and it's a good place to watch the English Premier League. Otherwise, there's not much spe-cial about this pub except that they have pretty damn good black and white pudding and Irish sausages (just some of my very unhealthy and hazardous addictions). They're not all that cheap, but it doesn't matter when someone else is buying. Thanks, Mike!

The Ear Inn
326 Spring St. @ Greenwich St.

Rumored to be one of the oldest bars in the city, the Ear Inn is, well ... old (built in 1817 old). And to prove it, it has loads of old photos and memorabilia scattered around it's interior. The decoration of the place comes off as a combination of a shipwreck and sideshow, which makes sense, considering it's original patrons were sailors and stevedores who worked the nearby boats when the Hudson's shoreline ran right by. The blue-collar clientele can still be found here, but so can a crowd consisting of hipsters, yuppies, and travelers. Some people come here for the shepherd's pie and $4 beers, some come for the live music (Sunday–Thursday), and others, like myself, come for the cool atmosphere and the weird shit on the walls (like a giant two-foot ear and an antique poster detailing the effects of alcohol and drugs on the body).

Milady's
160 Prince St. @ Thompson St.

The only impressive thing about Milady's is that it exists. It's about as un-Soho as possible, meaning it feels like a neighborhood bar with a decent jukebox, a pool table, regulars, beer signs, and sports on the tiniest bar TV ever. Who are these groups of cool-looking people drinking $4 Buds (very cheap for Soho) and eating average-priced bar food? Where do they come from? Where do they live? The world may never know. When I was last here I got this very drunk random Wall Street guy to by me a few drinks. The unfortunate part was that he ended up tagging along for the rest of the night and became the type of creepy drunk guy who is too wasted to talk, so he just hovers on the outskirts of all your conversations. Then, at some point a few hours later, I turned around and he was gone.

Nancy Whiskey Pub

1 Lispenard St. @ W. Broadway

When you walk into a bar at 7pm and the bartender is already drunk and being surly to someone on the other end of the phone, you know you're in a good bar. Then when you find out the bar food is super cheap ($2.50 for a personal pizza; a burger & fries for $5.25; 12 wings for $5.25), you know you're in a great bar. While the beers here are $4 ($2.50 at happy hour), Nancy makes it up by having the aforementioned cheap food and fucking shuffleboard. Hell yeah! By the looks of the place, it's a little rustic and even a bit rusty, but that just adds to its appeal. I mean it's a dive bar for fuck's sake; one with a cozy upstairs that you and your drunk friends can easily commandeer. Let me put it like this, it's the type of place where you might come one night, have a great conversation with someone not that attractive, drink too much Jameson, go home with that unattractive person, vow never to sleep with her again and end up becoming good friends with her because she's really cool. That's exactly the type of place this is. And yes, you end up sleeping with her once more.

The Patriot Saloon

110 Chambers St. @ Church St.

Recently liberated bras dangle from the ceiling, bearing silent witness to the mayhem below, while drunk young things struggle to hear each other's pickup lines over intolerably loud country music. Yes, this is a nightly scene here at the Patriot Saloon, a distinguished establishment where the bathroom is akin to a moist Petri dish and

hot female bartenders writhe and dance with each other, occasionally topless, on the bar. I don't generally like to get too technical, but in professional jargon, this saloon is what we in the industry call "a complete and utter fuckshow." What kind of volatile elements lead to such a deranged and wanton environment? The answer is simple: cheap drinks, very cheap drinks. Here one can procure a pitcher of Pabst Blue Ribbon for only $6, and pints of Stella and Guinness for $3.75 and $4, respectively. The also serve extremely inexpensive food like $1.25 burgers and 10 jumbo wings for $7. The ideology here is quite flawless; hire pretty and buxom women who flirt like strippers, encourage them to drink with patrons, give plenty of buybacks, and offer free shots to any female customer who dances on the bar. As if that wasn't enough, some genius of interior design hung a taxidermy alligator on a surfboard from the ceiling with bras dancing from its mouth just to show you how real party animals do it. I'm still seriously debating whether or not the Patriot Saloon is my own personal heaven or hell.

Raccoon Lodge
59 Warren St. @ W. Broadway

Like any solid dive bar with a woodsy cabin motif, the Raccoon Lodge is decorated with moose heads (I still think the plural should be "meese"), old tin gasoline signs, and the requisite suspended, upside-down, pink hippopotamus. This 25-year-old Tribeca mainstay also has a fake fireplace that becomes a fake fish bowl in the summer months and scores of hard hats (fire, police, construction) from 9/11. Best of all, it has PBR for $2.50. Strange and random bars attract strange and random patrons, so the crowd is part shirt-tucker stockbrokers, part beards and Misfits Ts, and part older, neighborhood people who hit on me and ask what I'm scribbling about. As expected with a place like this, the bartenders are damn cool and you can tell they strongly dislike entitled-feeling yuppies as much as I do.

Reade Street Pub & Kitchen
135 Reade St. @ Hudson St.

This place doesn't lie; it is a pub and it is on Reade Street. A mug of Bud is $3, a pint is $4 and the crowd is exactly what you'd expect it to be: after work people, locals, and the random, fat, 50-year-old drunk guy who tells you how much he likes your hat and how many "bitches he's got right now" (you know who you are). Actually this place is exactly what you'd expect in all regards. They just aren't big on surprises, I guess.

Shopping

While Soho is world famous for it's shopping, it isn't exactly known as a place to get shit for cheap. If you're looking for inexpensive things in this area, try Church Street in Tribeca. It's filled with cheap stuff like discount jewelry and luggage.

Girlprops

153 Prince St. btw W. Broadway & Thompson St.

Girlprops mostly just sells cheap and tacky jewelry and accessories. It's a lot like the chain Claire's that you see in every mall in the US, except that it doesn't do ear piercing and it's more risqué–it sells sexy leggings. Considering that feather boas here cost just $7.99, it's the perfect place to shop for costume party accessories or spice up your old drag queen outfit. I come here just to bask in its tackiness.

H & M

558 Broadway @ Prince St., *also* 515 Broadway btw Spring & Broome Sts.

See p. 211 (Midtown East) Did they really need two within two blocks of each other?

Housing Works Bookstore & Café

126 Crosby St. @ Houston St.

While Housing Works has thrift stores all over the city, this is their only bookstore. All 45,000 books and records have been donated and the money from the sales goes to helping homeless men, women, and children living with HIV and AIDS. I know this because it says so in big letters on the back wall. The place looks amazing, like an old library from a rich person's mansion that you see in the movies, and everything here is super cheap. Plus cute people hang out here, and if they are cute and hang out in a bookstore, they become hot. What more can you ask for in life than a good place to buy cheap books and meet cute people who like to read and hate AIDS? How about a place that also sells beer, has events, and gives out free condoms (because it would just be too ironic to get HIV from the hottie you met at the "Fuck AIDS" bookstore). Plus everyone who works here is a volunteer; so if you feel like pitching in, just ask how.

Kiosk

95 Spring St. btw Broadway & Mercer St.

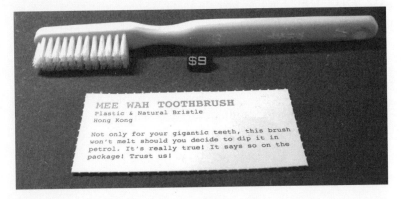

Kiosk totally gets it. It sees the grossness of our culture's obsession with hyper-consumption, which Soho has come to signify, and offers an alternative. Each piece in Kiosk is hand picked during the owners' travels and brought back to be sold in their shop. The items are chosen not because some fucking twit designer created them, but because they developed out of some actual need in whichever country they were found. And each item has a little blurb or story about it (kinda like this book). There are things like geisha cards, specialty kitchen knifes, a veggie peeler, kite-string spools, glass snuff bottles and suits made from feathers. Please go patronize this store to help ensure this gem will always be around.

Pearl River

477 Broadway between Grand & Broome Sts.

Everything that you've ever thought of as being associated with Asian people is carried in this store. They have birdcages, chopsticks, tea,

60-foot-long dragon kites, gongs, woks and even those awful Chinese instruments that sound like an injured bird getting beaten with an out-of-tune-violin. And they sell candy, too, delicious candy. There's also a 30-foot waterfall wall that leads you downstairs to where all the discounted stuff is. Everything said and done, Pearl River is really Asian lite; everything is made tolerable for white folks so they don't have to brave the madness of Chinatown.

Uniqlo
546 Broadway btw Prince & Spring Sts.

You know how the Japanese will import American subcultures like skateboarding and hip-hop, take them out of their context and then create an entire fashion movement centered around that subculture's aesthetic? And you know how sometimes it gets all screwed up and becomes a silly parody that makes everyone involved look stupid, while other times they do it so much better than us that it's scary? Uniqlo is an example of the latter. How is it possible to have so many ill t-shirt designs and sell them for only $15 each?

Sites & Entertainment

Evolution Nature Store

120 Spring St. @ Greene St.

When I was growing up, the San Diego Zoo had this two-headed snake which made the reptile exhibit doubly cool because it was also like going to a freak show. Topping a live two-headed snake is pretty hard, but Evolution Nature Store comes damn close by having a taxidermied two-headed calf. But that's not all this place has; there are alligator skulls, plaster human skulls from all eras of evolution, an ape skeleton, baby sharks, and I think even a baby human fetus skeleton in a jar! Easily the coolest store in Soho, the Evolution Nature Store been around for almost 15 years. And while it's too expensive for people like us to shop here, it's totally free to look around. Why is it that so much taxidermy ends up in my books? It's like I'm being haunted by tons of dead animals.

P.S. Do you know what a herpetologist is? No, it's not the person who diagnoses you at the clinic. It's someone who studies reptiles.

Ghostbusters Firehouse

14 N. Moore St. @ Varick St.

Sometimes, late at night, I worry that the EPA is gonna try to shut down the ghost containment facility in the basement again and paranormal activity will wreak havoc on the city. It's a terrifying thought.

Let There be Neon

38 White St. @ Church St.

By this point in the book, I haven't yet bombarded you with my fetish for neon lights. Just wait–you will be. I'd like to be buried here.

Museum of Comic and Cartoon Art

594 Broadway btw Houston St. & Prince Sts.

While MoCCA sounds like it might be a dating website for light-skinned brothas and sistas, it's actually the acronym for the Museum of Comic and Cartoon Art. Unfortunately the museum was closed for remodeling during my research, but it's set to reopen during the Fall of 2008 and will once again focus on teaching and preserving the awesomeness of comics and cartoons.

New York City Fire Museum

278 Spring St. btw Varick & Hudson Sts.

Located in a 1904 firehouse, this museum celebrates the long and interesting history of the NYFD. It's cool to see all the relics kept and maintained from the department's past, plus you get to learn stuff. Did you know that in the mid-to-late 19th century, many of New York's politicians started out as firemen? Being a fireman back then was like being in the Rotary Club now, except they got in a lot more gang fights and put out fires. The museum also has a very powerful memorial to those department members who died in 9/11. And it's only a *suggested* donation of $5 to get in, which really means you can pay whatever you want.

New York Earth Room

141 Wooster St. btw Houston & Prince Sts.

I am amazed that people are using this prime real estate for all this dirt. Who pays this rent? Whoever you are, I'd like to officially invite you to be a patron of the arts and help me pay my bills. Seriously, this shit is just ridiculous. Motherfucker rents a huge place in Soho and fills it with dirt ... if I did that shit in my place I'd get evicted, get fined for property damage and have fools saying shit like, "That dude Broke-Ass Stuart straight lost his mind. Did you hear he filled his whole apartment with dirt?" Shit, at least we don't have to pay to get in. P.S. It's on the second floor of a totally nondescript building and you have to get buzzed in.

Western Spirit

486 Broadway @ Broome St.

Even cowboys need a place to shop while they are in NYC and I guess Western Spirit is that place. While it's not cheap by any means, it's a great place to look around and try on coonskin hats. I met a 21-year-old Asian cowboy from East Texas who worked here, and who brought his horse with him when he moved to New York. Seriously. He stables it in Staten Island. When I walked in, Albert the Asian cow-

This is the only known photo of Albert the elusive Asian cowboy. Unfortunately, it's not enough hard evidence to put all the skeptics to rest.

boy was doing rope tricks, not to attract customers, but just for fun. I was so fascinated by him and asked him so many questions that I think I freaked him out. But really, that shit was like finding the Loch Ness Monster.

SOHO and TRIBECA

Grub-a-dub-dub
1. Café Duke
2. Ceci Cela
3. La Conquita
4. La Esquina
5. Lahore Deli
6. Ñ
7. Pepe Rosso
8. Ruben's Empanadas
9. The Soda Shop
10. Square Diner

DRINKS DRINKS DRINKS
11. Antarctica
12. Biddy Earlys
13. The Ear Inn
14. Milady's
15. Nancy Whiskey Pub
16. The Patriot Saloon
17. Raccoon Lodge
18. Reade St. Pub & Kitchen

Shopping
19. Girlprops
20. H&M
21. Housing Works Bookstore
22. Kiosk
23. Pearl River
24. UNIQLO

Stuffis to See and Do
25. Evolution Nature Store
26. Ghostbusters Firehouse
27. Let There Be Neon
28. Museum of Comic and Cartoon Art
29. New York Earth Room
30. NYC Fire Museum
31. Western Spirit

Free Food Bitches!!
32. Cupping Room Café

Street Meat
33. Calexico

17 year old models from Eastern Europe

Yet another famous person

Impenetrable herds of people spending more than they make

Paparazzi

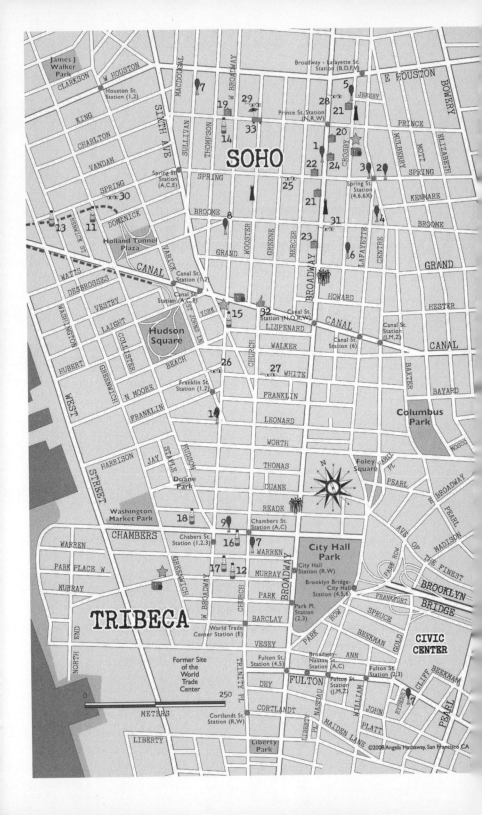

dear stuart.
4/4/06

hello, my name is paul alkaly and i am a huge fan of your work. i'm good friends with arik and those santa cruz kids that left early to go back home to LA. we are myspace friends, after all, so it's not like i'm a total stranger. anyways, usually when someone totally outshines me and puts me in my place (which is almost never, i'm amazing) i get very jealous and try everything in my power to bring misfortune to said person. i tell every girl he's trying to fuck he has an std, that sort of thing. but you, my friend, really really out did me. i've been saying for years how i would make an incredible guidebook. i'm a human thomas guide/lonely planet..i show everyone an amazing time when they come visit me in new york. it has become an artform, my calling card. except that i don't have a valuable asset to legitimize my work such as say ... hmmm ... i don't know ... my very own broke-ass stuart book? with such a book in hand i can achieve my dream of taking over the Wheeler dynasty in travel. so, bravo i say to you, bravo. now, since you have achieved this before i, it will be that much harder for me to do it myself. your book is amazing. it's really, really good. this is coming from someone who has read over 50 lonely planet guides, a few rough guides, and NFT guides for fun! i love armchair travel. i'm an armchair kind of guy. so i hope you take this as a complement. if you decide you want to do a guide to new york city, los angeles, or portland give me a ring. i'm not sure there is a better source of infor- mation available. in fact, if you put me in any country in the world, any time period, say ... rome 25 AD. i would be able to direct people to the coloseum, to get fucked at the vomitorium, grab a mean slice of pizza and achieve it all within a well planned day. what i'm trying to get at here is, you need me, i need you. Thank you very much for your time.

love. paul todd alkaly.

Lower East Side

These days the Lower East Side seems to be a neighborhood of cranes. Oddly shaped high-rise glass condos and hotels shoot towards the heavens, while greedy real estate developers stare at them, masturbating to the thought of how much money they're going to make. This is gentrification on amphetamines–quick and speedy without care for the ramifications. In fact, the neighborhood has changed so drastically in the past ten years that the National Trust for Historic Preservation put the *entire Lower East Side* on its 2008 list of America's Most Endangered Places. Let me repeat that, the *entire Lower East Side.* That's fucked up.

So what was it before? The Lower East Side was historically a working class neighborhood and the first stop for many immigrant groups on their path toward becoming part of America's cultural fabric. For most of the 20th century, it was a densely populated district filled with Germans, Poles, Italians and most famously Eastern European Jews, all living in crowded tenements and eking out livings in sweatshops and factories. As these populations became more prosperous and moved out of the neighborhood, they were replaced by other immigrant groups like Puerto Ricans and in more recent years, Chinese.

The last few decades of the 20th century were rough for the Lower East Side. For awhile it was as famous for its junkies and shooting galleries as it was for its immigrant past. Then, during the '90s, bars and restaurants began opening up in force, making the Lower East Side the crown jewel of downtown nightlife that it is today. Luckily, despite this neighborhood's hyper-gentrification, you can still find remnants of its unique past as the heart of New York's Jewish culture. Plus, if you're looking for cheap shopping, make sure to check out the Orchard Street Bargain District as well as some of the discount stores on Clinton and Delancey. The developers haven't figured out a way to make those upscale ... yet.

The **Lower East Side's** current boundaries are definitely E. Houston to the north and the East River to the east, and roughly Grand St. to the south and the Bowery to the west. Back before the mid-20th century though, the name Lower East Side also included the areas today known as the East Village, Chinatown, and Little Italy.

Food

Bereket Turkish Kebab House

187 E Houston @ Orchard

What's better than a delicious $6 chicken shawarma sandwich? A delicious chicken shawarma sandwich when you're drunk. Bereket is 24 hours, bitches!

Congee Village

100 Allen St. @ Broome St.

If a cheesy antique dealer teamed up with an Asian schoolgirl to design a moderately priced Chinese food restaurant in Disneyland, that place would look like Congee Village. You can't fucking resist now can you? What if I told you that they have oddly themed karaoke rooms that you can rent out with a group of friends? Yeah, it really is that sweet. The karaoke rooms vary in price by your group's size and the day of the week, but the good part is that you're not actually renting the room, you just have to meet a food and drink minimum. All I've gotta say is that this place just inspires shenanigans, so it's fun to see how much they will put up with before you get 86'd.

Doughnut Plant

379 Grand St. btw Essex & Norfolk Sts.

Did you ever think that you could afford something "designer" or "gourmet"? I never did until I went to the Doughnut Plant. While the goods here would be considered expensive if you held them to the standards of other doughnuts, you're still only spending $1-$2.50 for the best fried dough of your life. Plus the stuff comes in flavors you never thought possible: chai, lime, rosewater, roasted chestnut .... I wouldn't be surprised if they had an everlasting gobstopper flavor. The dude behind the doughnuts, Mark Israel, changes up the flavors every four to six weeks, so there's always something new and yummy for your cute little taste buds. Go to the Doughnut Plant and treat yourself to something fancy, and, while you're at it, get me a Tres Leche doughnut; they're disturbingly good.

P.S. Wanna know a random doughnut fact? In 1990, 90% of California's independent doughnut shops were owned by Cambodian immigrants. What you don't believe me? Google it.

Dumpling House

118 Eldridge St. @ Broome St.

Once famous because they sold five dumplings for $1, the Dumpling House has recently remodeled and much to everyone's chagrin (I love that word) now sells four dumplings for $1. You know that New York's property value has gone completely cuckoo when it starts to effect the price of dumplings. This shit is just getting ridiculous.

Essex

120 Essex St. @ Rivington St.

Normally if I put a $16 brunch in here you'd probably say, "Who does this motherfucker think he is? Talking about a $16 brunch and shit. Good for nothing bastard thinks that just because he sold a few books he's Donald fucking Trump ... shit ..." and normally I would totally agree. But this $16 brunch comes with booze! You get to choose between a Bloody Mary, a Mimosa, and a Screwdriver, and you get to make that decision three times (in fact they don't keep count so you can really get as many as you want)! This sweet deal is available on Saturday and Sunday from 10am–4pm, and then on Sunday evening they do a "sunset brunch" which is basically the same thing but from 4–8pm. See, would I lead you astray? Probably.

Guss' Pickles

85 Orchard St. @ Broome St.

They've been selling some of New York's best pickles since 1910 and you get two pickles for a buck. Yes, it's the simple pleasures in life that are often best for your word limit.

Katz's Deli

205 E. Houston St. @ Ludlow St.

It's not often in life that we get to take part in the best of something. I mean something that is so fucking good that every single authority on the matter ranks it in the top five of all time, like the movie *Casa-*

blanca or a 1965 Mustang. The hot pastrami sandwich at Katz's Deli is one of these. So I ask you, is $15 too much to pay for possibly the best sandwich on earth? How about when I tell you that it's so big that you have to take the second half home? I didn't think so. I would kill a motherfucker for one of those sandwiches right now.

Kossar's Bialys
367 Grand St. btw Essex & Norfolk Sts.

Kossar's Bialys looks a lot today like I imagine it looked back when it opened 65-plus years ago. The only differences are probably the spiffy new sign and the fact that instead of a middle age Jewish guy, there's a middle age Asian woman behind the counter. Sure the prices have probably changed too, but 70 cents for a bialy and 85 cents for a bagel aren't exactly what I'd call expensive. And guess what. They're the bomb, too. Fuck, is it still okay for me to call something "the bomb"?

Libation
137 Ludlow St. btw Rivington and Stanton Sts.

Saturday and Sunday from noon to 5pm, $19 gets you brunch and 3 drinks. It's not as good as the deal at Essex, but I figured you might be interested. Plus it's generally a little easier to get in here.

New Roma Pizza
116 Delancey St. @ Essex St.

There are about 38,000 great places in the LES to take someone on a date; New Roma Pizza is not one of them. Not that anyone would ever suggest that it was, but I know what it's like to see prices like $1.75 hamburgers, $3 baskets of wings and $2.50 organic whole-wheat pizza slices and think, "Jesus, I could totally afford to bring someone here on a date. I wonder if that cute Puerto Rican girl at the bank likes buffalo wings ...." The closest this late-night place will ever come to being a date spot is when you meet someone at a bar and stop in for a slice on the way home (so you don't end up puking all over her bed).

Russ & Daughters
179 E Houston @ Orchard St.

Okay so you moved to New York from _____ and back there you really didn't know a lot of Jewish people. Sure you went to that Rubinstein kid's bar mitzvah in seventh grade, but other than him and a couple of Chinese kids, your home town was as WASPy as it gets. Now you're in NY, dating a Jew, you're about to meet his/her parents for the first time. You wanna make a good impression. That's where Russ & Daughters comes in. Open since 1914 and having been run by four generations of the Russ Family, this is as old school New York Jew as it gets. Here's a tip from a fucking Jew (me) to someone who's fucking a Jew (you); buy your possible future in-laws some bagels and get some of Russ & Daughters' famous lox, herring, and cream cheese (tofu cream cheese if they're vegan) to go along with them. As long as you don't say, "I hear this is what you people eat," you should be golden.

Tiny's Giant Sandwich Shop
127 Rivington St. @ Norfolk St.

It's a wonderful thing to sit inside this square-shaped sandwich shop and peer out its big windows, hoping for a glimpse of the madness that once existed in the Lower East Side, but which now rarely seems to surface. While more and more sleek and shiny crap pops up around it, Tiny's seems intent on doing a rare thing in modern day Manhattan– provide generous helpings of good food at real people prices. I got a big-ass, excellent grilled chicken sandwich on a toasted bun for $4.75. Word! The staff here is super friendly, the rotating art exhibitions are usually pretty good, and did I mention that you could get a big, filling sandwich for $4.75?

Yonah Schimmel's Knishes
137 E. Houston St. @ Forsyth St.

Knish is a Yiddish word that roughly translates to "the best $3 you've spent in ages." What, you don't believe me? Then go to this spot and see for yourself. You can get pretty close to full from just one knish, and they've been hand-making yummy Jewy goodness here since 1910. It's hard to beat that.

Bars

151

151 Rivington St. btw Clinton & Suffolk Sts.

This basement-level bar, vaguely decorated like a nightclub VIP room in a Blaxploitation movie, is definitely one of the more solid places to drink in the Lower East Side. It's rarely too crowded, a Bud is $4 (which is unfortunately par for the course in the LES), and the music of choice is mostly punk and rock n' roll. One time my girl and I came here after seeing the amazing Kelli Rudick (www.myspace.com/kellirudick) play at the Rockwood Music Hall, and, although the bar has no particular leanings regarding sexual orientation, it must have been bi-night. "Why?" you ask. Because at one point when I walked away from the bar to chat with friends, the guy my girlfriend was talking to said, "Was that your boyfriend? He's hot! I wanna suck his cock and fuck you at the same time." Then a bit later on, while my lady and I were talking in a corner, some random girl approached us to inquire about a lost jacket and began casually stroking my arm. No we didn't end up in any orgies that night, but it made me think that if there are such things as bi-bars, they must be awesome because *everyone* ends up getting laid.

Home Sweet Home

131 Christie St. near Delancey St.

The chandeliers, concrete floor, brick walls and plastic cups all add to the ambience of this super-hip hangout, but anybody you ask will tell you that it's the taxidermy sprinkled in amongst all this stuff that really gives Home Sweet Home it's certain *je ne sais quoi*. You can always spot Home Sweet Home from the outside; not because of its sign (there is no sign), but because there is almost always some hipster kid standing outside smoking. This is particularly conspicuous because all the surrounding businesses are Chinese. But what I like about the hipsters here is that they all dress like they belong in *Vice* magazine's "Do" section as opposed to its "Don't" section. It's not like gross hipster overkill. The dance floor here is pretty big, and since there is always a DJ and never a cover charge, this spot can get pretty crackin'. My only comment is that I wish the drinks were a little cheaper.

Iggy's
32 Ludlow St. @ Rivington St.

Iggy's is kinda like a mix between a punk rock dive bar and an Irish pub, where different drink specials happen every night depending on who is bartending. For example, when Pirate Mike is working, PBR is $2, and, on most nights you can get a shot and a beer for $5. The music also varies by who's working. Some nights it's punk, others you hear Joy Division. Last time I was there I met a couple guys from Denmark who couldn't stop talking about how much they like railing girls from Amsterdam. One corner smelled faintly vomity (it *is* a dive bar after all), and that night I first heard one of my new favorite songs. It's called "She Rides" by Danzig. Go listen to it right now. Danzig is totally underappreciated.

Lolita
266 Broome St. @ Allen St.

Lolita is not exactly super cheap (they charge $4 for Yuengling), but it's pretty cheap for how "hip" it is. One side of the place has a big brick wall, and last time I was here, it was covered with vaginal-looking paintings. The crowd is generally a good mix and it's not overly bridge-and-tunnel, even on the weekends. This, combined with the great music, gives the place a groovy vibe. I went here one time with a friend I knew from back in SF and he ended up spilling his guts about the various female friends of mine he had sex with. There were some pretty good stories, including one about him fucking another friend's sister. Chalk that one up in the blackmail category for Stuart.

The Magician
118 Rivington St. @ Essex St.

For someone like me, who constantly waivers between feeling like an anachronism and feeling like I'm at the center of everything happening right now, the Magician is the type of place Match.com would hook me up with if I dated bars instead of women. Black and white checkered floor tiles, art deco ceiling lamps, vintage coat racks, and a couple of big windows with blinds make the bar look like something from an old noir film set in Los Angeles. Yet the crowd is (obviously) of this era. Even when busy, the patrons are always a nice assortment of everything the LES has to offer. The $4 Buds don't make it the cheapest bar, but the way the joint is set up, you always end up meeting some pretty cool people. Make sure to check out the old black and white pictures to see what the Lower East Side used to look like.

Motor City Bar
127 Ludlow St. @ Rivington St.

Yet another themed bar; this time the subject matter is America's most economically fucked big city, Detroit (sorry New Orleans). Did you know that Detroit's motto is *Speramus Meliora; Resurget Cineribus*, which translates to "We Hope For Better Things; It Shall Rise From the Ashes"? The fucked up thing is that it has been Detroit's motto since 1805, seriously. But hey, at least this bar is pretty good. PBRs are $3, there's tons Detroit memorabilia, and there's a half-naked girl dancing in the window on busy nights. Also, if your "type" is someone who wears lots of black and has many a tattoo, then you'll be happier than a fatty at an all you can eat buffet.

Parkside Lounge
317 E. Houston St. @ Attorney St.

The first time I came to the Parkside was with my girlfriend from fifth grade, her current boyfriend, and some friends of theirs. (She got me a Bo Jackson baseball card for Valentine's day when we were 10. How cool is that?) One of the best parts of living in New York is that so many random people from your life come through, and on those occasions, it's always a good to know of places with $3 PBR on tap and $5 well drinks. The Parkside is just such a place. Sure it's a little beat up looking inside, but that just means it's loved. What also makes it cool is that there are performances every night of the week that range from stand-up to bluegrass to experimental hip-hop. I guess what I'm saying is that the Parkside is really good at being a really good bar.

The Skinny
147 Orchard St. @ Stanton St.

The Skinny does not have black lights or a fog machine. Paul felt it was an important thing to inquire about and I had to agree with him. There is no such thing as knowing of too many places with fog machines. Despite that little shortcoming though, we came to the conclusion that the Skinny was a pretty decent place to hang out on a weeknight. The bartenders are super cool, PBRs are $2, there's never a cover, there's always a DJ, and if you're a lady looking for a little lady lovin', there's almost always a fair amount of lesbians hanging out. But I advise you not to go during the weekend, because they up the price of everything and just like the rest of the LES, the douchebaggery index reaches an astounding level. A fog machine would fix everything.

St. Jerome's
155 Rivington St. btw Clinton & Suffolk Sts.

Sorry about the streaked lights. The prospect of $2 Budweisers made my hands tremble from excitement.

I had a roommate when I first moved to New York who occasionally played records here. One night she came to my room and said, "Hey I'm gonna go DJ at this place called St. Jerome's tonight. Do you wanna come?" When I answered that I was too poor, she told me that not only would she pay for the car ride (she had to carry her records) but that St. Jerome's served $2 Buds until midnight, every night of the week. I think you've read enough of this book to know what my answer was to that; I ended up drinking a lot of $2 Buds. Since then, this small bar, with the comfy booths, low lighting, old school movies and a vagina chandelier (yes, you read that correctly), has become my go-to spot in the LES. The crowd here is always friendlier than they look and the bartenders appreciate it when you talk a little shit to them. I don't know who the hell Saint Jerome is, but the man sure knows how to run a drinking establishment (note to all you other saints: it's time to step up your game!).

Welcome to the Johnson's

123 Rivington St. @ Essex St.

This great LES dive feels as if someone opened a bar on the set of *That 70's Show* and invited all of his friends to come get wasted (including the one that always gets so drunk that he pisses on the carpet). It's also a good place to run into all your random broke-ass friends. My girl and I were here one night and ended up bumping into my friend Heather, who I've also crossed paths with in San Francisco and Barcelona. Good times! Especially since PBR is $2 and well drinks are $4. Long live the dive bar in all its glorious forms.

↓

Shopping

A.W. Kaufman Designer Lingerie

73 Orchard St. btw Grand & Broome Sts.

Honestly I don't even know if this place is well priced or not, but I couldn't resist putting it in here. Judging solely on the window display, I'd have to say the "unmentionables" sold here are more Golden Girls than Sex in the City. It's looks like lingerie for Hassidic Jewish women. I guess even if you're having sex through a hole in a sheet, a gal wants to feel sexy.

Bluestockings

172 Allen St. btw Stanton & Rivington Sts.

Even though I had been meaning to check out Bluestockings ever since the 4am Lower East Side night I first walked by, it wasn't until after a drunken bruncheon at Essex that I finally made it in. We came because my girlfriend's friend needed to buy a new Diva Cup (www. divacup.com), which is a little reusable silicone cup one can put up in her va-jay-jay* during her period, instead of using tampons or pads (which are bad for the environment). While the Diva Cup lost my interest fairly quickly, the amazing reading material that Bluestockings carries kept me entranced until we had to leave. They carry all kinds of books on topics like anarchism, feminism, the prison industrial system, anti-capitalism, queer and gender studies, and basically anything else that belongs in a great revolutionary bookstore like this. Plus they have a groovy organic café and do tons of cool events. Truthfully, Bluestockings reminds me of a lot of bookstores in San Francisco, but I'm damn glad it's here in New York.

Economy Candy Market

108 Rivington St. btw Essex & Ludlow Sts.

An entire store piled from the floor to the ceiling with candy. No worries, this is America; we all have free dental insurance. Right?

This is the most ridiculous word I've ever heard.

Essex St. Market

120 Essex St. btw Delancey & Rivington Sts.

Started in 1940, by Mayor Fiorello LaGuardia to get the pushcarts venders off the claustrophobic clusterfuck of the Lower East Side's streets, the Essex St. Market has become a center for affordable gourmet food. Now I'm not gonna sit here and say everything here is dirt cheap, but because it's a city building, all the purveyors benefit from city subsidies which allows their food to be a lot cheaper than anything you'll find at other gourmet food stores. And what's even better is that the market has a lot more than just cheesemongers, fishmongers and whatever other things that can be monged! There's a smoothie place, an outdated electronics stall, an art gallery, a joint that makes really weird cakes, a religious iconography botanica, and a British tailor who looks like he's 300 years old. Even if you're not gonna buy anything, it's a great place to wander around, especially when you stop in for a free sample at Roni-Sue's Chocolates.

New Era Factory Outlet, Inc

63 Orchard St. @ Grand St.

This is one of quite a few places in the area where you can get really inexpensive menswear. You can get a three-piece suit for as little as $99! It'll be interesting to see how long stores like this are around though; the Orchard Street Bargain District will probably not have any bargains at all in 10 years. If you're a developer, you can suck my dick.

Ted's Formal Wear

155 Orchard btw Rivington & Stanton Sts.

I found Ted's the way that I often find the stranger things that end up in these books: by wandering around. As soon as I walked in, I realized that if someone wanted to pick one thing that perfectly encapsulated the changes the LES has gone through in recent years, it would be Ted's Formal Wear. Ted started the store over 30 years ago as one of the many places in the Orchard Street Bargain District to get a decent price on dressy clothes. Eventually his son Charlie took over the family business and recently began selling rock n' roll T-shirts along side the cummerbunds, bow ties, and cuff links. Charlie told me the shirts are selling so well, he might just stop ordering the fancy clothes altogether. The shirts start at $10 and are some of the coolest rock T-shirts I've ever seen. Go see for yourself.

Sights & Entertainment

ABC No Rio

156 Rivington St. @ Clinton St.

Remember when you moved to New York and you thought places like the Village and the Lower East Side would be filled with really cool, artistic people doing unique and creative things? Then remember how you realized the battle for Manhattan was lost, that the assholes had won, and that most of the people doing these amazingly creative things were all actually living in Brooklyn? While all these things you felt were true, I'm happy to tell you that there are still some strongholds of creativity that have weathered New York's new blandness, and one of them is ABC No Rio. This former squat (which is now there legally) is a social center and community resource for all of us who want to do things outside of the normal means of production. They have a darkroom, a silks-screening studio, a computer lab, and even a zine library, all of which are available for free or for very little money. Beyond these things, ABC No Rio also has gallery, studio, and work space, and also hosts weekly punk matinees and provides a kitchen for NYC's Food Not Bombs. And, fucking AND!!! the people there are super supportive and helpful to newcomers. I'm not kidding when I say that ABC No Rio is the perfect example for the case against capitalism.

Cake Shop

152 Ludlow St. btw Stanton & Rivington Sts.

Remember that time in college when you and your buddies were sitting around smoking a blunt, talking about what you would do if you found a pot of gold, and you said, "You know what I would do, man? I would open up this café right, and in the back there'll be a fucking record store! How dope does that sound? Wait, wait, wait even better! Downstairs will also be this sick music venue with a full bar, and upstairs in the café, hey pass that shit fucker, upstairs in the café we'll sell mostly vegan pastries." It really was a damn good idea, and some-

one with more motivation than a stoner actually made it a reality and called it Cake Shop. Cake Shop rocks, and since it has free Wi-Fi, it's actually better than the place you imagined when you were stoned. But don't worry; the fact that the Salvation Army probably furnished it and the decor is mostly X-mas lights, photos and record covers, means that it looks a lot like the apartment where you first thought of the concept.

The Mercury Lounge

217 E. Houston St. btw Ludlow & Essex Sts.

When I was in Ireland I became really friendly with some guys from a band called the Thrills. While they're huge in Europe (they've opened for U2), they're relatively unknown here in the States, so when the band came to New York, they played the moderately priced and intimate Mercury Lounge. My girl and I had a 4am flight the morning after the Thrills show because we were going to SF for the big book release party for *Broke-Ass Stuart's Guide to Living Cheaply in San Francisco* (which was fucking awesome!). Normal people would be content seeing the show, having one with the band afterwards, and then going home to catch a little sleep before the flight. But me, I'm a fucking idiot. I convinced myself and my girlfriend that it would be way better to party with the band all night, catch a cab home in time to change clothes, and then go to the airport. Needless to say, by the time we got to JFK, we were both crashing, and I had to pace up and down the terminal for fear that I'd fall asleep and we'd miss our flight. Since I don't sleep on planes, I ended up getting pretty sick and couldn't talk for a few days. Yeah, I'm a winner ... ugh.

New Museum

235 Bowery @ Prince St.

People are excited about the New Museum. It just opened at its new location on the Bowery at the end of 2007, and for a lot of New York art people (meaning rich art snobs, not your talented friend in Bush-wick), this is a breath of fresh air. Besides it being housed in a boxy building that's being heralded as architecturally brilliant, it showcas-es the hot new shit of the art world; the type of art that's supposed to upend the current establishment. The museum's mission statement is simple: "New art. New ideas." Sounds like something you can dig? If your answer is "Hell, yes!" then go on Thursday nights from 7–10pm when admission is free (it's normally $12).

Rockwood Music Hall

196 Allen St. btw E. Houston & Stanton Sts.

In a town where there's practically a cover charge to go to the liquor store, Rockwood Music Hall does something beautiful and unthink-able: it charges nothing for admittance. Sure the drinks in this tiny place aren't the world's cheapest, but fuck it, the music here is almost always amazing, and like I said before, free. But if you do wanna sup-port the musicians, buy a CD or toss a couple bucks in the urn that gets passed around after each set.

The Slipper Room

167 Orchard St. @ Stanton St.

Let's face it, burlesque is hot, and, in its own way, classy too. You've got a stage where pretty girls dance and perform to great music while stripping down to a pair of glittery pasties and panties. And what's so cool about the Slipper Room is that it feels so old school and unique that, as a guy, you don't feel pervy for being there. In fact there's tons of girls there to see the show, too. I mean, how could you not want to hang out in a low-lit place with blue-and-red-checkered floors and plush booths made from fake gator and snakeskin? Sure there are minor drawbacks, like a $5 cover, $4 PBRs and $6 mixed drinks, but look at it like this: where else can you see superb burlesque most nights of the week? It's not a rhetorical question; I've already been 86'd from Scores and Flashdancers and those aren't even burlesque.

It's true. If we go out to dinner, I'll finish before you and then try to eat some of your food too. Photo by Nicki Ishmael.

LOWER EAST SIDE

Grub-a-dub-dub
1 Bereket Turkish Kebab House
2 Congee Village
3 Doughnut Plant
4 Dumpling House
5 Essex
6 Guss' Pickles
7 Katz's Deli
8 Kossar's Bialys
9 Libation
10 New Roma Pizza
11 Russ & Daughters
12 Tiny's Giant Sandwich Shop
13 Yonah Schimmel's Knishes

DRINKS DRINKS DRINKS
14 151
15 Home Sweet Home
16 Lolita
17 The Magician
18 Motor City Bar
19 Parkside Lounge
20 The Skinny
21 St. Jerome's
22 Welcome to the Johnson's

Shopping
23 A.W. Kaufman Designer Lingerie
24 Bluestockings
25 Economy Candy Market
26 Essex St. Market
27 New Era Factory Outlet, Inc.
28 Ted's Formal Wear

Stuffis to See and Do
29 ABC No Rio
30 Cake Shop
31 Mercury Lounge
32 New Museum
33 Rockwood Music Hall
34 The Slipper Room

Free Food Bitches!!
35 Boss Tweed's
36 Iggy's

Herbivore Friendly
37 Teany
38 Tiengarden

Someone enjoying the best sandwich in the world

High-rise condo going up

Puke pile from Saturday night's binge drinking

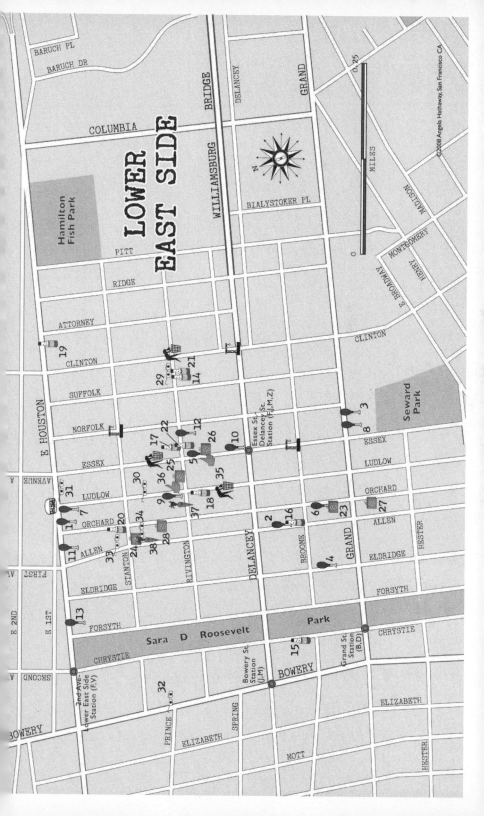

East Village

You can hear the death rattle in the lungs of the East Village. After spending the last half century as the standard by which all things cool and radical were measured, this neighborhood is quickly becoming the thing it has always railed against: ordinary. Now don't get me wrong, the East Village is still happening and teeming with some of the best cheap restaurants and bars in the nation. But the neighborhood that incubated the Beats, birthed punk, and added grit and gravel to rock n' roll, is nothing more than the shadow of the hero it once was. It's like watching Muhammad Ali in the last fights of his career: something very special is at the end of a long and glorious run.

Originally considered part of the Lower East Side, the East Village got its current name in the early 1960s when it metamorphosed from a dodgy, working-class neighborhood of Eastern European and Latino immigrants to the home of artists, writers and musicians from the burgeoning counterculture (the name "East Village" was derived from the fact that it was directly east of Greenwich Village). Around this hotbed of bohemian lifestyle and maverick ideals grew a community of bars, restaurants, shops and venues created by and for the odd assortment of people who called the neighborhood home. St.

Mark's Place became the center of this scene and its characteristically quirky shops still inspire teenage goths and punks to loiter all day in an attempt to tap into the neighborhood's edgy past. Nobody has the heart to tell them that the growing presence of NYU, the gentrification of Alphabet City and the cleaning up of the Bowery has effectively sanded down that edge to something far safer and more dull.

Despite these changes, though, the East Village is still the East Village. The abundance of cheap food, drinks and activities means it's still the best place in Manhattan for a broke-ass to have a good time. You can still eat amazing meals from all parts of the world for less than $10, find dirt cheap drinks (if you know where to look), and the neighborhood's history of going against the grain can be seen on any street corner. But as penny loafers, blazers, striped shirts and $2,000 rents replace Chuck Taylors, leather jackets and T-shirts, let's hope the neighborhood retains the soul that made it our hero in the first place.

As for what constitutes **the East Village**, its the space between E. 14th St. to the north, E. Houston St. to the south, the Bowery/4th Ave. to the west and the East River to the east.

Shut the fuck up:

Look I get it; I missed your favorite spot in the East Village. Do you know how many dope, cheap things are in this neighborhood? I could probably have written an entire book on this hood alone. So because of that I'm leaving this first entry blank, and you can write your own review of that place where you passed out drunk in the bathroom with your pants at your ankles and half a bag of coke on your upper lip. Then you can go to brokeassstuart.com and post the story yourself:

_____

_____

_____

_____

_____

Food

Atlas Café
73 2nd Ave btw. 4th & 5th Sts.

If you dream of a world where veggies and meaties can stop their endless war and come together to share a table, or some wine, or even a goddamn gargantuan menu, then Atlas Café is your utopian vision come to fruition. Really, the menu at this diminutive restaurant takes up an *entire* wall, and it's not like 11th grade English class when you would change the font to make the paper look longer; no this shit is dense, too. Most restaurants say that they have something for everyone, and those places are fucking liars. This one really does. The menu has lobster ravioli, vegan couscous, sweet and savory crepes, grilled chicken paninis and even *vegan fucking soft serve!* The Vegan Oreo Milkshake (peanut butter, Oreos, bananas, tofu ice cream, soy milk and chocolate) is seriously dope. And the part that makes this little beauty absolutely broke-tastic is that almost everything on the menu is under $7. The Atlas Café is really one step closer to Peace in the Middle Feast (ugh … and I just took that one step too far).

B & H Dairy & Vegetarian Restaurant
127 2nd Ave. @ St. Mark's Pl.

This skinny little diner with the long lunch counter is perfect for all you veggies and Semites out there who love greasy spoon diners but are well, veggies or Semites. While there isn't any meat served here, they do have challah French toast for $4.50 and potato knishes with veggie gravy for $2.75. Sounds good right? I'm just weirded out by the fact that there's a vegetarian greasy spoon diner. It's like vegetarians think they're real people or something.

BAMN!
37 St. Mark's Pl. @ 2nd Ave.

What I thought was some weird imported idea from Japan (like a food version of those hotels the Travel Channel always shows where people sleep in little capsules) was apparently really common in New York back in the day. Basically you put some coins in a machine and then open the compartment to grab your food. The grub isn't half bad (it's supposedly made fresh every 15 minutes) and nothing costs more than $2. I don't know if it's the pink lights, the cheap prices or the fact that most people who eat here are drunk, but the nighttime vibe here is kinda like someone was throwing an irony party. Regardless, it's hard to pass up $2 teriyaki burgers and mozzarella sticks in a pink place bumping Tupac.

Birdies

149 1ˢᵗ Ave. btw 9ᵗʰ & 10ᵗʰ Sts.

I didn't start eating vegetables until my 20s. I'd tolerate simple things like carrots and lettuce, but that was about it. While I've gotten a lot better, there are still ones I completely despise (I'm looking at you, onions and cauliflower). Needless to say, I've got a fairly shitty diet, which is why Birdies is great. They've taken it upon themselves to make fried chicken slightly less awful for your body by using only free-range, no-antibiotic chicken. And it's cheap, too! For $5.95 you get three big pieces of chicken. What was that? You don't eat meat? Never fear, Birdie is looking out for you, too (Birdie is actually the owner's grandma). They have an entire veggie "chick'n" menu for those of you who are less meat inclined. So now you have no excuse. See you there.

Elvie's Turo-Turo

214 1ˢᵗ Ave. @ E. 13ᵗʰ St.

I grew up with mad Filipinos (and was arrested with two of them) so I have a certain place in my heart for *lumpia*. The big dishes here are $9 and the small ones are $5. But I prefer getting a few side orders like the giant lumpia ($1.50) and bbq chicken skewers ($2.50). Personally I like that all their straws came from the recently closed Popeye's next door.

Jennifer Café

On the corner of E. 4ᵗʰ St. & 1ˢᵗ Ave.

I had been itching to try this place out for a while because the prices (three tacos for $5) reminded me of taquerias back in California, and the employees were from Vera Cruz. This matters because most Mexicans in NY come from Oaxaca or Puebla, whereas most Mexicans in San Francisco come from the Yucatan and Vera Cruz. So basically I was hoping that it would taste like SF Mexican food. Anyway, the verdict is that it's pretty damn good; not California good, but damn good. However, they have no seats and they use way too much Styrofoam, which is bad for the environment. Mother Earth is a sexy bitch!

Kate's Joint

58 Ave. B @ E. 4th St.

While this big, hip veggie/vegan joint may not be the cheapest thing in this book, it makes up for it by being really, really good at being a big, hip veggie/vegan joint. The menu is huge, the food is tasty, the music is good and they have a full bar. You can even wash your fake meat/fake cheese Philly cheese steak down with a $2 PBR. (Did you hear that? That was the sound of thousands of vegan hipsters squealing with joy.) Dude, they can even make fettuccine alfredo with fake cream. Make sure you stop in during their happy hour (Mon–Thurs, 12–9pm) for cheaper drinks and daily food deals.

Kenka

25 St. Mark's Pl. btw 2nd & 3rd Aves.

Oh Kenka ... Kenka ... Kenka ... Kenka. You are one of the weirdest fucking places I've ever eaten in in my entire life and for that, I salute you. I'm sitting here in front of my computer trying to find the proper words with which to describe you and the only thing that keeps popping into my head is "bull penis". Yes, bull penis. You sell bull penis. To be eaten. By people. For $5.50 a pop. And yet there is more to your menu than just penises, squid beaks and cow tongues; there's also the drawing of a guy sticking a revolver up the ass of a bound, half-naked chick. While I'll admit that I am just pointing out some of your more ... er, colorful qualities, it must be noted that *everything* on your menu is amazingly cheap. Most of your food (including your far more normal dishes) rings in at around $5–$7 and you sell beers for $1.50 each or $8 a pitcher. That my friend is beautiful; almost as beautiful as the scores of vintage bondage-porn posters that line your sacred walls or the rules written on the bottom of your menu saying "No fighting, masturbating, having sex or drugs. You will be ejected." Kenka, you're my kind of place, and I just wanted to say thanks for the cotton candy that you give out at the end of the meal; it helps to get rid of the lingering bull cock taste.

P.S. For those interested, I think Kenka is only written in Japanese on the outside sign, which can make it harder to find when searching for it.

Maoz
59 E. 8th St. @ Mercer St.
See p. 172 (Union Square)

Otafuku
236 E. 9th St. btw 2nd & 3rd Aves.

Otafuku is a tiny Japanese fast food spot where the only seating is a single bench outside. The specialty here is *takoyaki,* a type of octopus dumpling, but noodles and pork dishes round out the small menu. As strange as it all sounds, people seem to love this shit, and there can sometimes be a line. But Otafuku has you covered; they put their own trash can out on the curb with menus pasted all over it so you can ponder what to eat while you refrain from being a litterbug.

Papaya Dog
239 1st Ave. @ E. 14th St.

Not nearly as awe inspiring as the one on p. 124 (West Village)

Panna II and Milon
93 1st Ave @ E. 6th St.

What do Panna II and Milon have in common with KRS-One and MC Shan, Dr. Dre, Easy-E, Jay-Z and Nas? Mad beef, that's what! There are various rumors as to which of these cheap and tasty Indian/Pakistani/Bengali restaurants was there first and who copied whose "motif", but there is no doubt that the employees at these two eateries will do anything to get you into their spot and not their neighbor's. I've been grabbed, prodded, harangued, goosed, tickled and massaged, sometimes by the two competitors at the same time. And while I'll have to admit I do like being fussed and fawned over, I'm always afraid a fight is gonna break out over little, old me. I bet these guys share a kitchen and are probably just beefin' to sell more food, just like Kanye and 50 beefed over records. Regardless, you should check out these spots because the food is cheap and good and the décor is that of a psychedelic Christmas party. Make sure to tell them that it's someone in your party's birthday. Trust me on this one.

Punjabi

114 E. 1st St. btw 1st and 2nd Aves.

If Craigslist were a real place that only catered to cab drivers who hailed from the Indian subcontinent, that place would be Punjabi. Flyers offering various services abound, while Hindi tapes and DVDs sit stacked behind the counter ready for some homesick cabbie to purchase them. But me, I'm not an Indian cab driver (nor am I a Pakistani or Bengali one) so I go to Punjabi for the dirt-cheap 24-hour grub. Here samosas go for a buck while the most expensive plate you can buy comes out to three roti and two veggie choices for $5. If it's not too cold or wet outside, you'll find me chowin' down on the stoop next door with the rest of the kids.

Sushi Park

121 2nd Ave. @ 7th St.

If you eat here for dinner, they give you 50 percent off all your sushi, sashimi and maki. Seriously. Fuck atmosphere, fuck drink prices, fuck all the other dumb shit that I talk about; they sell sushi here for 50 percent off. And it's actually good, too! I don't know how they do it. The only catch is that you have to order a minimum of something like $14 worth of food–but really, who cares? It only comes out to seven bucks anyway. I just want to thank Sushi Park for helping to nourish the Broke-Ass Revolution.

Tuck Shop

68 E. 1ˢᵗ St. btw 1ˢᵗ & 2ⁿᵈ Aves.

I've never been to Australia, but if Tuck Shop is any indication of anything, then meat (and veggie) pies are pretty popular down there. Ranging from $3–$6, these hand held food thingies are decent sized and while they may not be able to make you groaning-in-the-corner-balled-up-in-the-fetal-position full, they will definitely hold you over between meals. And just to keep with the Aussie theme, the toilets here flush backwards and the owners sometimes import vegemite to sell. Okay, I lied about the toilet thing.

Yaffa Café

97 St. Mark's Pl. between 1ˢᵗ Ave. & Ave. A

No write up about the East Village would be complete without the inclusion of Yaffa Café. I love the fuck out of this place, but not for the usual reasons. The food isn't really that amazing and the prices are just a tad more expensive than what I'd consider cheap. So what makes this place so great? It's got mad soul. And I don't mean "soul" in the way kinda racist white people use the word to describe hip things created by black people. I mean soul in the sense that there's something ineffably cool about Yaffa Café. It's a 24-hour joint that has excellent wallpaper (zebra, floral, and even that faux Victorian one with the velvet designs), cow-print tables, leopard-print seats, random hanging beads and off-colored X-mas lights. It's kinda like what I imagine the inside of Cyndi Lauper's vagina to look like. And since the restaurant is on St. Mark's and is "open all nite", you get an awesome variety of people who dine here. So here's my advice: next time you're having a late night in the East Village, stop in for a bite at Yaffa. You might just see me there.

Bars

7B (Vazacs Horseshoe Bar)

108 Ave. B @ 7th St.

Remember that part in *The Godfather II* when the guy comes up behind Frank Pentangeli and says, "Michael Corleone says hello" and then starts to strangle him, but a cop comes in and it turns into a shoot out? Yeah, that was filmed here. Apparently the real name of this spot is Vazacs Horseshoe Bar, but everyone just calls it 7B because it's on um ... 7th and B. Ugh, I really wish I could get it together today and tell you that this bar is awesome because PBR is $3, the bartenders manage to be both sweet and surly, the horseshoe-shaped bar is giant, and there are private booths as well, but I just can't find my funny right now. You know what I mean? I guess all I can say otherwise is that the bar is always busy; it can be a little too college-y later on in the week and *play Big Buck Hunter!*

Ace Bar

531 E. 5th St. @ Ave. A

Yes, the rumors are true. Ace Bar has a Skee-ball league. League nights equal many drink specials, which in turn equal many drunken people. The competition gets pretty fierce and tempers can fly; Skee-ball is not a gentleman's sport. It's cutthroat, goddammit! You've been warned.

Blarney Cove

510 E. 14th St. btw Aves. A & B

The bartenders here are *super* New York. They speak with thick local accents and spit out homespun witticisms like "shit or get off the pot". That's what one gruffly said to some drunk college kid who ordered too slowly. PBR here is $3 a pint, well drinks are $4, and the white-and-green, candy-striped wallpaper kinda makes me want to lick it and see if schnozzberry tastes like schnozzberry. But I think licking this wallpaper would make me come down with some old school Oregon Trail-style disease, like diphtheria, and get me kicked out and beaten up, too. Considering that the vibe is totally blue-collar, old-man bar, there is a surprising amount of cute young things here on the weekend nights. It's actually mind-boggling.

Blue & Gold Tavern

79 E. 7th St. @ 1st Ave.

There must be some type of conspiracy going on because otherwise, all the things that I know to be true in this world would be suddenly proven false. When I first saw the prices at Blue & Gold I harangued the bartender saying, "There has to be something wrong here. Is the person in charge of writing the drink prices on the chalkboard so utterly dyslexic that he (or she) jumbled up every single number up there? Jesus, if you're gonna employ the kid for this line of work, at least pay so he (or she) can take some classes to help with his (or her) learning disabilities. Otherwise, you're just a dick for getting your jollies by laughing at another person's misfortune." Then I realized that while the bartender was actually dyslexic, the prices were written correctly and it was I who was apparently the dick. But come on, if you walked into a bar in Manhattan and saw Maker's Mark for $4, Skyy for $3 and Red Bull and vodka for $4, wouldn't you think there was something going on? Other things you should know about this place are that the pool table is red, the jukebox is good, there are weird family photos on the back wall, and that it gets way too packed on weekends.

The Boiler Room

86 E. 4th St. @ 2nd Ave.

Do you know how hard it is to find a good, cheap, gay, dive bar in New York? There are plenty of bars that are any combination of good/cheap/gay/dive, but not really that many that comprise all of these traits. Trust me, I've spent *a lot* of time in *a lot* of bars in this city. What makes Boiler Room a good, cheap, dive bar? A pool table, touch screen games, and strong $3 well drinks after 10pm. What makes Boiler Room a gay bar? Guys blowing each other in the bathroom.

Cheap Shots

140 1ˢᵗ Ave @ 9ᵗʰ St.

Maybe all bars should do this. Like, instead of naming your bar "Arctica", you should name it, "Cheesy Bar with Moderately Priced Drinks and a Whole Lot of Bridge and Tunnel Fuckfaces." It would save everyone a whole lot of time. Thankfully, Cheap Shots had this foresight and gets straight to the point; they sell cheap shots at this establishment. In fact, everything they sell here is cheap. Shots are around $2; you can get a shot and a beer for like $5, pitchers of Yuengling are $8 and every night of the week they have some type of ridiculous deal, like Mondays when $10 gets all you can drink domestic beer. And if you show up on your birthday, you drink for free. Because of the prices, the clientele ends up being everything from hipsters to frat boys to the random Chinese lady who sells cigarettes from her little cart.

Continental

25 3ʳᵈ Ave. @ 9ᵗʰ St.

Continental was once on the second tier of legendary New York rock clubs; kinda like a step down in legendariness from CBGB or the Fillmore East (Bill Graham's Fillmore East, not that fake one currently at Irving Plaza). But now the music is over at Continental and all we have to console us are ridiculously cheap drinks. How ridiculously cheap? They sell five shots for $10, every night of the week. That's almost sadistic. And every night in the early part of the week has some type of special like $1 Buds. Even on weekends the prices are good considering that all shots are $2.50 all the time. But there's more to Continental than just cheap hooch. There's also the sweet collection of vintage illuminated beer ads, there's the cute bartenders and then there's Trigger, the eccentric bar manager who always wears one of those straw hats people wear in rice paddies in Asia. He's hard to miss.

Cooper 35

35 Cooper Square @ 3ʳᵈ Ave.

This is basically a college spot with an outside patio that has $4 drinks and free edamame every day but Friday and Saturday. The inside is pretty nice, almost bordering on classy and I think their bar food is pretty cheap too. There's not much else to say, so I won't.

Crocodile Lounge
325 E. 14th St. btw 1st and 2nd Aves.

Put your hands out in front of you and imagine they were holding a personal-sized cheese pizza. Can you see it? If this were the Crocodile Lounge, there would be an actual pizza in that space, which means that you would have just bought a drink, been given a ticket, played some Skee-ball, and then redeemed that ticket for that free, cheesy round thing now balanced in your palms. But chances are you're not in the Crocodile Lounge, are you? This means that you're actually sitting in the subway staring at your hands and salivating. Do you know how creepy that looks?

Croxley Ales
28 Ave. B btw E. 2nd & E 3rd Sts.

What is it about the prospect of Buffalo wings that can drive a man to do foolish things? Is it the anticipation of holding, smelling, and tasting those crispy little devils that drives us to give fate (unyielding heartburn) the middle finger? Or is it the belief that through sheer tenacity (beer) we can conquer any challenge, overcome any obstacle, and climb any mountain, even if that mountain is a heaping pile of crispy fried and delicious Buffalo wings? Croxley Ales exploits this flaw in the human genome by selling 10-cent wings on Mondays and Wednesdays with the condition that you purchase a beer (which only costs $4). The exploitation is in the fact that the minimum order of wings is 20; a few too many for a man riding solo, despite what his ego says. I found this out the hard way. And if $2 for wings is too much for you, drop by on Friday from 5-7pm and get those fuckers for free.

Doc Holliday's
141 Avenue A @ E. 9th St.

Statistically speaking, if you go to Doc Holliday's on a Tuesday night there is a 64.8 percent chance that you'll end up in jail. These are numbers, baby, and numbers don't lie. Since Tuesdays are all you can drink Bud Light ($7 from 8–11pm), ending up in the drunk tank is simply a cold, hard lesson in getting your comeuppance. Blacking out, dancing on the bar, going home with someone uglier than you, getting in a fight, getting head in the bathroom, going home with someone better looking than you, getting bruises/scrapes/cuts you don't remember, and puking on your new shoes are also forms of what your mother would call, "getting what you deserve". Sounds like fun doesn't it? And if you're a female (genetically or otherwise) and can't make Tuesday night, Monday is "Ladies Night" where the fairer sex gets to drink all the tap beer and well liquor they want for $5 from 8–11pm. Needless to say, Mondays are a big lesbian night at Doc Holliday's.

Grassroots Tavern
20 St. Mark's Pl. btw 2nd & 3rd Aves.

Just as the taste of Budweiser on draught (served here for $3 a pint) has the unmistakable flavor of a high school kegger, the musty odor of the Grassroots Tavern has that hard-to-forget smell that can mean only one thing: dive bar. And if the aroma isn't enough to make your brain register "cheap place to get drunk with unsavory characters", then the wall-to-wall wood, embossed tin ceiling, and angry at the world bartender will. Given that the Grassroots has been around for over 30 years, I'm willing to bet that it saw a lot of punk rock mayhem in the '80s. These days, though, the crowd is a good mix of college kids, old man drunks, devoted darts players and hip kids wearing fingerless gloves. Other than the cheap drinks and the dilapidated darts trophies, my favorite thing about the bar is that on weeknights, the place is big and empty enough that you and your friends could have as many tables as you'd like. Who's down to play some motherfucking dominos?

Holiday Cocktail Lounge
75 St. Mark's Place btw 1st & 2nd Aves.

This is a classic and perfect dive bar where the prices ($4 whiskey, $3 beer) and atmosphere reflect what this neighborhood was (bohemian and working class) instead of what it's becoming (a cluster-fuck of gentrification). If you read the poster-sized story on the wall you'll learn that the current owner bought the bar in 1965 (it's been a bar since 1936) and that both Leon Trotsky and W.H. Auden used to drink here. The jukebox is great and has dope shit like Dr. John, Ray Charles and Johnny Cash. Whether I'm sitting at the crescent-shaped bar or at one of the back booths, I always think to myself that I wish this bar were closer to my house (which I never actually had while living in NY because I moved about every two months). The best time to stop by is during the day when you're guaranteed to get served by the 90-something-year-old owner.

Karpaty Pub

142 2nd Ave. @ 9th St.

I ended up at Karpaty Pub one night while I was doing some bar research with a random guy I worked with for a week. It was Monday, so it was dead, and the only people in the place were the owner, who just sat in the back texting someone, the bartender, and a guy who was very excited to tell us that Blues Traveler once played there. There are many things that make Karpaty Pub a very strange bar. For example, if one wishes to use the bathroom, one must go through a back door into a random business building, past a Ukranian restaurant and down some stairs. It's also a meeting place for NYC's Libertarian Party and has been host to a few Dungeons & Dragons games. How do I know? The fairly cute and very nerdy bartender (she was wearing a Star Wars T-shirt, un-ironically) proudly told us because she was the one responsible for bringing these activities to the bar. As much as I love D&D, the highlight for me was that the Buds are always $2. This holds true even on weekends when the place is packed with the youngest looking crowd of 21-year-olds you'll ever see. Catch my drift?

Mona's

224 Ave. B @ E. 13th St.

Any bar with a framed photo of the Band from the inside cover of *Music from Big Pink*, is automatically cool in my eyes. That album is just too good. Seriously, "Tears of Rage" might just be a perfect song. I mean, Richard Manuel sings like a grown-ass man and he can't be over like 23. Fucking brilliant! But you know what else makes this a cool bar? $2 PBRs, a great jukebox, and a big back room where the spaces between the brick walls are covered in murals.

Mars Bar

25 E. 1st St. @ 2nd Ave.

Have you ever come across someone who is such a total fucking asshole that they're proud of being an asshole? In fact, they're so proud of being one and doing such overtly asshole-ish things, that they end-up becoming a parody of an asshole. Like they'll do or say something fucked up, not because they necessarily mean it, but because that's what assholes are supposed to say and do. You follow me? Well if Mars Bar was a person, it would be that person. If you've never been there, Mars Bar is pretty much the last of the old East Village/Lower East Side punk bars. It smells like shit, the walls are completely covered in graffiti, the jukebox only plays punk, the shots are poured huge, and the patrons are old, surly or both. These are all good things that help make a respectable dive bar. But when you ask the bartender for some soap (because some big punk fucker licked your friend's face, uninvited, and she wants to wash off the gross saliva) and the barkeep answers, "This is the Mars Bar, man. There's no soap in the Mars Bar," that's when you know the place has become a parody of itself. Really dude? Are you fucking kidding me? There's no soap because this is the Mars Bar? If I hadn't defused the situation, saliva guy would've had a bottle broken over his head. If there's no soap in the Mars Bar, how do you clean blood off the seats and floor?

McSorley's Old Ale House
15 E. 7th St. @ Cooper Square

Founded in 1854, McSorley's is New York's oldest bar. Its slogan is, "We've been here since before you were born." Are you kidding me McSorley's? You've been here since when my ancestors were getting raped and pillaged by fucking Cossacks. No shit you've been here since before I was born. And you know what, McSorley's? I love you for it. I love that your walls are crammed with photos and memorabilia from over 150 years of dedicated drinking. I love that your chandelier probably hasn't been dusted since when they used to call WWI "The Great War". I love how your urinals are weird and old and bigger than some of the apartments in this strange city that you and I both inhabit. And you know what else I love about you, McSorley's? I love that you only serve two drinks, light beer and dark beer, and that they're both delicious and only cost $2.25 each. Who cares if it wasn't until 1970 when you begrudgingly let women through your hallowed doors because of some namby-pamby Supreme Court case? You've had Abe Lincoln, John Lennon and Woody Guthrie hang out at your tables! Who needs chicks, right? I guess what I'm trying to say McSorley's is that you might be the best bar in the world, except for Friday and Saturday nights when your sublime atmosphere gets screwed up by too many guys who's favorite band is Sublime.

Odessa Bar
117Ave. A btw St. Mark's & 7th Sts.

I've always said that being human means existing in the space between one's heart and one's mind. Everyone is at a different level of the spectrum, but we're all there somewhere. Odessa is one of those spots that my heart knows should be in the book, by my mind says, "I don't know motherfucker ... they sell Budweisers for five bucks!" The rest of the conversation goes like this:

> Heart: But *all* the beers at Odessa cost $5, even Guinness.
> Mind: Yeah, but we mostly drink shitty beer because we're poor. Remember?
> H: This spot is an East Village classic and the food is cheap, too. We can get appetizers like perogis for as little as $3!
> M: Other things like steaks and seafood are over $10 though.
> H: Come on, man, it's a dark, 24-hour Ukrainian diner with a bar. You're not gonna get fucking seafood. This is where you end your night with a beer and some greasy food before going home.
> M: Alright fine, you win. Put it in the damn book. Just so you know, it was the dark, 24-hour Ukrainian diner part

that won me over.

H: I knew it would.

What, you don't personify your heart and mind so that they can argue about beer and late night food? What kind of weirdo are you?

Phoenix

447 E. 13th St. @ Ave. A

If you're a gay guy who's more into M.I.A. and American Apparel than Madonna and Armani Exchange, Phoenix might just be your new favorite bar. Most of the boys here are alternative and artsy, which can be a very welcome change if you've been spending too much time cruising in the West Village or Chelsea. And there are great drink specials every night, which helps everyone get drunk and frisky. Hooray for drunk and frisky!

Sophie's

509 E. 5th St. @ Ave. A

This is a great East Village dive bar with a solid, mostly local, regular crowd. It's low lit and the art on the walls was undoubtedly made by some of the aforementioned stalwarts. It has the requisite Big Buck Hunter and pool table, but more than anything it's got a nice worn, lived-in feel that lets you know how much this place is loved. $3.50 for most of the beers makes me love it, too.

Shopping

East Village Cheese
40 3rd Ave. @ 10th St.

Okay, even though the things that you purchase here eventually make it into your belly, I'm putting it in the Shopping section because it's not a restaurant, you shop here for stuff, and this is my book so I can do whatever the fuck I want. East Village Cheese carries all kinds of goods like anchovies (yuck!), pesto (yum!), and plums (meh), as well as other things that I won't bother to emote about like bagels, jellies and pasta. But the reason to go there is for the cheap cheese. This joint always has weekly specials where they sell great cheese for only $2.99 a pound. And if you're a vegan or cheese gives you the shits, you can buy soy cheese for only $3.59 a pound. Chalk one up for the lactards!

Enchantments Inc.
341 E. 9th St. btw 1st & 2nd Aves.

Every girl who, in high school, saw the movie *The Craft* and then spent the next three months really wanting to be a witch, pretty much dreamed of hanging out in this place. It's spot on; you walk in here and the Cowboy Junkies play in the background while a couple of black cats skitter around, and somebody prepares candles and blends oils in the "Magickal Apothecary" in the back. But while you can find botanicas all over the Latin parts of New York, the 25-year-old Enchantments is the last occult store in the city. Apparently what separates the two is that the traditions represented in botanicas are all tied to Catholicism, where those of the occult are not tied to Christianity at all. That being said, you can still take care of most of your Voodoo/ Santeria/Yoruba needs here as well as getting a Tarot reading. I was surprised at the diversity of the clientele (New York never ceases to amaze me); one woman was carrying a Louis Vuitton bag and looked like she was on her way to a big meeting.

Kim's Video
6 St. Mark's Pl. @ 3rd Ave.

If I had gone to high school in New York, I would have spent all the money I didn't spend on drugs at Kim's Video. It's like this place is a physical incarnation of imdb.com (Internet Movie Database) combined with a sweet used record store. The used stuff is generally under $10, unless it's mad rare. And in terms of movies, their selection is fucking ridiculous. Plus, if for some reason they don't have what you want, they'll find it.

Love Saves the Day
119 2nd Ave @ E. 7th St.

This is the coolest store ever because instead of remaking things for nostalgic value (like Urban Outfitters) they have the real deal. There's a bin of random action figures that, while not being in mint condition (and occasionally missing an appendage), only cost $3.50 per toy. And, of course, there are random novelty tchotchkes like Jesus action figures, but who wants one of those when you can buy original GI Joes, Teenage Mutant Ninja Turtles and My Little Ponies. (I always preferred Barbie dolls myself because you could take off the clothes and have Ken do her from behind. Seriously, that's all I did with my cousin's Barbie dolls when we were kids. Not just from behind, but well, you get the picture. I've always been a perv.) And you know what else? They also have the old rubber non-movable WWF wrestler toys (can you say Jimmy "Superfly" Snuka?) and the old school Star Wars toys too. I'm getting too nerdy for you right now, aren't I? Well don't worry; they also have great vintage clothes and costumes, too. So anyway, stop buying ironic knockoffs and go indulge yourself in your childhood at Love Saves the Day.

Pageant Book and Print Shop

69 E. 4th St. btw 2nd Ave. and Cooper Sq. (Bowery)

Pageant has tons of cool unique prints and maps that are not inexpensive at all. So why would I put it in this book? I'm glad you asked. They have a box of super cool shit that only costs from $1–$5. That's why sucka! I love shit like this. I'm a nerd.

The mixtape place on the corner of St. Mark's and 3rd Ave

If you love hip-hop, these little places are gems. The legality of what they sell is probably, uh "not very", but shit, if you want a leaked hip-hop album, you can get it for like five bucks. I got the new Lil' Wayne shit and it is fire!

Sights & Entertainment

Walk around and check out all the little community gardens throughout Alphabet City (from Ave. A east to Ave. D and 14th St. south to
Houston St.) like the super cool Kenkeleba House Gardens and also
check out the marble cemetery on E. 2nd St.

Bowery Poetry Club
308 Bowery btw E. 1st & 2nd Sts.

Get some culture in your sinful, barhopping, greasy spoon eating life
goddamn it! Quit your backsliding ways and feed your brain with
some of the amazing events that go on here nightly. Sure there might
be a cover, but it's almost always below $10 and most often in the
$5–$7 range. And just in case you feel like getting culture *and* backsliding, you can get a PBR for $3. Who said you can't have it all? Big-
ups to the guy who runs this place: he put a Broke-Ass Stuart sticker
on the front window.

Charlie Parker's House
151 Ave. B @ Tompkins Square Park

I wanna ask you a big favor. When I die, will you run around and
spray paint "Broke-Ass Lives!" all over town? Pretty please? When
Charlie Parker died they did it for him (except they called him "Bird"
instead of "Broke-Ass"). That's not too much to ask is it? Good, I
didn't think so. Anyway, Bird lived here in the early '50s at the height
of his career, and, while I doubt you can go in and see the place, you
can walk by and say, "Did you know Charlie Parker lived there?" And
people will think you're cool because you know stuff.

The Lakeside Lounge
162 Ave. B btw 10th & 11th Sts.

Come for the free nightly music, stay for the $6 PBR and well shot
special. Or just get a can of Blatz. "Milwaukee's finest beer" is only
$2. I have to tell you, though, that it's not really as fine as it claims

(you can do finer, Milwaukee). There's a decent-sized crowd most nights from all over the city, including the Upper East Side Austrian housewife who told me that she was unhappy with her husband and needed a new man like me. I, of course, turned her down; my girlfriend wouldn't really approve of me cheating on her.

New York Marble Cemetery

E. 2nd St. btw 2nd & 3rd Aves.

This easy to miss graveyard was incorporated in 1831 as New York's first public nonsectarian cemetery. It's one of the coolest cemeteries in the city, and you've probably walked by it a million times without noticing it was there. It's free to visit, but they keep to a pretty set schedule. Check out their website for times.

Rapture Café and Books

200 Ave. A btw 12th & 13th Sts.

I was walking around the East Village with the Gaslamp Killer, who was in town to play a show, when I first came across Rapture. The fact that it was a café and a bookstore impressed me, so I stepped inside and was surprised to see that they also sold zines, booze and food; all of which are very close to my heart. How could I not love this place? They also have live performances of poetry and music as well as book readings and motherfucking BINGO! Make sure to check their calendar to see what they've got going on because it's always interesting and unusual.

Red Square Apartment Buildings

250 E. Houston @ Ave. A

While there is nothing cheap about living in these perfectly located luxury apartments, the building's coolest feature is free. Just look up at the top of the building and you'll see the giant statue of Vladimir Lenin. One of the people involved in the creation of the building found this statue in Russia after the fall of Communism and thought it would look great on top of his new luxury building. Further adding to the irony, Lenin's arm is raised towards Wall Street (the center of American capitalism). Isn't it amazing how anything subversive can be swallowed up by mainstream culture, stripped of its meaning and sold to the masses as kitsch or a commodity? What's next, Che Guevara's face on T-shirts?

Russian & Turkish Baths

268 E. 10ᵗʰ St. @ btw 1ˢᵗ Ave. & Ave. A

The Russian & Turkish Baths, opened in 1892, is one of the gems of
New York City. It's the cheapest spa treatment you'll ever get in the
US; $30 gets you a full day's use of facilities that include the Redwood
Sauna, the Aromatherapy Room, and the extremely hot Russian Sauna. The admission also includes bathrobe, swimsuit, soap, towel, flip-
flops and razors, should you need them. I came here with a buddy of
mine who was interested in making a Broke-Ass Stuart TV show. We
wanted to shoot a Benny Hill–type scene here where a mixture of hot
girls in bikinis and old fat Russian guys (both groups are well represented here) would be chasing me from room to room. Unfortunately,
that particular TV show didn't work out, but hopefully one will soon.

Tompkins Square Park

All that nature stuff between Aves. A & B and E.
10ᵗʰ & 7ᵗʰ Sts.

Daniel D. Tompkins was the US vice president under James Monroe
and the New York governor who abolished slavery in the state. He's
been dead since 1825, so he probably hasn't heard the good news:
there's a park named after him and there hasn't been a riot there
since 1988! It's now a lovely park that, despite the occasional heroin
OD, has become a safe place for even people with strollers to stroll
through. Not like those pesky '70s and '80s when the park was filled
with squatters, junkies and vagabonds. My personal favorite time to
be in the park is during Wigstock, an outdoor drag festival held in the
summer. They also have a year round farmers' market on Sundays
from 8am–6pm and a weekly needle exchange.

Yoga to the People

12 St. Mark's Pl. btwn 2ⁿᵈ Ave. and 3ʳᵈ Ave.
(Cooper Sq.), 2ⁿᵈ Fl.

My last experience with yoga was in San Francisco where I did a free
trial session at a place that turned the room to temp 105° and the
humidity to 40 percent. They call this style Bikram yoga, but I call it
smelling like funky-ass feet. I couldn't handle the heat/stench/muscle
pains so I left halfway through the session. (Go ahead, call me a
pussy. I know you're gonna do it anyway.) But lately I've considered

trying yoga again. And if I were to do it, it would be at Yoga to the People. First of all, being the Pinko bastard that I am, any name that involves "to the people" immediately piques my interest. Then once I found out that they're actually doing something amazing and for the people, I knew I had to include them in my book. At Yoga to the People classes are by a $10 suggested donation, but here they really do mean *suggested* and you can give anything you want. That, my friends, is beautiful.

This was taken at the Bowery Hotel. When I found out that one of the guys in the group I was drinking with was Radiohead's manager, I discreetly told the server to put all my drinks on his tab. Thanks guy! Photo by Victoria Smith

EAST VILLAGE

Grub-a-dub-dub
1 Atlas Café
2 BAMN!
3 Birdies
4 Elvie's Turo-Turo
5 Jennifer's Cafe
6 Kenka
7 Otafuku
8 Panna 2 and Milon
9 Papaya Dog
10 Ruben's Empañadas
11 Sushi Park
12 Tuck Shop
13 Yaffa Café

DRINKS DRINKS DRINKS
14 7B (Vazacs Horseshoe Bar)
15 Ace Bar
16 Blarney Cove
17 Blue & Gold Tavern
18 The Boiler Room
19 Cheap Shots
20 Continental
21 Doc Holliday's
22 Grassroots Tavern
23 Holiday Cocktail Lounge
24 Karpaty Pub
25 Mars Bar
26 McSorley's Old Ale House

DRINKS DRINKS DRINKS (ctn'd)
27 Mona's
28 Odessa Bar
29 The Phoenix
30 Sophie's

Shopping
31 Academy Records
32 East Village Cheese
33 Enchantments Inc.
34 Kim's Video
35 Love Saves The Day
36 The Mixtape Place on the Corner of
   St Marks and 3rd Ave
37 Pageant Book and Print Shop

Stuff is to See and Do
38 Bowery Poetry Club
39 Charlie Parker's House
40 The Lakeside Lounge
41 New York Marble Cemetery
42 Rapture Café and Books
43 Red Square Apartment Buildings
44 Russian & Turkish Baths
45 Tompkins Square Park
46 Yoga to the People

Free Food Bitches!!
47 11th St. Bar
48 Aroma Kitchen & Wine Bar
49 Cha An
50 Cooper 35
51 Crocodile Lounge
52 Croxley Ales
53 Cucina Di Pesce
54 D.B.A.
55 Nevada Smith's
56 Standings
57 The Thirsty Scholar

Herbivore Friendly
58 B & H Dairy & Vegetable Restaurant
59 Café Viva Natural Pizza
60 Hummus Place
61 Kate's Joint
62 Lan Café
63 Maoz
64 Pukk
65 Punjabi

Street Meat
66 From Atlantis With Love
67 Mud Truck

15 year old Goth kids

Someone who just got a tattoo

Looming spectre of gentrification

West Village/ Greenwich Village

Greenwich Village was originally separate from New York City. But in 1822, an epidemic of yellow fever sent the city's wealthy scurrying northward, turning what was once a pastoral hamlet into New York's original "new hot neighborhood". Dotted with picturesque townhouses, the original street plan still exists in the part of Greenwich Village west of 6th Avenue (aptly called the West Village), making for strangely meandering streets that occasionally cross thoroughfares they run parallel to in other parts of the city. Though this helps to make the area truly charming, it creates maddening frustration when trying to find a particular address.

While Greenwich Village was first considered a bohemian quarter in the early 20th century, it wasn't until the Beats began hanging here in the 1950s that it truly became identified as a home for alternative lifestyles and ways of thought. The poetry and jazz of the '50s gave way to the coffee shop folk revival of the early '60s, which in turn gave way to rock n' roll. By the time the '70s hit, the Village was the center of gay life in New York, and it was here that the Gay Rights movement began after the Stonewall Riots erupted in 1969.

Today the Village is a strange place indeed. NYU and Washington Square Park are surrounded by streets like Bleecker and MacDougal that are densely packed with buzzing college bars and small music venues, while the main drags of the West Village (W. 4th St. and 6th and 7th Aves.) are a mixture of sex shops, brunch places, tattoo parlors, and some of New York's hottest restaurants. The demographic is just as varied. NYU frat boys and homo-thugs wait in line together at Papaya Dog, while an old gay couple strolls by hand in hand walking their little Chihuahua. Because of NYU's student population, Greenwich Village has a fair amount of well-priced bars and restaurants, but the further west you go, the more expensive it becomes. Sometimes I feel like every time I come back to the West Village, the prices are higher than the time before, and I weep from nervousness that I may not be giving you the best book. Then I remember how awesome I am and my tears dry instantly.

For those of you wondering what constitutes Greenwich Village and what makes up the West Village, Greenwich Village runs from 14th St. south to Houston St. and 6th Ave. east to 4th Ave./the Bowery. The West Village has the same north/south boundaries, but runs from 6th Ave. west to the Hudson River.

Food

Dojo

14 W. 4th St. btw Broadway & Mercer Ave.

You can get mad full here for $4.25. Sure the food tastes a little card-boardish but chances are you don't care because you're really poor from paying $40,000 a year at NYU.

Esperanto Café

114 MacDougal St. btw Bleecker St. & W 3rd St.

Imagine how a really cool café in the Village should look. That's exactly how Esperanto looks. They've got comfy places to sit, rustic-looking things on the walls and even a phone booth (but instead of a phone inside, there is a computer, so you can use the Internet for free). And if you have a laptop, you can just steal Internet from one of the surrounding neighbors. If you're looking for eye candy, there's always hot NYU students hanging out here, and, if you like the sound of Hebrew (ear candy?), I think everyone that works here is Israeli. It might be a hiring policy.

Galanga

149 W. 4th St. @ 6th Ave.

While not being amazingly cheap, Galanga is really good considering that the entrees begin at only $8.50. It makes a great first date spot, unless of course your date is down for Papaya Dog. If that's the case, you either have a keeper or a junkie, both of which will lead to an exciting night.

Joe's Pizza

7 Carmine St. btw 6th Ave. & Bleecker St.

This classic West Village pizza place sells delicious slices for $2.50. They're so good that it's actually hard to stop at just one. It's crazy popular with tourists, locals and broke-asses alike.

Kati Roll Company

99 Macdougal St @ Bleeker St.

See entry on pg 186

Mamoun's

119 MacDougal @ W. 3rd St.; also at 22 St. Mark's Pl. btw 2nd Ave. & 3rd Ave.

Invariably, the first two suggestions people make when I tell them about my book are the Alligator Lounge (p. 343) and Mamoun's. I've come to the conclusion that there are hundreds, if not thousands of broke-ass New Yorkers living solely off these two places—which makes total sense. At Mamoun's you can get a fucking delectable falafel for $2! Word. And I even think falafels are healthy for you, but I'm not sure. I'm not nearly as good at knowing what's healthy as I am at knowing what's cheap and delicious. There are other $2 falafel places on MacDougal, but Mamoun's is the best.

Panino Giusto

551 Hudson St. @ Perry St.

Very simply, Panino Giusto is a small and rustic-looking spot where you get your panini on. If you don't know what a panini is, that's pretty weird, but I'll tell you anyway: it's an Italian-style, warm, toasted sandwich. What makes it Italian style? The fact that it's got an Italian name. That's it. As for the restaurant, it's well priced (most of its delicious paninis are in the $7.50 range), and it has a big community table at which you can sit and talk shit with other patrons. Me, I like the joint because it's a mellow place to sit and read the paper in the afternoon.

Papaya Dog

333 6th Ave. @ W. 4th St.

So cheap and *so* not exactly amazing. It's one of those things that's not even amazing when drunk. It's better at that point, teetering on the edge of being good, but still not amazing. But then again, I don't eat the hot dogs (sorry to admit I don't like them unless they are wrapped in bacon) so maybe I don't have a proper reference point. But Papaya Dog is special because of its location. Late at night, it becomes the epicenter of West Village drunkenness. Everyone from homo-thugs to frat boys congregate here for $2.50 burgers, $1.25 dogs, $2.50 mozz sticks and of course papaya juice. Sure there are other Papaya Dog locations, but none as surreal as this one; it's practically a place of entertainment.

Papaya King
200 W 14th St. @ 7th Ave.

See p. 273 (upper east side)

Pardo's
92 7th Ave. South btwn Grove & Barrow Sts.

Hey look, an actual classy establishment in one of my books! What's the world coming to? This Peruvian restaurant has fantastic traditional rotisserie chicken cooked with 14 spices. Considering the location and that it's super nice inside, I'm blown away that you can get a half chicken for $6. It's almost like I feel guilty that they might have accidentally underpriced themselves. If you're curious as to the story behind this place, just look to the back wall. It's written on there real big.

Pepe Verde
559 Hudson St. @ Perry St.

Other than the one exposed brick wall, almost everything in this tiny Italian spot is a slightly offensive shade of green. But the food is good and well priced, especially for the neighborhood. Pasta dishes begin at $5.95 and the lunch special (11am-4pm) is big, filling and only costs $7.95. My favorite part though is that their to-go menu says:

<u>NO-DIET-COKE</u>
<u>NO-SKIM-MILK</u>
<u>NO-DECAF-COFFEE</u>
<u>ONLY-GOOD-FOOD</u>

Is it me, or is the to-go menu basically saying, "Don't be a fucking pussy!"

'SNice

45 8th Ave. @ W. 4th St.

'SNice looks kinda like a cross between the Disneyland ride "Thunder Mountain" and the way that hip coffee shops looked in movies in the 90's. Besides trying to figure out what the fuck I'm talking about, another reason to visit this cool vegetarian café is that nothing on the scrumptious menu costs over $7.50. Also, there are books and board games to occupy you, and they have something that not enough cafés in New York have–free WiFi. Goddamn, I love free WiFi.

Sweetheart Coffee Shop

69 8th Ave. btw W. 13th St. & Greenwich Ave.

I love empanadas more than I love most things on earth; they are the perfect food. This tiny place sells authentic Argentinean ones for $2.25, which is much cheaper than at Ruben's. What do you think of that, old Rube? And you can get two empanadas and a soda or coffee for $4.95.

Westville

210 W. 10th St. @ Bleecker St.

A cute and tiny place, Westville is supposed to seem like a random restaurant in the countryside instead of a spot in the middle of Manhattan. It's pretty hard to imagine yourself out of the West Village though when you look out the window and see a man in hot-pink biker shorts walking his Chihuahua, who also happens to be wearing some type of hot-pink sweater dealie. The food is pretty good, and is well priced for the neighborhood, but that just means that it's scraping the ceiling of what might be considered "cheap". I guess I'll let you be the judge of that. All I know is they earned major points with me because they have Tapatio as their hot sauce. If you don't know what Tapatio is, your life will be much better once you do (hint: look in the glossary).

Bars

1849

183 Bleecker St. btw MacDougal & Sullivan Sts.

1849 is themed like a gold rush saloon where flat-screen TVs, guys in backwards ball caps and non-plussed Russian waitresses are mixed in amongst the red plush velvet couches and taxidermy. Because it's a total college hang out, they have tons of deals throughout the week, like 20-cent wings and half-price drinks for happy hour, $2 Coronas and $2 shots of Cuervo on Tuesdays (yes, they call it "Loco Tuesdays") and 20-cent wings till the kitchen closes on Wednesdays. They also have DJs Thursday–Saturday and live music Sunday–Wednesday. If you can't handle all that crap, just take your cheap drinks and wings and go play pool upstairs.

Corner Bistro

331 W. 4th St. @ Horatio St.

When I first discovered this place, I told Paul I found an amazing gem of a dive bar in the West Village that would be perfect for the book. When I told him it was the Corner Bistro, he and the two girls sitting at our table laughed in my face. Of course my reaction was, "Eat a bag of dicks, fuckfaces," which they responded to with more laughter (my insults are never very convincing). Apparently the "discovery" I had attributed to my finely tuned, broke-ass sensory perception, was really quite famous, bordering on being world-renowned. Paul hammered this point in by telling me, "It's like coming to me and telling me that you found this great place called the Chelsea Hotel." Regardless of my newbie naïveté, I can tell you that this place hits pretty much every great bar benchmark: $2.50 Budweisers, $3.50 Stellas and $5.75 for one of the best burgers you've ever had. Plus it looks like someone completely forgot to gentrify it. It has exposed brick walls, old wooden booths, a register that whirs when used and a jukebox that plays nothing but jazz and blues. And the best part of this is that none of it is ironic; it just is this way. What? That's not enough for you? It also manages to attract hotties of all persuasions, too. If you see me there, buy me a drink.

Cubbyhole
281 W. 12th St. @ W. 4th St.

While I might not be gay, the fact that I have the gayest family in the world and that I do lots of bar research means that I go to a fair amount of gay bars (which are actually amazing places to meet straight women). One thing I've noticed in all this gaiety is that most queer bars in big cities are focused on either gay men or lesbians. Cubbyhole is cool because it's a good mixture of both gay and lesbian. The vibe here is always super friendly and the spot is always decorated all kinds of crazy for different seasons. I went in here around Christmas and was afraid someone was gonna wrap me up and dangle me from the ceiling.

Down the Hatch
179 W. 4th St. btw 6th & 7th Aves.

Hopelessly collegiate, this place has foosball, beer pong and lots of guys who have no idea how much they overuse the word "bro". Normally the cheapest beer is a $4.50 Bud, but never fear, they have so many deals throughout the week that it's almost never "normally". For example, on Wednesdays you'll get $8 pitchers and half-price pints, and Thursdays they serve $3 beers and shots. In fact, Down the Hatch is so proud of their drink deals that they have hand painted wooden signs proclaiming these deals all over the walls. But you know what? Places like this need to exist, so cheese dicks have some place to go when they wanna dress down, wear flip-flops and drink till they hug their buddies and say, "I'm not a fag, but I love you, bro."

Four-Faced Liar
165 W. 4th St. btw Cornelia & Jones Sts.

This bar is named after a clock I've been to in Cork, Ireland. But that's not why I come here. I come because the PBR is always $2 and in this neighborhood, the cheapest beer is often $5. Otherwise it might be a bar I would overlook. But since it's never too busy, it's a good place to hang out with someone you actually want to talk to. You can usually get a seat.

Johnny's Bar

90 Greenwich Ave. @ W. 12th St.

This darkly lit gem of a bar in the West Village is so small that if you farted the entire place would most likely smell it. Despite the threat of farts though, the bar's size is certainly one of its more charming features. That combined with affordable drinks ($4.50 Newcastles/$3.50 shot of the day), friendly patrons and weird shit on the walls (license plates, foreign currency, stickers, etc.) makes Johnny's Bar one of my personal favorites in the West Village.

Kettle of Fish

59 Christopher St. @ W. 4th St.

Set, Kenny and I were walking by here one night when a board saying "$3.50 beers" sucked us in like a tractor beam. I came to some conclusions about Kettle of Fish that night. The first is that it's a strange bar. The second is that I like the place. And the third one is that it completely jams my gaydar. My gaydar is pretty damn good; I lived in San Francisco for many years, and my family could be a case study for the existence of a gay gene, but it's hard to make sense of this place. Are those older, single, guys sitting at the bar as gay as they seem? Are those groups of men and women sitting at the tables actually going home to have penis-in-vagina sex? I have no clue what is gong on here. Does this have anything to do with the fact that Kerouac used to hang out here (note the photo by the bar of him chilling outside)? He played for both teams right? And why is part of the back room set up to look like someone's entire living room? Also, why is it that during a televised sporting event, it's like this is a completely different bar? I guess I'll never know.

McKenna's Pub

245 W. 14th St. btw 7th & 8th Aves.

McKenna's is basically a regular pub with grub and cheap drinks, like $2 PBR cans. It's not really a favorite of mine, but it will do in a pinch, and it's better than anything in the Meatpacking District. (I abhor that place). The crowd here is a good mix of gays and lesbians, random drunks, and B&T people who don't know any better places to go. Last time I was here was during fleet week, so there was a ton of sailors here (which always seems extra gay to me, but that's probably just because of all the Halloweens spent in SF).

Peculier Pub

145 Bleecker St. @ Thompson St.

You ever had a friend who you thought was super cool but you could only hang out with occasionally because his friends were an awful reflection on the human race? That's how I feel about Peculier Pub. From Sunday to Wednesday this is just about a perfect bar. Come Thursday–Saturday though and the joint is so packed with obnoxious fuckwits that you want to do *seppuku,* that Japanese form of suicide where you stab yourself in the guts. But I'm a glass-half-full type of person so I'll now focus on the good stuff: a beer list with over 200 selections from around the world (mostly $4.25 microbrews) and a grub menu where most things cost $5.25 and the calories are listed next to the price (which caused my girlfriend to take an abnormal amount of time choosing her food). But the décor is really the icing on the cake: church pews for benches, wooden tables scratched thoroughly with graffiti and mosaics made from beer caps. Yes, that is "Starry Night" created from beer caps on the back wall ... genius, I know.

Pieces

8 Christopher St. @ Gay St.

I'd actually be disappointed if a bar on the corner of Gay Street didn't have a bathroom mirror positioned to let you watch your cock while you pissed. But Pieces isn't one to disappoint, so the one bathroom that actually does have a closing door (and a sign that says "one at a time"), has the aforementioned, uh ... cock reflector. The bathroom mirror is not the only thing that let's you feel like a star; Pieces also has karaoke on Saturday nights. And if craigslist is too high-tech for your "Missed Connection" needs, come to this spot on Thursday for its "Post Office" night. This is where everyone gets a numbered "Hello my name is ..." sticker that corresponds to a cubbyhole where you can deposit messages like, "I like your Marc Jacobs shoes" or "Let's go use the cock mirror". And for those of you who don't care about any of the rest of this shit, the drinks are pretty well priced, too.

The Stonewall Inn

53 Christopher St. @ W. 4th St.

While it's not necessarily the cheapest bar around ($5 beers), the Stonewall is a landmark and something that you should stop in and pay your respects to (by which I mean, have a drink there). On June 28th, 1969, police raided the Stonewall, which was then the largest gay bar in the US. The ensuing riots are considered as the moment when the Gay Rights movement began in earnest. While it has had many lives since then, the Stonewall Inn is now a dive where drunk drag queens sit on the bar singing show tunes. But then again, maybe I was just lucky enough to catch it on a good night.

Ty's

114 Christopher St. btw Bedford & Bleecker Sts.

I think the best way to describe Ty's is cheap beers and cheap bears. They sell $2 cans of Miller and Bud to old hairy guys in leather who've been drinking there regularly since the bar opened in 1972.

White Horse Tavern

567 Hudson St. @ 11th St.

Okay, let me just get this out of the way now instead of agonizing for the next 35 minutes about the coolest way to squeeze it in: after raging (get it?) and drinking 18 whiskeys at the White Horse Tavern, Dylan Thomas collapsed and died. The year was 1953 and this bar has pretty much been one of the more happening spots in the West Village ever since (except on weekend nights when the crowd becomes overly bridge and tunnel). When the weather permits, the White Horse has an outdoor patio that is absolutely crackin', especially on Saturday and Sunday afternoons. Nothing on the pub grub menu costs more than $7.25 (okay, maybe one thing does) and the beers are all averagely priced. Indoors feels (and smells) like an authentic Irish pub, and of course, there are photos of the bar's most famous dead patron all over the place. Basically what I'm saying is that this is a pretty good place to be.

Wicked Willy's

149 Bleecker St. @ Thompson St.

When I first moved to New York, I was living in Carroll Gardens, Brooklyn. While the neighborhood was beautiful, bordering on idyllic, my particular building was a rundown and dilapidated piece of shit brownstone that on any given night had five to ten people sleeping in it (depending on whether the couch guy was there and how many people had brought home someone to fuck). Anyway, in my three-month tenure there, one of my roommates actually went through more jobs than I did, and one of these jobs was bartending at Wicked Willy's. The way she described it was, "Hell! I fucking hate working there. It might be the worst place on earth." In my opinion, she might have been a little overzealous, but I will say there are only a few reasons why you should drink at this nautically themed, beer-pong playing, college bar. The first is if you are looking for cheap drinks; they have ridiculous drink specials every night of the week. The second is if you wanna hang out with people who are turning 21 and who scream "Wooooo!" every time their buddy takes a shot. The third is if you are looking to hook-up with drunk 21-year-old-ish people screaming "Wooooo!" (attn: gay men who like fucking boys who wear Abercrombie and swear they are "straight"). Needless to say, Wicked Willy's fills its roll and I applaud it for that.

P.S. DO NOT go here on a weekend night. There is a cover charge and the drinks are literally $3 more expensive than during the week.

Shopping

Left Bank Books

304 W. 4ᵗʰ St. near Bank St.

While buying rare books is, shall we say, way the fuck beyond my means, perusing them isn't and that is why I'm including Left Bank Books. The guy, who owns this small and cluttered store, does actually sell some books that aren't rare, but his specialty is first editions and signed copies. Dude even has some Victorian-era first editions and a first edition, first issue Rudyard Kipling book for a whopping $16,500! For some strange reason he wouldn't let me touch it. Regardless of how poor you are, if you like books, then Left Bank Books is an excellent place to check out; especially since the owner is a strange guy with cool stories about famous poets.

Chess Forum and Village Chess Shop

219 & 230 Thompson St. (respectively) btw Bleecker St. & W. 3ʳᵈ St.

I wonder how long these shops have been sitting across the street from each other (I'm too lazy to find out). I almost wanna imagine that its some age old rivalry that goes back to the old country, where two grand chess masters both came to America and set up chess shops near each other out of sheer spite. That's probably not the case, but how else would you explain it?

P.S. I just found out that there is a rivalry here! The guy who owns Chess Forum used to work at the Village Chess Shop (or the other way around) and now they hate each other. Who doesn't like a good feud?

McNulty's Tea & Coffee

109 Christopher St. btw Bedford & Bleecker Sts.

Fragrant and ancient, McNulty's Tea & Coffee seems like something out of a completely different century, which it is. It was established in 1895 and has been in this location since the 1920s. Is this place for real? I almost expect them to be making strange potions in the back and selling them as "Professor McNulty's Famous Magical Cure-All". Other than the actual tea leaves and coffee beans, everything in this store has probably been here since it opened, and this goes for the old guys who work here, too.

National Wholesale Liquidators

632 Broadway @ Bleecker St.

Crap. Lots and lots of crap.

Oscar Wilde Bookstore

15 Christopher St. @ Gay St.

For a long time, the signature at the end of my emails was the Oscar Wilde quote, "We are all in the gutter, but some of us are looking at the stars," which perfectly describes my life. I'm not sure how much you know about the man and I'm not gonna sit here and write his biography, but I will tell you that besides being a quote genius, Oscar Wilde is also one of the first modern gay heroes/martyrs. This, to me, is perfect because the Oscar Wilde Bookshop is the world's oldest gay and lesbian bookstore (I bet they did that on purpose). While they might not actually be the cheapest booksellers in New York, you gotta support them simply for having the balls to open up in 1967. The staff here is super friendly and the store has everything from magazines to books on critical thought to fiction ... sexy butt-lovin' fiction (sorry I had to throw *something* crude in there).

Unoppressive Non-Imperialist Bargain Books

34 Carmine @ Bleecker St.

Can you think of a better name than this for anything else in the world? Me neither. I like it so much I wanna name my first kid Unoppressive Non-Imperial Bargain Books and just call him/her UNIBB for short. Has a nice ring to it huh? I mean what else can I say about this place that the name hasn't already told you? Nothing, other than my usual "support independent businesses" rant. Are you tired of hearing me say that yet?

Urban Footwear

351 6th Ave. btw W. 4th St. & Washington Pl.

This photo kinda feel like those pictures you used to see at the mall where you'd unfocus your eyes and a picture would pop out.

For some reason half of the inventory here is always super discounted. This is pretty much the only place I buy shoes in New York. Just last week I got a brand new pair of ill ass New Balances for $40.

Sights & Entertainment

Wander the streets and see what you find.

The Cage

W 4th St. @ 6th Ave.

Wanna see people play basketball better than you can do anything in your life? Come here on a nice day.

The Forbes Collection

62 5th Ave. @ 12th St.

When I was in 4th grade, a touring collection of Fabergé eggs came through San Diego and, as a field trip, my class went and saw them. I thought they were so cool that I asked for Brut cologne (yuck!) for Hannukah because a company called Fabergé made it. I guess I hadn't put together the fact that the company had nothing to do with the 19th century jeweler that had made the gorgeous eggs for the Russian Tsars. So anyway, the reason I originally went to see the Forbes Collection (besides that it was free) was because I'd read that they had the second-biggest collection of Fabergé eggs in the world. Unfortunately I arrived about four years too late and the whole set of eggs had been sold ☹. I went in the gallery anyway and looked at the collection, which included tons of toy soldiers and boats, one of the original versions of Monopoly and a whole bunch of Olympic Medals. Still the whole thing was *meh* compared to my memories of the Fabergé eggs.

P.S. Where do you get a whole bunch of Olympic medals? What kind of junkie athlete sells their gold medals?

LGBT Community Center

208 W. 13th St. @ 7th Ave.

Established in 1983, the Center in the West Village is the second biggest Lesbian, Gay, Bisexual, and Transgender (LGBT) Community Center in the world. It provides dozens of services to New York's

Queer community like, Alcoholics Anonymous, yoga classes, reading groups, and teen drop-in hours, as well as bringing in world-class speakers and educators. Another cool thing about the Center is that they have a bathroom painted by the late Keith Haring to celebrate the twentieth anniversary of Stonewall. And wow, there is a lot of sexy-time going on in that mural.

The Triangle Shirtwaist Factory
29 Washington Pl. @ Greene St.

Once a scene of a horrific fire that led to major labor reforms, this place is now an NYU building for biology or chemistry or some other useless major.

Washington Square Park
The big fucking park in the middle of the Village

The words *Washington Square Park* bring so many images to my mind: old guys playing chess, hot young things studying for their NYU classes, smelly homeless guys mumbling to themselves, David Lee Roth getting busted for buying weed, and buskers playing music for money. Originally used as a burial ground for poor people and a place to hold executions, WSP is now arguably one of the best places in New York to while away a sunny afternoon. Whether lying in the shady grass reading, watching pretty girls sunbathe in the big empty fountain or marveling at the humongous marble arch, I love hanging

in this park. And one of my absolute favorite things that ever happens in the city, happens here on summer nights: A huge and motley crowd congregates around some random guys with guitars, hand drums, and even the occasional horn or electric bass, and everyone sings classic songs like "Sittin' on the Dock of the Bay" and "My Girl". And the best part is that nobody is really doing it for any reason other than the love of doing it. There's nothing better than harmonizing with a dude who doesn't have any teeth.

WEST VILLAGE — GREENWICH VILLAGE

Grub-a-dub-dub
1 Dojo
2 Esperanto Café
3 Galanga
4 Joe's Pizza
5 The Kati Roll Company
6 Mamoun's
7 Panino Giusto
8 Papaya Dog
9 Papaya King
10 Pardo's
11 Pepe Verde
12 Sweetheart Coffee Shop
13 Westville

DRINKS DRINKS DRINKS
14 1849
15 Corner Bistro
16 Cubbyhole
17 Down the Hatch
18 Four-Faced Liar
19 Johnny's bar
20 Kettle of Fish
21 McKenna's Pub
22 Peculier Pub
23 Pieces
24 The Stonewall Inn
25 Ty's

DRINKS DRINKS DRINKS (ctn'd)
26 White Horse Tavern
27 Wicked Willy's

Shopping
28 Chess Forum
29 Left Bank Books
30 McNulty's Tea & Coffee
31 National Wholesale Liquidators
32 Oscar Wilde Bookstore
33 The Strand
34 Unoppressive Non-Imperial Bargian Books
35 Urban Footwear
36 Village Chess Shop

Stuffis to See and Do
37 The Cage
38 The Forbes Collection
39 LBGT Community Center
40 The Triangle Shirtwaist Factory
41 Washington Square Park

Free Food Bitches!!
42 Bar 13
43 Dell'Anima
44 El Cantinero
45 Spain Restaurant

Herbivore Friendly
46 Gobo
47 Hummus Place
48 Quantum Leap
49 Red Bamboo Vegetarian Soul Café
50 'SNice
51 Taim
52 Temple in the Village

Street Meat
53 Dessert Truck
54 Mud Truck
55 N.Y. Dosas

Some college kid who just bought this book

Buff guys with little dogs

Girls who really think they are living the "Sex and the City" life

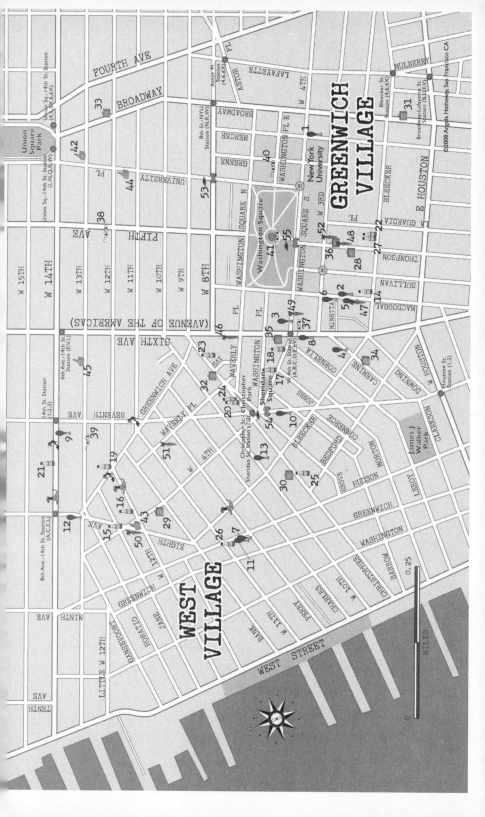

Basic Tips for Making Survival More Likely

Tipping: I can't stress how **important** it is to leave a good tip. For people who wait tables or bartend, tips are a major part of their income because their hourly wage is absolute shite! Having been a server for many years myself, I can't tell you how insulting it is when I work very hard to please someone only to receive a crappy tip. Therefore, I will give you a rough guide to tipping: tip your server 20 percent. How hard is that? I guess 18 percent is acceptable, but anything less sucks. If you're in a bar, tip a buck a drink. Consider yourself as being a patron of the arts. Most of the servers and bartenders I know only do it because it gives them enough freedom to pursue what they really want in life, so this means that by tipping well you're helping artists, writers, actors and other creative people survive. How's this—if you think tipping 20 percent is too expensive, then just get your food to go and leave a couple bucks. Basically what I'm saying is, bad tippers shouldn't be allowed in restaurants or bars. Also, if you take a cab, the standard tip is 10-15% unless you're going for a really long ride (maybe to the airport). There, I'm glad I got that off my chest.

Sleeping: You're gonna have to go it alone on this one. What do you want me to do, write a review of your future apartment? I can't do everything. What I will do, though, is give you the resources so you can help yourself find a place to sleep. And worst comes to worst, there's always Central Park.

If you're looking for an apartment, Craigslist.org is really the only way to go. I've found every place I've ever lived on Craigslist. If you're trying to sign a lease, look for a place that advertises "no broker's fee" because brokers are basically vampires who want a piece of your money. Unfortunately you just might have to pay one, unless you are simply moving into a room in someone's place or you get lucky. Just for the record, I'd like to say that the use of brokers is completely archaic in the era of Craigslist. But then again the religion of New York

City is the almighty dollar, which is also the reason that fair housing rights like rent control are virtually nonexistent. Don't believe the hype; there are only 50,000 rent controlled units in the entire five boroughs, and you would have had to be living in that unit since the 1970s for rent control to be in effect. I love New York, way more than a t-shirt could ever express, but the housing laws are simply unfair and are going to lead to the gentrification of this entire city.

If you just plan on being here for a little while and want a decent hotel at a good price, try hotwire.com. My dad uses it every time he travels, and he often gets shit like a four star hotel for a third of the price you would regularly pay. I'd imagine that three and two star places would also be substantially cheaper.

If you want to go an even cheaper route, try staying at one of New York's 50-plus hostels. I prefer to stay in hostels when I travel because it's the best place to meet amazing people from all over the world … and have sex with them. But it's also a great way to make lasting friendships. I've got friends and places to stay all over the world thanks to hostels. If you have enough loot, an ideal way to stay in one of these is to rent a private room. That way you get the privacy of a hotel and the social benefits of a hostel. You can read about them and book online at sites like *hostelz.com, hostels.com* and *hostelworld.com* Another option is *couchsurfing.com,* which is a site where you can meet people around the world who might let you stay at their place for free. I actually haven't done it yet, but I know tons of people who have and I generally hear amazing things. You can also volunteer your couch as a place for a traveler to sleep.

I hope all this was helpful to you. Finding a place can be really fucking shitty. Good luck.

Dumpster Diving: This is for those of you who spent your last pennies on this book. Dumpster diving is the practice of going through trashcans and dumpsters, generally from commercial businesses, and taking the things that were thrown away. As the old saying goes, "One man's trash is another man's treasure". A lot of my friends who dumpster dive do it behind big markets like Key Foods and Trader Joe's, where you can find a lot of edible produce. Also check out the dumpsters used by bakeries, bagel stores, and specialty food places like Gourmet Garage. Bring some bolt cutters in case those scoundrels have locked up their dumpsters. Also, if this anticapitalist lifestyle sounds appealing to you check out *freegan.info* to learn more about alternative ways.

Food from Vendors at Street Festivals: After a street fair or festival ends, go up to some of the food booths and find out what they're doing with all the food they didn't sell. Sometimes you can score some free food or they might sell it super cheap. During Bay to Breakers in SF one year, we stumbled across the finish line party, and since the venders were packing up, they sold us $8 sausages for $1 each. At the time I thought that maybe they were angels sent from heaven to help us with our drunken journey. But in retrospect I think they were just trying to get a few last dollars.

Food Court Discount: If you're in a food court, tell the cashier that you work in the mall. There is almost always a discount for people who work in the shopping center. This is true for most of the food courts I've ever been in.

Restaurant Week: This is for if you're feeling flush with extra money. Restaurant Week happens a few times a year, and it allows you to dine at some of the better spots in the city while getting a three course prix-fixe meal for about $25 at lunch and $35 at dinner. It's definitely a worthy splurge if you've got some extra bread to spend. For details about which restaurants are participating go to *www. nycvisit.com/restaurantweek.*

Bodegas: I know this should go without saying, but bodegas are your best friends. They are where you can get cheap sandwiches and hot food at any hour of the day, buy beer until 4am, and hear the local neighborhood gossip. Become buddy-buddy with your bodega guys because they are *always* around and are thus the constant eyes and ears on your block. Be good to these people, too, because, I know this sounds crazy, but one day it will save your ass. Trust me on this one. Even if you don't believe me, be good to them anyway, because they are hard working folks who deserve your respect.

Buybacks: One thing you can say about bartenders in this city is that they are fantastic about giving buybacks. A buyback is when, after you buy a few rounds, the bartender buys the next one. When it happens, it's usually after the third or fourth round. There are a few things you can do to help make sure you get one. Here are some tips: 1) Try to order from the same bartender all night long. 2) Always tip at least a buck a drink. 3) If it's not too busy, try to chat a little with the barkeep. 4) Keep your orders simple and try to order the same things all night long. 5) As with anything, always try to be nice. If you do all these things, it greatly increases the chances of the bartender remembering you and thus buying you a round.

Get a Student ID: Who cares if you're not a student anymore? You still want student discounts right? While the days are over when you could just walk down the street in the East Village and be offered to have a fake ID made for you (this happened to me when I was 16), you can still get a real student ID at STA Travel. Just go in there and ask about a packaged trip and before you go, tell them that you've got to think about it but that you'll be back. At that point they'll probably try to sell you an international student ID; if they don't, just ask if you can get one. Most of the time they never bother to check if you're actually a student.

Discounted Theater Tickets: If you're in school, still have your old student ID, or just got the good people at STA to make you one, you can get discounted theater tickets from the box office. While every theater has a different policy regarding student discounts, most of them put aside a handful just for those people who represent our nation's bleak, I mean bright, future. To get a hold of these, you can look up student rates at *www.broadwayworld.com* or just Google the name of the show you want to see and the words "student tickets" or "lottery".

Another good way to get discount tickets is to sign up for mailing lists that give you discount codes for when you buy online. There are tons of these mailing lists, but I warn you that each generates a fair amount of email for your inbox. Go to the following sites if you're interested in being on the list: *playbill.com, broadwayworld.com, broadwayinsider.com, smarttix.com, telecharge.com, broadwaybox. com, nytimesticketwatch.com.*

And of course there is TKTS in Time Square, the South Street Seaport (199 Water St. @ Fulton St.), and now Downtown Brooklyn (1 MetroTech center at corner of Myrtle Ave & Jay St.) which sells discounted tickets for day of shows, on a first come, first served basis. This can mean *long* lines, especially in the Time Square location. Thanks to Producer Laura for hipping me to all this good stuff!

Volunteer Ushering: Want to see a great show for free? Volunteer to be an usher. Many theatres and music venues would rather have someone do it for free than pay someone, so if there is a show you're interested in seeing, contact the venue it's playing at to inquire about ushering. More often than not, Off Broadway shows need ushers, but there are still some Broadway theatres that do this as well.

Seeing a Live TV Show Taping for Free: You know how when you watch *David Letterman, The Daily Show,* or *The Colbert Report* there is always a live audience? Well my friend, that can be you! Just figure out the show you wanna see, go to their website, and either fill in the proper form or call the number they give. It's that easy. Now lets cross our fingers and hope that I can get interviewed on *The Daily Show* one day. That's a reasonable goal right?

Free Kayaking: Did you know that you can kayak on the Hudson River for free? Just check out The New York City Downtown Boathouse's website, *www.downtownboathouse.org* and learn all about their free kayak lessons and trips. Just try not to get any of the water in your mouth. It will probably kill you.

Free Concerts and Free Movies: There are tons of free concerts and movies that happen during the year, especially during summer, all throughout New York. That being said, I can't possibly list all that shit, and even if I did, you'd end up just going to the web anyways to verify my listings. So I'm gonna make this easier for both of us; just go to *freenyc.net.* They're really good at listing stuff. You could say that's what they do.

Showpaper: Bands like the Yeah, Yeah, Yeahs and TV on the Radio were playing sweaty smelly parties in lofts and warehouses before they made it big. While some of the spaces these groups played may not be around anymore, the DIY music scene they came out of is still going strong and Showpaper is your free key to finding out where and when. Keeping it lo-fi by specifically not having a website, Showpaper can be picked up in bars, restaurants, and stores all over New York and the surrounding areas (yes, even in Jersey). To find out where to get a copy into your grubby little hands visit their myspace page at *myspace.com/showpaper.* I love this type of shit!

Photo by Krista Vendetti

Free Smell Goods: I'm a cologne junkie. I just love the stuff. I'm not sure if people know this or not, but you can get perfume/cologne for free. Just go to a department store or Sephora, pretend you want to buy some fragrances, and then ask them if they have samples. They always do, and they will give you tiny take home bottles for free. So please *stop* smelling bad. This is the 21st century for fuck's sake. You know who you are.

Free Haircuts: If you can't afford an expensive ass New York City haircut, you can always go to one of the salon schools, like Bumble and Bumble, and get your hair cut for free or at least super cheap. The list of places that do this is incredibly long, so luckily *New York* magazine has already listed it for us on their website. Just go to *www.nymag.com/guides/cheap/haircuts* and check out their suggestions, or just google "free haircuts new york."

Don't Get STDs or Preggers: If for some absurd reason you haven't been able to fit prophylactics into your budget, NYC has your wang or your friend's wang covered. Most bars in the city have little things that look like tip jars, filled with free condoms, and you're encouraged to take a few with you. And you know what? They aren't half bad either. They're a whole hell of a lot better than anything I've ever gotten at Planned Parenthood. Those shits are like having sex with a Ziploc bag on your dick.

Historical Markers: Always stop to read these plaques. Sometimes they're lame, but sometimes they are amazing. How much of a rush are you really in?

Free Wireless: Most of the parks in NYC have free Wi-Fi. Just bring your laptop, log on to *nycwireless.net* and voila! You're ready to post a missed connection about that sexy motherfucker you just saw on the train. The site also has a map of all the public places (not just parks) that are free Wi-Fi accessible. I'm a big fan of the Internet. It's pretty amazing that we live in an age where the answer to 99 percent of your questions can be obtained just through Google.

Google on Any Phone: If you don't have a fancy pants phone (Blackberry, iPhone etc.) this will be the coolest thing you read all day. Let's say you're out for the night and meeting up with some friends at the Levee in Williamsburg, but you don't remember where it is. Just whip out your telephono, send a text message to g-o-o-g-l (466-45); in the body of the text, enter the name of the place you're looking for like this: The Levee Brooklyn NY. Then press send. Within seconds, Google will text you back with the address and phone number. And the best part is, it costs the same as a regular text. Sweet huh?

311: Whether you're searching for a job, reporting a broken street light, getting more food stamps, or simply narc-ing on your neighbor, 311 is the number to call. It's a pretty nifty idea that streamlines tons of city agencies into a single operation that can help you with just about any query, in almost 200 languages. 311 is sweet, but you know what I find ridiculous? How 911 isn't the same in every country. Don't you think that the UN should have figured out some universal number so that if you're in Paraguay getting chased by a bloody mob, you'll know who to call without getting the "wrong number" message?

Lost or Stolen Metrocard: Here's some good advice, use your credit/debit card when buying an unlimited ride metrocard. I say this because if your card gets lost or stolen, you can call (212) 638-7622 (212-METROCARD) or 311 (remember that little guy from 25 seconds ago?) and give them your debit/credit number, and they can reimburse you for the remaining days. They will do this three times a year for you. Tell me you love me. Come on, tell me ...please?

Library Card: I know this sounds silly, but people always forget how awesome libraries are. Not only can you borrow millions of great books, but you can also borrow CDs, DVDs and other media too. Hell, you can just borrow a CD you like and rip it straight to your iTunes, giving you free music.* Plus library cards are free themselves.
*Publisher's note: Broke-Ass Stuart in no way endorses music piracy. He is simply speaking hypothetically.

Broke-Ass Stuart's note: Don't listen to them. I totally endorse all forms of piracy as long as no one gets hurt or killed. There's nothing wrong with stealing from the rich. They probably had to do something crooked to get where they are.

Apple Discount: I made the switch to Mac a couple years ago, and I've gotta tell you, I'm never going back. My Mac is SO much better than any PC I've ever had. If you're ever considering switching yourself, go talk to someone in the store to figure out exactly what you want, and then buy it online. If you do that, you can get the student discount by just clicking a box that says you're a student. They never verify this. This discount gives you like 10–15 percent off. Not bad, right? I'm not sure if you can do the same with other Apple products, because I haven't tried, but I don't see why you wouldn't be able to.

Spirit Airlines: If you've done some traveling in Europe, you know that they have crazy cheap airlines like Ryan Air and Easy Jet, on which you can get flights for like $5 plus taxes. In the States, we're not as lucky, unless of course you live in a city that Spirit Air flies to. It just so happens that New York is one, which means that Spirit Air might become your new best friend. Go to *www.spiritair.com* and sign up for their email list. You can choose up to five airports to receive deal notifications from, so choose La Guardia and Long Island MacArthur airports, and they will send you deals every week. You can get flights to beautiful places like Peru, Costa Rica, Jamaica, the Virgin

Islands, Puerto Rico and even Detroit, for like $50 round trip (including taxes). Can I get an Amen?

Chinatown Buses: Yes, the famous Chinatown Buses. These fuckers are the cheapest way to get from one city to another on the East Coast. You can get roundtrip tickets to DC or Baltimore for $35, Philly for $20, and Boston for $30. Each route has multiple operators and each operator has it's own streetside pickup spot. Check out *www. chinatown-bus.org.* On the website they tell you where to catch each bus, how much it is, and they even allow you to pre-purchase your tickets because sometimes that's the only way you can get on one of these crowded buses. Safety is not guaranteed.

Taxi Cabs: Sometimes it's late and you've been drinking or you're tired or both, and you just don't want to deal with waiting for the fucking train. If you do decide to take a cab, you need to know that, by law, the cabbie has to take you where you want once you're inside the vehicle. If home is Brooklyn or Queens or something, hop in the car as soon as it pulls up, that way the cabbie can't drive off when he/she hears that you aren't going somewhere in Manhattan. This happened to me many times until someone finally hipped me to the law. And if they won't drive you through White Castle on the way home, try offering to buy them some fries. That usually works.

Affordable Health Care: Don't die, because getting sick or broken is so expensive. The City of New York has locations like the (in)famous Bellevue Hospital, which provide affordable and in some cases free, health care to those of us who can't afford proper insurance. I have a feeling that going into any further depth could get me sued for some type of wrongful death thing, so I'll just give you the website and let you figure out the details yourself: *www.nyc.gov/hhc*

Paul and I did three more shots before we became total drunken messes and got 86'd from yet another bar.

Chelsea

The High Line running through Chelsea serves as a distinct reminder of the neighborhood's industrial past. Back before the art galleries moved in and before buff Chelsea boys strutted down 8th Ave. with their tiny dogs, Chelsea was a center for warehouses and meatpacking factories, where longshoremen and factory workers toiled during the day and "decent citizens" avoided at night. Though it sits unused and decaying today, the High Line was originally a set of elevated train tracks that functioned as a way to bring freight directly to and from the various industries populating Manhattan's Westside waterfront. Luckily though, New York has learned from its past (attn: Penn Station) and instead of tearing down the High Line, it has set forth plans to turn it into an elevated park that will run from Gansevoort St. north to 30th St. While this will be the final crowning note of a 30-plus-year transformation from industrial wasteland to hip cultural Mecca, you can still catch whiffs of grit in the high 20s and low 30s (streets) west of 10th Ave.

But Chelsea's unglamorous past is not something most people think about often. Instead they focus on what this neighborhood is today: the beating heart of an affluent gay community and a densely packed ghetto of art galleries. People come from all over the world to bask in the radiance of both these cultures, sometimes walking away with a fine piece of art, but more often satisfied with having gotten a fine piece of ass. Chelsea's historic district of 19th century townhouses (centered in the low 20s between 8th and 10th Aves.) is yet another collection of beauty worth wandering around and ogling.

And then there's the Meatpacking District, absolutely the worst part of New York City; I fucking despise that place. It's social Darwinism at its worst, meaning that it's just one alpha-male-douchebag-with-blown-out-hair-and-a-skintight-Armani-shirt after another, each trying to out shine the rest with his supreme douchebaggery. Oh God I loathe it there; so much so, that I chose not to include any of its establishments in this book. Every single time I went there (and there are more instances than I'd like to admit), I went because I knew I'd be drinking for free. It's amazing what I'll endure for free booze.

Chelsea's borders are W. 30th St. in the north to W. 14th St. in the south, and from 6th Ave. in the east to the Hudson River in the west. The Meatpacking District technically straddles Chelsea and the West Village, but it doesn't matter anyways because it can suck my dick.

Food

Billy's Bakery

184 9th Ave & W. 21st St.

I heard a rumor once that Billy's Bakery leaves day-old cupcakes outside the store and anyone can take them for free. I can't corroborate this rumor, but if it is true, and some diabetic homeless person kills himself eating these free cupcakes, how much time do you think Billy would do? Any lawyers in the house? Regardless of Billy's possible upcoming manslaughter case, I can tell you that this shit is astoundingly good. But as the Great New York Cupcake Debate* rages on in cyberspace, I'll let you in on a little secret. While a cupcake in this cute 1950s-looking bakery will set you back $2, the real score is the $4 slice of cake; it's literally 1/8th of a cake! The icing is so sweet that my teeth are still tingling.

Chelsea Thai Wholesale

75 9th Ave. btw 15th & 16th Sts. (in the Chelsea Markets)

Because this eatery sells Thai cooking products like Sriracha (mmm … Sriracha) and is decorated with various photos of Thailand, it ends up looking like a mixture between a Thai bodega, a noodle house, and a travel agency. Personally, I wouldn't care if it looked like the public restroom at the Port Authority, as long as it continued to sell heaping plates of food for less than $8.

Cola's

148 8th Ave. @ W. 17th St.

You know you're in New York when you're getting served a $6.95 lunch special at a decent Italian restaurant by a Bengali guy who used to be an

---

This really exists.

astrophysicist back in his home country. While the prices at this 1940s-looking spot jump a couple bucks at dinnertime, the huge, oxidized-copper lion bust, behind the espresso bar, doesn't move an inch. Why would it? I don't know either, it just sounded like something I should say.

D'Aiuto Baby Watson Cheesecake
405 8th Ave. @ W. 30th St.

Goddamn these people are cocky about their cheesecake. Everything in here, from the articles and plaques on the wall, to the signs proclaiming "Best Cheesecake in New York" lets you know that these folks think theirs is the dopest around. I gotta admit it's pretty damn good, and it's rich and thick, just like I like my women. In fact, the only shitty thing about this $3 cheesecake is that the lady behind the counter wouldn't give me a glass of water. She wanted me to buy a bottle, which I *had* to do because otherwise I would've choked to death. So I didn't give her a tip, and I generally tip everybody. Just because I'm a broke-ass doesn't mean I'm a cheap-ass.

F&B Gudtfood
269 W. 23rd St. @ 8th Ave.

With such a clean, corporate, recently-built-by-Ikea look to it, it's surprising how well priced Gudtfood is. Their angle is taking unhealthy and expensive European classics like fish and chips, Swedish meatballs, and steak frites, and making them cause slightly less shock and awe to your body and wallet. And they seem to be doing a fairly decent job of it, too; a whole chunk of the wall is covered in articles about the place and its famous veggie dogs. What actually impressed me the most, though, was that they were playing Gil Scott-Heron when I was there. It's pretty hard to get cooler than that.

From Earth to You Café
252 10th Ave. btw 24th & 25th Sts.

All the sandwiches at this busy lunch spot are $6.75 or under, except for the smoked salmon sandwich that is $315. Just kidding, it's $8. While everything here is fresh, the bagels, marinara sauce and yogurt are all made on the premises, which means that if you had a pizza bagel, topped with yogurt, the whole thing would be homemade. The only things cheesier than this review are the lines the rotund guy behind the counter spits to all the female customers.

La Taza de Oro

96 8th Ave. @ W. 15th St.

The name of this place should be changed from La Taza de Oro (The Cup of Gold) to El Plato de Arroz y Frijoles (The Plate of Rice and Beans) because you can get a huge helping of the stuff for roughly $3. In fact, the closest I saw to anything resembling gold in this place was a crucifix dangling from a construction worker's neck. Come here for the 1970s-colored lunch counter and the daily rotating menu of $7 Latin favorites. Don't be fooled by their slick advertising campaign and come expecting the cups of gold. You'll be sorely disappointed.

Lobster Place

75 9th Ave. btw 15th & 16th Sts. (in the Chelsea Markets)

Dude you can get oysters here for as little as $1.10! I recommend buying more than one though because there is a one-time 60-cent shucking fee per purchase. They also have fresh sushi (then again who wants their sushi not fresh?), but it's not that cheap. The place is mostly a fresh fish market.

Pita Hut

225 W. 23rd St. btw 7th & 8th Aves.

This small, halal hole in the wall specializes in vegetarian food. I know this because it says so in large letters on the awning. It also sells sandwiches for under $6 and serves up healthy juice drinks. Really, that's all you need to know.

Poppy's Terminal Restaurant

329 10th Ave. @ W. 29th St.

Poppy's is a hidden classic. It's the type of old school spot that reminds me of pre-Giuliani New York; as if he forgot to send his gentrification goons to clean up this gritty block. I get giddy when I find places this hot. A signed photo of Steve Buscemi looks down from its place nestled amongst the sports memorabilia on the wall, while blue-collar workers sit around and talk about how it's so cold outside that they can't find their dicks.

Come nighttime, the place fills up with freaks, weirdos, club kids and lost souls; the types who are born to gravitate towards 24-hour joints in oddly empty parts of Manhattan. Sure, part of what attracts, the patrons, day and night, is the cheap chicken wings, burgers, gyros and beer. But the other part of it, whether they realize it or not, is that it reminds them of a place they used to know. It's like looking at a photo of a friend that was taken back before they got that nose job that now makes them look so pretty.

Punjabi Food Junction

301 10th Ave. btw 27th & 28th Sts.

Any eatery that sells tall boys of Colt 45 unironically is fucking a-ok in my book. Remember those old Colt 45 ads with Billy Dee Williams saying, "Don't let the smooth taste fool you"? Well don't worry Billy Dee, I haven't been fooled. I know that shit fucks you up. That's why I'm washing it down with these delicious samosas. Hell, I may even go big and start in on that $7, all-you-can-eat buffet, because you know what? This place is 24 hours. I can sit here for as long as I want (or at least until the owner gets tired of me talking to an imaginary Billy Dee Williams and kicks me out). Billy Dee, you and I are some classy motherfuckers...

Tebaya

144 W. 19th St. btw 6th & 7th Aves.

I know I'm supposed to sit here and tell you about how you can get eight delicious Japanese-style chicken wings from this small place for $5.75, and that they sell other things like burgers and shit, but I'd rather tell you about Gregory Isaacs. Now I really don't know much about him other than that "Night Nurse" is my favorite song this week. I'm listening to it right now. You should, too.

Bars

Barracuda
275 W. 22nd St. btw 6th & 7th Aves.

When asking my gay friends for good cheap spots in Chelsea, they almost unanimously recommended Barracuda. As one friend put it, "They have *strong* mixed drinks for $6 and the hottest bartenders who give lots of buybacks." It's pretty hard to argue with that. And as if that weren't enough, the kick-ass drag show in the backroom makes it one of the best cheap gay bars in New York.

Blarney Stone
340 9th Ave. @ W. 30th St.

Mostly populated by working class, middle age, black folks who work nearby at the main post office, the Blarney Stone is a solid dive bar serving $3 pints of Bud. The Irish bartenders and the patrons all seem to have known each other for years, but that doesn't stop them from being welcoming and friendly to the strange-looking Jewish kid scribbling in his notebook at the end of the bar. Maybe that's because we're all yelling out wrong answers at the giant flat-screen that's playing trivia from something called "the Bar Network". Or maybe it's because I was drunk enough to buy a Lotto ticket here and tell the whole bar that if I won, I would take us all to Vegas. Regardless, Joe Frazier and Hank Aaron look down on us from their framed photos, disapprovingly.

Deno's Party House USA (aka Bikini Bar)
393 8th Ave. btw W. 29th & 30th Sts.

Deno's Party House USA is the poor man's Hawaiian Tropic restaurant. The food is barely edible and the decorations consist of some potted plants, a shit load of mirrors, a pool table, and some Ukrainian and Russian girls in bikinis. Generally speaking, the only people in this place, other than the girls, are frightening looking Eastern European heavies, total creeps, and the occasional hostel kid who got lured in by the promise of a free drink if he showed his out of state ID. If you do decide to come here, and you're not researching a travel guide or selling bikinis, let me give you a word of advice: don't try to mac on the bartenders; it just makes you one of the creeps. I know what you're gonna say, but listen—creeps are like junkies and hipsters in that they think everyone else is one, but deny it themselves. Plus, I think this place might be a front for a brothel, which means just sit back and let the action come to you.

The Eagle
554 W. 28th St. btw 10th & 11th Aves.

I consider myself to be a fairly knowledgeable and well-traveled person. I'd like to think that I'm hip to a lot of different subcultures and that I know enough about them that I can pick up on most of the slang. But when I came to the Eagle, I was totally surprised by the entire subculture within the Bear/leather community, which is in itself already a gay subculture. I learned that, not only are there Bears (big, hairy lumberjack-looking guys), there are also Otters (skinny, playful, hairy guys), Wolves (aggressive, muscular, hairy guys) and Cubs (younger guys who are growing into Bears). Since when is being gay like being in the Cub Scouts? Do Wolves eventually become Webelos? Are there merit badges for safe sex and reach arounds? If you identify as one of these woodland creatures, or just wanna see them at play, stop in at the Eagle on a nice Sunday for their rooftop beer blast. You might just get to pitch a tent.

Flight 151
151 8th Ave. btw 17th & 18th Sts.

While the theme here has something to do with WWII fighter pilots (I think) it comes off a little half-assed, and the various airplane parts scattered around the room actually remind me of the TV show *Lost*. It's probably not a good thing if your theme bar reminds people of the worst-case scenario of your themed subject. But overall it's actually a decent bar; it sells $3 PBR pints, has crayons so you can draw on the butcher paper and express your sexual frustration in pictures, and has an Internet jukebox. Which brings me to this point: I'm all for Power to the People, as long as they don't get to choose the soundtrack. How do so many people have such bad taste in music? The real reason to come here, though, is because they have different shit going on every night—like "flip night" on Tuesdays where they flip a coin and you get to call it for a free drink. Can you say drunk?

Peter McManus Café
152 7th Ave. @ W. 19th St.

When you walk into Peter McManus Café and see the stained glass cabinets and the liquor shelves sagging from age and use, and notice that the bar is built into the wall and the clock is built into the bar, you can immediately feel that it's the oldest family-run bar in the city.

The wooden phone booths and the 1930s tile floor only add to this feeling, and then when you peek into the back area and see the big vinyl green booths, you realize you're in love. For anyone who's worth a damn, there is nothing better than finding a bar as perfect as this. Just ask the patrons, who range from guys in suits to guys in coveralls, and hip kids to complete drunken messes, and they'll tell you the same. I came here with my girlfriend Krista and a fellow Lonely Planet writer named Becky, and we all sat around drinking $3 pints of Bud and munching on cheap bar food. We all walked away thinking the same thing: this place is a total gem.

Rawhide
212 8th Ave. btw W. 20th & 21st Sts.

Remember in '80s movies when someone would get tricked into going to a bar and they wouldn't realize where they were until they looked up and were surrounded by really butch gay guys? I think all those bars were based on Rawhide. I mean you can't get any more butch than a darkly lit bar with blacked out, one-way windows, cartoon leather porn on the walls, a motorcycle suspended over the pool table, and buff male go-go dancers. I mean even the pinball machine is butch–it's designed by Harley-Davidson. The bartender here was a huge shirtless Bear wearing an unbuttoned denim vest, whose big beer belly had enough hair on it to make three wigs for kids with leukemia. I always wonder where guys like this would work if they weren't bartenders at the Rawhide.

Red Rock West Saloon

457 W. 17th St @ 10th Ave.

The bartenders here are always either drunk and surly, drunk and flirty, or drunk and violent, but, two things are for certain: they're always drunk and always showing cleavage. Because of this penchant for potion that the girls behind the bar seem to share, the prices tend to fluctuate by how much the bartender likes you and how much she feels like charging. While most of the girls are just hard drinkers, some of them are completely insane. I saw this one bartender bully a guy into bending over repeatedly, to get spanked, repeatedly, in front of his girlfriend, before she would give him his change back. And the thing was, it wasn't even being done playfully, it was downright vicious, like she was trying to humiliate him. The scene was awkward to say the least. The nightly crowd who comes to revel in this madness ranges from Hell's Angels to famous actors, and the bartenders, never wanting to disappoint, will take to dancing on the bar in boas and wigs if there is ever a dull moment. There generally never is.

Shopping

W. 30th St. between 6th & 5th Aves. is apparently the fur coat district, just in case you want to look like Ghostface.

192 Books
192 10th Ave. btw W. 21st & 22nd Sts.

192 is a fairly small bookstore with a decent selection of books in general, and a big selection of art books. It's not exactly super cheap, but I try to include as many indie bookstores as possible because, well, motherfuckers gotta know.

Chelsea Market
75 9th Ave. btw 15th & 16th Sts.

Did you know that Nabisco is actually short for National Biscuit Company? Well now you do, which makes you that much better of a Trivial Pursuit player. The Chelsea Market, which is kinda like a mall where the entire thing is the food court, is built in the old National Biscuit Company factory, which accounts for its really cool industrial look. Some of the eateries are pricier than others, but there are excellent inexpensive options throughout (like Chelsea Thai Wholesale and Lobster Place, both previously mentioned). Some places give out free samples of food and booze, and there are also weekly events like Salsa lessons on Tuesdays and Tango lessons on Fridays. Rumor has it that the entire complex is haunted by the ghost of some Vanilla Wafers that mysteriously disappeared in the 1930s.

The Flower District
6th Ave. btw 26th & 29th Sts.

Okay, so you really fucked up this time. Not only did you forget your anniversary, which also happens to fall on her birthday (which you also forgot), but you didn't close the front door all the way, allowing her cat to run out and get hit by a car. It's gonna take *a lot* of flowers to make up for this one, right? Well the Flower District just might be your salvation my friend. The trick is though, you gotta get here really early, like between 7 and 8am, otherwise all the good shit will be gone. I know it sucks, but if you tell her you got up at 6am just to get her flowers, it might earn you extra points. Then again, it might not.

PB Cuban Cigars

265 W. 30th St. @ 8th Ave.

Even though I'm not a smoker, I like to treat myself to a nice cigar a few times a year. I believe that smoking, like anything else, is fine when done in moderation*. That's where PB Cuban Cigars comes in. They hand roll their cigars on the premises while old school New Yorkers sit around the comfortable couches talking shit about sports, stocks and when they used to be able to get their dicks up. And you'll never guess how cheap these hand rolled boutique cigars are. Come on, guess. They start at $2.50! Can you believe that? Next time you stop in there, tell them Broke-Ass Stuart sent you. They'll probably say, "*Quien?*" but do it for shits and giggles anyways.

TekServe

119 W. 23rd St. btw 6th & 7th Aves.

You can check out the mediocre fish tank and also all the cool old radios on the wall, but we all know the reason you're here–to get your Apple gear fixed. TekServe is way cheaper than the Apple store. They only charged me $50 to replace my iPod battery. Also peep the old columns that hold up the ceilings of this cast iron–style building. And the weird fake stuffed leopard and shark hanging on the wall.

There are also a few counters apparently made from old Macs. Yeah we all know this is just a poor attempt at making this place seem less like a computer store than it is.

Apparently my liver won't stop laughing at the thought of me doing anything in moderation.

Sights & Entertainment

Chelsea Art Museum
160 11th Ave. @ W. 22nd St.

Chelsea Galleries
mostly in the 20s along 10th & 11th Aves.

Wouldn't it be nice to have enough money to be able to collect art? Sure I've got a couple great pieces that have been given to me by friends, but how amazing would it be to be able walk into a place and be like, "Yes, *dahling*, I think that piece would really bring together the living room at our summer cottage. Call Jeeves and have him bring the car around." That's the type of shit that happens everyday at the Chelsea galleries, a consolidated mass of galleries that display the hottest, newest shit in the art world. Of course some are better than others, and I'm no art critic, so you're best bet is to take a day, stroll around this area, and figure out which galleries you like best. You can get an idea of what's going on, including art openings (free wine and cheese), by checking out www.galleryguide.com. And, if you are an artist and would like to add to my meager collection, drop me a line; I love getting presents!

Photo by Nicki Ishmael

Chelsea Hotel
222 W. 23rd St.
btw 7th & 8th Aves.

I became enamored with the Chelsea Hotel the very first time I heard Leonard Cohen's beautiful "Chelsea Hotel No. 2". I was 15 at the time, and any hotel where people were getting head on unmade beds sounded pretty awesome to me. It wasn't until I got to college that I found out that the song was written about Cohen's short affair with Janis Joplin, which makes the

Photo by Nicki Ishmael

song even cooler. Built in 1883 as one of the city's first private apartment co-ops and made into a hotel in 1905, the building's name is technically the Hotel Chelsea, but nobody calls it that. Besides the absolutely stunning architecture and design of the building, the Chelsea Hotel is important because it has pretty much been the beating heart of New York's Bohemian life for as long as anyone cares to remember (although in modern day New York it's becoming ever more impossible for up and coming artists to afford to stay there). Most of the 400-plus rooms are taken by long-term (sometimes decades) guests, and about 100 of them are available for short stays. Truly amazing things have happened in this hotel: Bob Dylan wrote "Sad Eyed Lady of the Lowlands" here, Sid Vicious killed Nancy Spungen in room 100,

Dylan Thomas was staying here when he drank himself to death, and Leonard Cohen met Janis Joplin in the elevator and they became lovers. The list of people who've lived or stayed here is staggering; Jimi Hendrix, Mark Twain, Jean-Paul Sartre, Jack Kerouac, Tom Waits, Joni Mitchell, Frida Kahlo, Patti Smith, and Stanley Kubrick, just to name a few. Part of what allowed the magic to happen here was that the Bard family ran the hotel, but unfortunately Stanley Bard was recently ousted. Many fear the new management plans to turn it into a boutique hotel, which would, in effect, ruin this special place.

P.S. Thanks again to Glennon Travis for letting me use the Chelsea Hotel for a photo shoot.

Rubin Museum of Art
150 W. 17th St. btw 6th & 7th Aves.

The Rubin Museum is sweet because it's so specific. They're like, "Hmmm … what hasn't been done yet? Modern art? Nope, taken. Medieval art? That's been done, too. How about art from the Himalayas dating from the 12th century onward? Perfect! You ain't got shit on us now Guggenheim, you fucking peckerhead!" While admission is generally $10, they knock the price down to $7 if you are a student or an artist (trust me, just say you're one). And on Friday nights it's free from 7–10pm. What also makes this place great is that they have a bar (well they call it a "café") that does a two-for-one happy hour, with a DJ, from 6–7pm on Friday nights. That way you can get "enlightened" before you check out all the dope art.

Upright Citizens Brigade Theater
307 W. 26th St. @ 8th Ave.

The Upright Citizens Brigade Theatre has a philosophy I can dig. They don't think people should have to pay a lot of money to see awesome comedy. They've been putting on New York's best and funniest improv and sketch comedy since 1999 and they always charge less than $10 for admission. In fact, many of their shows are either free or only $5. And the coolest part is that you can see some really big names there like Mike Myers, David Cross, Will Ferrell and Tina Fey. And for all you aspiring actors out there, (I'm looking at you girl-who-just-moved-here-yesterday-from-Nebraska-and-will-eventually-work-at-Coffee Shop) they also teach comedy and improv. I love this place and you will, too.

CHELSEA

Grub-a-dub-dub
1. Billy's Bakery
2. Chelsea Thai Wholesale
3. Cola's
4. D'Auito Baby Watson Cheesecake
5. F&B Gudtfood
6. From Barth to You Café
7. Lobster Place
8. Pita Hut
9. Poppy's Terminal Restaurant
10. Punjabi Food Junction
11. La Taza de Oro
12. Tebaya

DRINKS DRINKS DRINKS
13. Barracuda
14. Blarney Stone
15. Deno's Party House USA (AKA Bikini Bar)
16. The Eagle
17. Flight 151
18. Peter McManus Café
19. Rawhide
20. Red Rock West Saloon

Shopping
21. 192 Books
22. Chelsea Market
23. The Flower District
24. PB Cuban Cigars
25. TekServe

Stuffis to See and Do
26. Chelsea Galleries
27. Chelsea Hotel
28. Rubin Museum of Art
29. Upright Citizens Brigade Theater

Free Food Bitches!!
30. Rocking Horse

Herbivore Friendly
31. Blossom Vegan Restaurant

Bear (Come on, who doesn't like bears?)

Gay couples with adopted Cambodian babies

Someone telling their friend "Oh my God! You look so fierce in those new Diesel jeans!"

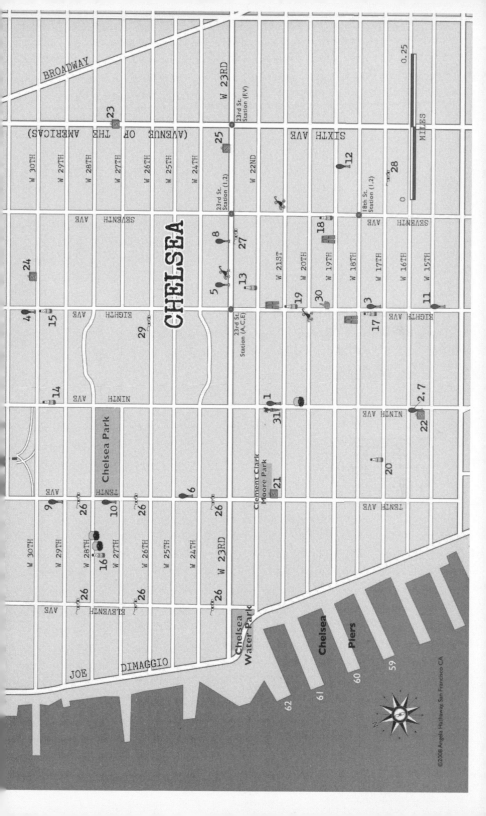

Union Square & The Flatiron District

Union Square has always been a meeting point. The first Labor Day parade happened here in 1882, and many pro-Union rallies were held in the square during the Civil War. But what's funny is that it's the meeting or union of two roads, Bloomingdale Road (now Broadway) and Bowery Road (called 4th Ave. here), that gave this square it's name, not the fact that it was the site of pro-Union demonstrations. Union Square isn't really a neighborhood in itself though; it's actually part of the Flatiron District. But no one ever says "Oh I'm going to the Flatiron District", they say, "You know, over by Union Square".

But that might be because the area only began being referred to as the Flatiron District (after it's most famous landmark, the Flatiron Building) in the 1980s, or because it doesn't have any real specific and unique characteristics. Sure it's got a few prominent features like the Met Life Building and Madison Square Park, but otherwise it's just a collection of offices (mostly publishing and advertising), restaurants and residences.

Roughly speaking, the boundaries of the area are Irving Pl./Lexington Ave to the east, 6th Ave. to the west, 27th St to the north, and 14th St. to the south.

Food

Andy's Deli
873 Broadway @ 18th St.

I used to get breakfast sandwiches here on the way to some fucking job that I hated and only worked at for three weeks. There are tons of spots like this, but this one holds a special place in my heart, because I remember always walking into work eating my breakfast sandwich and bumping the Clipse in my headphones being like "Fuck this place! I'm quitting as soon as I find a new job." It also sells flowers outside in case you really piss off your girlfriend.

Azuki Sushi
239 Park Ave. South btw 19th & 20th Sts.

See p. 227 (Hell's Kitchen)

Barocco Kitchen
42 Union Square East @ E. 17th St.

A medium-sized place right at Union Square where the average price for a gourmet sandwich is $7, and all of them come on home-baked bread. The narrowness of the place makes it really easy to walk right by it, but that in turn makes it a good place to avoid the madness on the streets and have a quiet cappuccino, if you're into that sort of thing.

Eisenberg's Sandwich Shop
174 5th Ave. btw E 22nd & E 23rd Sts.

If you can't tell by the name, this formidable old school diner from the 1930s is a Jewish style deli specializing in sandwiches. Sandwiched (see what I did there?) between Lucky Jeans and Jamba Juice, Eisenberg's has what those corporate cum-rags will never have: soul. Old black and white photos of New York line the walls, while people from all walks of life sit at its long lunch counter and order from a menu where everything is less than $10. They also have daily specials like fried fish filet and mac and cheese on Fridays, which is what I had. I know I should start eating better. I'll start tomorrow, I swear. The fact that places like this still exist makes me happy.

Ennju
20 E. 17th St. btw 5th Ave. & Broadway

Despite the recent bump in prices, Ennju is still a rocking spot to get cheap grub in this expensive neighborhood. A freshly made spicy tuna roll is about $5.25. The sushi is made in front of you assembly line style, like at a health food store, and then put on the rack to be bought. If you happen to read Japanese, they have a library of comics (are these the manga I hear so much about?) for you to peruse as well as a couple of newspapers and magazines. The rolls range from $5 to $10 and you can get noodle soup and *donburi* for around $8. Too bad I don't know what *donburi* is.

Latin American Restaurant
29 W. 26th St. btw 5th & 6th Aves.

Names like this kill me. It's like they just couldn't be bothered to think of something else to call it. It's like naming a restaurant Italian Food. (Believe it or not, one of the world's biggest telescopes is actually called the Very Large Telescope. These people can design a way to see light years away, yet can't think of anything better than Very Large Telescope.). But you know what? Creative names usually mean expensive prices, and I'd rather have a $5.99 pork chop with rice and beans than a creative name any day. And just to let you know they're serious about their prices, there's a giant three foot by five foot menu in the window to show you that they aren't fucking around.

Mandler's
26 E. 17th St. @ Broadway

Mandler's is the best sausage fest I've ever been to...sorry I couldn't resist. They serve breakfast all day and the best of these is the $3.95 omelet with sausage (of course), tomato, cheese, onion (yuck), bread, butter and jam. Hell of a deal Mr. Mandler, hell of a deal. The original Mandler's sausage is 9 ½ inches (I'm not gonna put a joke here, but feel free to), and you can also get a Mandler's special like sausage pasta. If it's your first time, try the sausage sampler (four half sausages of your choice, cut up real small), which is what I got. They also have the mustard bar with more types of mustard than I care to list and there are crazy colored chandeliers that look like they came from a psychedelic haunted house.

Maoz Vegetarian

38 Union Square East btw E. 16th & 17th Sts.

Good, cheap, veggie falafel.

Rainbow Falafel

26 E. 17th St. @ Broadway

An impossibly tiny spot that slangs great balls of fried chickpeas, Rainbow Falafel, and sits in what appears to be an alcove under a really cool beaux-arts-looking arch. Then again, I might have just made up the beaux-arts thing because I don't really know what that is. It sure sounds good though. They also sell candy bars that are dispensed from the wall. A falafel sandwich here runs you $3.50, which is not quite Mamoun's prices, but still damn cheap.

Shake Shack

in Madison Square Park

People line up for Shake Shack like they're in Moscow in 1981. But I guess a gourmet burger for $3.50 might be worth waiting for. Then again, you can also just call (212) 889-6600 and pick up your order—but it has to be for over $25 and you can only do it in winter time (people dying from frostbite while waiting in line is bad for business). This is the only Danny Meyer restaurant you or I can afford to eat at, so let's get it while we can.

Sirtaj

36 W. 26th St. @ Broadway

Everything is $7 or under. There's little to no décor but they don't want you to be distracted from the flavor. Right?

Bars

119 Bar

119 E. 15th St. @ Irving Pl.

119 might be one of the most perfect bar setups I've ever seen. It's really low lit, with a substantial amount of wide-open space, and lots of seating in the form of booths and couches. Then there's also a small, snuggly backroom, with a few worn and comfy couches that are perfect for little bit of drunk smoochin' (or dry-humping like the couple I saw there last time). The walls are wood paneled and the only things hanging on them are Victorian-looking round lights and a giant blow-up of Frank Sinatra's mug shot. But you're not here to stare at the walls, you're here to play some pool, drink some booze, listen to the bartender's iPod, talk some shit, and then pass out on your friend's couch and piss yourself. You know who you are. One time I was here and got into a really interesting conversation with a bartender who told me that, at one point, she was the number one female amateur boxer in the US. She also informed me that boxing is the only Olympic sport that doesn't have a women's competition. I informed her that she could probably kick my ass. She agreed.

No Idea

30 E. 20th St. btw Park Ave. South @ Broadway

While they don't take Disney Dollars at No Idea (I asked), they do put a name on the board everyday, and if it's your name, you drink for free. I don't bother looking though, because I know it's gonna be like those tiny license plates with names on them in Chinatown that never said "Stuart". Many people who toil in the surrounding area use No Idea as an after work spot, and if you do decide to pop in and it seems packed, keep heading to the back; there are, surprisingly, two more rooms back there. Make sure to take note of the poster of the periodic table on the wall; it has to be one of the biggest I've ever seen. Who needs a periodic table that big?

Old Town Bar & Restaurant
45 E. 18th St. @ Broadway

If you haven't figured it out by now, this book is just as much about the search for glimpses of old New York as it is about finding cool, cheap things to do. Something about this city, the way it pushes, prods, and screams at all your senses, has absolutely absorbed people's attention for centuries. And now, with the hyper-commercialization of *everything*, more and more of the things that make this city special are in the process of disappearing. Luckily, Old Town Bar and Restaurant isn't one of them. Not much has changed in this joint since it opened in 1892. Sure, owners have come and gone, prices have gone up, and alcohol has gone from legal, to not, to legal again, but otherwise things look the same. The embossed tin ceiling is still here, as are the light fixtures, dumbwaiters, mahogany and marble bar, giant urinals, tile floors and the booths (including the one that still flips up from back in Prohibition days when this was a speakeasy). I guess what I'm saying is that there's something simply poetic about the way this bar looks. Just ask any of the famous writers whose signed book covers hang on the wall*. If for some reason I haven't hooked you yet, I will when I tell you that the entire food menu is under $10. See you there.

Revival
129 E. 15th St. btw 3rd Ave. & Irving Pl.

I like bars that believe one happy hour isn't enough for the common man and, therefore, make a second happy hour later on in the night. Revival is just such a place. From 11pm–1am on weeknights, happy hour does a second victory lap, just to prove its stamina (and test yours). While Revival is open year long, the best time to go is during the warm months when they open up their lovely back patio. Otherwise you'll be stuck inside with the weird colonial scenes that are painted on the walls.

Any room for one more book cover?

Shopping

W. 26th between Broadway and 7th Ave has lots of places to get brightly colored ball caps and oversized XXXXXXXL shirts of Biggie and Coogi gear.

Past Madison Square, going north, on the side streets, there are lots of stores with cheap clothes at negotiable prices. The clothes are probably all made in questionable conditions, but what's not these days? That's how I assuage my conscience.

Abracadabra Superstore
19 W. 21st St. @ 5th Ave.

When you walk into a place that's playing ABBA, and you overhear one clerk asking another, "Can we rent out these clown shoes?" you know there's a high probability you're in the best store ever. Between the fluorescent purple, pink and green carpet (think Hammer pants from elementary school), the wig gallery, the feather boa gallery, and the giant stuffed monsters (Abominable Snowman, Orcs from *Lord of the Rings*), the only thing that could possibly make this place more complete would be if they employed a magical midget. It's like Abracadabra Superstore is equal parts Halloween store, drag queen depot, and studio back lot. And this place is huge! There are two floors overflowing with shit you've never imagined before. Is it cheap? Not really, but any place that has a sign saying, "Adult Costumes for Rent Downstairs" is my kind of place (truthfully though, the idea of secondhand "adult" costumes kinda gives me the heebie-jeebies).

Academy Records & CDs
12 W. 18th St. @ 5th Ave.; *also* at 415 E. 12th St. btw 1st Ave & Ave. A, 96 N 6th St. btw Bedford Ave. & Berry St.

I walked out of here having spent $12 for the DVD of *A History of Violence* ($4) and the Smiths album *The Queen is Dead* on CD ($8)! Are you fucking kidding me? That's awesome! You can also get full TV seasons on DVD for way cheap; *Lost* was $25. While the selection of used DVDs and CDs is pretty sweet, the real focus here is on classical music LPs, meaning that most of the clientele is old guys with a smattering of crate-digging beat producers. Be sure to check out the other locations if you're looking for nonclassical vinyl. But this is the only one that sells DVDs.

Books of Wonder
18 W. 18th St. btw 5th & 6th Aves.

Whether you knocked up your girl a couple years ago and now have a rug-rat, have a thing for Dominican nannies, or are just simply a pederast, Books of Wonder is a great spot to be. This is a giant book-store filled with every kid's book imaginable. It has a small gallery of framed prints from famous children's book authors and a café called Cupcake Café. Can you guess what they sell there? There's also a col-lection of old and rare books like some of the old school Oz books.

H & M
111 5th Ave. @ E 18th St.
See p. 211 (Midtown East)

Revolution Books
9 W. 19th St. btw 5th & 6th Aves.

Selling subversive literature and posters, this sizable, nonprofit store has all the right values (morally and price wise). There's tons of lit-erature by cats like Bob Avakian (the head of the American Commu-nist Party) and Noam Chomsky, as well as big Mao posters and shit from the Chinese Revolution. This is definitely my type of store, and I love the fact that it's so close to Union Square (for symbolic reasons). The workers here are all volunteers, which is fantastic, but what's funny is that they are a little paranoid. When I was taking photos of the place, one of them loudly said, "Please make sure you do not photograph any employees or patrons." Don't worry buddy, I doubt the FBI is worried about this place. Communists are the least of their concerns these days. Revolution Books has lots of events, so make sure to check the schedule on their website.

Skyline Books
13 W. 18th St. @ 5th Ave.

Solid used bookstore that smells like one (this is definitely a good thing). It sells mostly hard covers, many of which are art books and books on stuff like art and communism. There's also a $2-books cart outside.

Sights & Entertainment

Flatiron Building

175 5th Ave. @ Broadway

Designed by Daniel Burnham (that dude from Erik Larson's book *Devil in the White City*), the Flatiron Building was originally called the Fuller Building when it was completed in 1902. Although you probably can't go in unless you have some type of business there, you can stand outside and take photos of it to post on MySpace with captions like, "Look, I live in New York and you don't!" It'll make your friends back wherever the fuck you're from totally jealous.

Madison Square Park

btw W. 23rd & 26th Sts. and 5th Ave. & Madison

Filled with statues, monuments and plaques, and surrounded by famous buildings, Madison Square Park is a lovely green oasis in the center of the bustling city. It's a great place to chill and read a book, or access free Wi-Fi on a nice, sunny day. But of all the neat things in this park, my favorites are the big metal trees (which look like they've been hit with one of Willow's magic acorns), and the statue of William H. Seward. Rumor has it that when Randolph Rogers, the man who made Seward's statue, was commissioned to do the gig, he just took the body mold from the Abe Lincoln statue he had recently done in Philly's Fairmont Park, and added old Seward's head. That sounds like some lazy-ass shit that I would do.

Museum of Sex

233 5th Ave. @ E 27th St.

For a museum to make it into this book, it pretty much has to be a place with suggested donations or have a free day. While the Museum of Sex has neither of these, it does have a $3 off coupon that you can print from its website. I just like this museum so much that I had to put it in here, even if it's not super cheap (with the coupon admission is still $11.50). It's a museum about sex! My girlfriend Krista and I came here during the Kink exhibition, which was all about different fetishes. Holy shit there are some freaky people out there. Dear reader, I don't care what kind of depraved shit you're into–I saw things that would top it. There are fetishes out there that would make Charles Manson squirm (like the one about injecting saline into someone's scrotum so it blows up to be the size of beach ball ... wow). The permanent collection is also pretty amazing, showcasing the history of porno flicks, which began when film began, and an entire display of various masturbatory devices. If you're uncomfortable with "deviant" sexual practices then maybe this just isn't your type of museum. But me, I'm a total perv, so I felt right at home.

Tibet House

22 W. 15th St. btw 5th & 6th Aves.

The Tibet House is an institution dedicated to preserving Tibetan culture. Because of this, it's both an office space and a gallery with art running right by people's cubicles. I was looking at some art while overhearing someone make dinner reservations for 12 people. I hope they went to Sumile Sushi (154 W. 13th St. btw 6th & 7th Aves), because that's the best sushi place in the city, and it's right around the corner. The gallery rooms have breathtaking tapestries and statues that are mostly from people's private collections and gifts from monasteries. The collection here ranges from modern creations to pieces that date back to the 15th century, and the best part is it's totally free to check out! They also do lectures and classes here, including a free meditation class on Tuesdays. An added plus is that the people who work here are super nice (maybe that Dali Lama fellow is rubbing off on them), so if you've had enough of New York's signature rudeness, stop in here. It's refreshing.

Union Square

btw E. 14th & E. 17th Sts. and Union Sq. West & Union Sq. East

While living in New York, Union Square was pretty much the center of my world. I lived in Brooklyn off the L-train, I worked in the West Village off the L-train, so pretty much when I had time to kill I often found myself in Union Square. There's just so much to see here; gorgeous people walking by, skaters trying to land kick-flips, artisans selling their wares, film school kids shooting shorts, and a fantastic farmers market that happens Monday, Wednesday, Friday, and Sat-

I don't even like vegetables, and this guy makes me want to buy a vegetable peeler.

urday, year round. Then there's Joseph Ades, a 70 something year old British man, in a tweed coat, who *Vanity Fair* called "The Gentleman Grafter". Known to most of us as "that old British guy who sells the vegetable peelers", Ades is possibly the best salesman in New York; he makes enough money selling $5 veggie peelers from Switzerland that he lives in the Upper East Side and drinks expensive champagne every night. Although he does his spiel and demonstration all over the city, you can often find him in the north west corner of Union Square. Considering that I started off selling $5 zines from a backpack, this guy is my fucking hero.

UNION SQUARE and FLATIRON DISTRICT

Grub-a-dub-dub
1 Andy's Deli
2 Azuki Sushi
3 Barocco Kitchen
4 Eisenberg's Sandwich Shop
5 Ennju
6 Latin American Restaurant
7 Mandler's
8 Rainbow Falafel
9 Shake Shack
10 Sirtaj

DRINKS DRINKS DRINKS
11 119 Bar
12 No Idea
13 Old Town Bar & Restaurant
14 Revival

Shopping
15 Abracadabra Superstore
16 Academy Records & CDs
17 Books of Wonder
18 H&M
19 Revolution Books
20 Skyline Books

Stuffis to See and Do
21 Flatiron Building
22 Madison Square Park
23 Museum of Sex
24 Tibet House
25 Union Square

Free Food Bitches!!
26 Tarallucci e Vino

Herbivore Friendly
27 Maoz Vegetarian

Street Meat
28 World's Best Sandwich Truck

People who want you to sponsor a kid in Africa

Really hot girl going to work at Coffee Shop

Kid who has been trying to land a kickflip for 3 hours

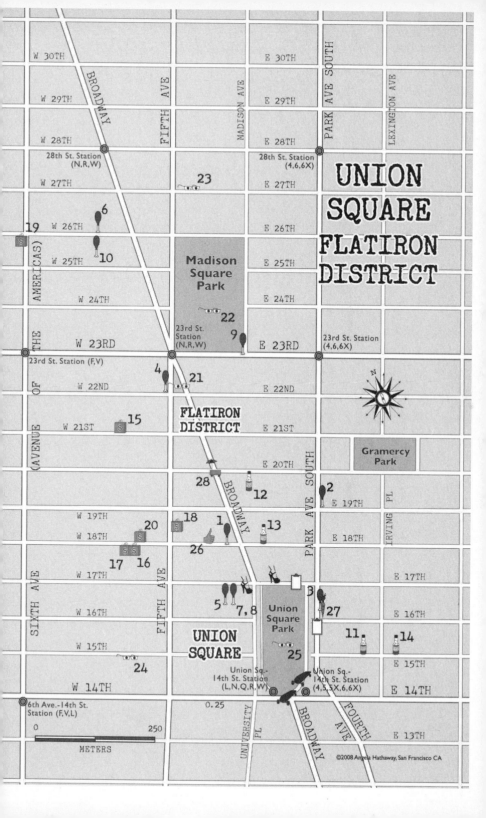

Gramercy Park & Murray Hill

Gramercy Park is named after the fenced in, private park of the same name. Only the people who live in the surrounding area are given a key to the park, so they are the only ones who have access. I personally think this is ridiculous, greedy and extremely bourgeois, and I'd love to scale the fence one day and take a shit on the grass, just to prove a point (what that point is though, I'm not quite sure). But from the outside, the park does look beautiful and complements the exquisite buildings that surround it. The rest of the neighborhood follows suit, largely a collection of lovely brownstones with the occasional highrise sprinkled in. On a whole, the neighborhood is fairly tranquil (by NY standards) with most of the activity taking place along the main thoroughfares like 3rd Ave. and Irving Pl. The boundaries for the neighborhood of **Gramercy Park** are E. 14th St. to the south, E. 23rd St. to the north, Irving Pl. to the west, and the big ass housing complex known as Stuyvesant Town to the east.

Murray Hill, on the other hand, is far from serene. Largely populated by a self-absorbed post college crowd probably still paying dues to their respective fraternities and sororities, this neighborhood was originally the home of a prominent 18th century Quaker merchant family named Murray (hence its name). These days though the main drags are lined with bars and restaurants pandering to the needs of the area's young residents, while the architecture consists of many large apartment buildings and a few pockets of charming brownstones. While coming here for a bite to eat is grand, I try to avoid the bar scene as much as possible. What is it about middle-class white guys in collared shirts that make them wanna fight so much? Come on, are their lives really that tough? The boundaries of Murray Hill are approximately E. 40th St. to the north, E. 30th St. to the south, Park Ave. to the west and the East River to the east.

Since the north part of Gramercy ends at about E. 23rd St. and the south part of **Murray Hill** goes till around E. 30th St., there's a little pocket between the neighborhoods affectionately known as Curry Hill. There's an amazing amount of Indian, Pakistani, and Bengali restaurants here, generally focused around Lexington Ave. I personally just call that part of the city "delicious".

Food

Called Curry Hill because of all its hamburger joints. I've written about some good curry spots below, but I didn't want to make the whole thing just about food from the Indian subcontinent. So here are a few other good cheap choices:

Curry & Curry India Restaurant
153 E. 33rd St. @ Lexington Ave.

Curry Dream
66 W. 39th St. btw 5th & 6th Aves.

Chennai Garden
129 E. 27th St. btw Park & Lexington Aves.

Carl's Steaks
507 3rd Ave. btw 34th & 35th Sts.

Some heretics, who are apparently not afraid of death at the hands of vicious and rampaging mobs of Philadelphians, claim that the steaks served here are better than those in Philly. Other people, with a greater desire to live out the rest of their days without losing their Philly visiting privileges, just claim that it's the best in New York. Personally, I believe the best one in this fine city is made by a man named Ali who works the graveyard shift at the Big Apple bodega in the eastern part of Williamsburg. I'd also like to visit my dear friends in Philly again without receiving hateful and vengeful bodily harm, so I'm not going to venture far enough to say Ali's are better than anything in the 'City of Brotherly Love'. That being said, Carl's $6.50 cheesesteaks are pretty fantastic. So is the plaque commemorating Babe Ruth's trade to the Yankees (from Boston), which calls the Yanks "the best team ever".

Joe Jr. Restaurant

167 3ʳᵈ Ave. btw E. 16ᵗʰ & 17ᵗʰ Sts.

While it's not one of the absolute gutter cheap spots in this book, Joe Jr. is mad reasonable and the food is damn solid. $6.20 for a burger and fries is pretty good, right? Like I said, not dumpster diving cheap, but totally reasonable. The best part though is that it looks exactly like the type of old New York coffee shop that you see when you watch movies like *Taxi Driver* and that one movie where Woody Allen plays the little neurotic Jewish guy. In fact the guys who hang out on the corner in front of Joe Jr. (and occasionally inside) look exactly like the degenerate, mildly homicidal guys who used to drive cabs in this town.

The Kati Roll Company

49 W. 39ᵗʰ St. btw 5th & 6ᵗʰ Aves.; also at 99 Mac-Dougal St. btw Minetta Ln. & Bleecker St.

Kati rolls are like delicious, skinny, Indian burritos. And while I know that it's of course not really a burrito, doesn't the idea of blending Indian and Mexican foods sound heavenly? I can just imagine it, chicken tikka fajitas or tandoori carne enchiladas ... mmmm ... I just drooled on my keyboard. Enough of this nonsense, some dreams never come true. Back to the Kati Roll Company, whose walls are decorated in what appears to be 1970s Indian movie posters on one side, (the poster from the Indian version of *The Matrix* is more recent and possibly hand drawn) and a lot of orange paint on the other. The food is excellent and cheap; a chicken tikka roll is $4.50 and you get two for $8. Just don't get too excited like me and eat part of the wrapping.

Katsuri

83 Lexington @ E. 26ᵗʰ St.

When you walk into Katsuri, the first thing you think to yourself is, "This place is either gonna be the best meal in ages, give me dysentery, or both." Then the second thing you think is, "If it *doesn't* give me dysentery, knowing about this place is gonna give me so much street cred with my friends." And how could it not? It's literally a big room, furnished solely with plastic tables and chairs and a TV playing a Bengali channel. Other than that, there's just a soda machine, the counter and 35 cab drivers from Bangladesh. That's it. I'd been walking by this place forever, wanting to check it out, but it wasn't until Paul, Tobias, Michelle and I were out doing bar research one night that I finally made it in here. Michelle and I shared a huge meal we couldn't finish for less than $10 and it was spectacular. Needless to say, it was easy to get a cab afterwards. And no, I didn't get dysentery.

The Famous Chicken Place

592 3rd Ave. @ E. 39th St.

There's really not much you can say about this place other than it's a cheap hole in the wall. In fact, I think they're exaggerating when they call it famous, so I'm just gonna go ahead and list off various foods and their prices. Half a charcoal broiled chicken: $5.85; nine piece buffalo wings with fries: $7.75 ($6.55 w/o fries); quarter rack of ribs: $7.95 and comes with two sides (good traditional Southern shit like mac and cheese, corn, and falafel!); burger with fries and coleslaw: $6. But, oh snap! They got cheap healthy options, too! You can get a whole-wheat chicken wrap for $5.95.

Mark Café

125 E. 23rd St. btw Park Ave. South & Lexington Ave.

When I first popped in to check out this place, I had just regrettably paid $3.50 for a mini burger (roughly the size of a small cell phone) around the corner at the New York Burger Company. Seriously, fuck the New York Burger Company–go to Mark Café instead. While this spot may be lacking that corporate sheen that its around the corner neighbor pulls off so well (Mark's actually has zero atmosphere unless you count televised Mexican soccer games as ambience), who cares? It's not that I'm opposed to ambience; I generally just can't afford it. Which is why Mark Café rocks–it hits the spot for the right price; a solid-sized burger *and* fries for $5.50. My left nostril is bigger than that fucking mini burger was.

Minar's Taj

5 W. 31st St. @ 5th Ave.

It's all about Southern Indian food here at Minar's Taj, and when talking about Southern Indian food, one must include dosa. If there is a god, he/she/it definitely had a hand in the creation of this delicious, toothsome crepe. Dosa starts at $4.50 here and comes with coconut chutney and sambar, a pea and vegetable stew made with tamarind. Very fucking toothsome.

Spade's Noodles, Rice & More
557 3rd Ave. @ E. 37th St.

Spade's serves decent Chinese food at decent prices. In this lifestyle that we live, that's about all we can ask for. The place looks like it crept out of Chinatown when no one was looking and made sure to bring all the weird hanging roasted birds with it. There's a shit ton of variety here and a good 80 percent of the menu is under $10.

Sunburst Espresso Bar
206 3rd Ave. btw 18th & 19th Sts.

Cool jazz plays on the speakers, while people sit between the dark red walls eating $7.50 wraps, paninis and salads and using the free Wi-Fi. This is an average afternoon at Sunburst, a place where you can get shit done and possibly meet some attractive people who are also trying to get shit done. It's the type of place that would totally play Sade (pronounced "Sha-day"), and if they do, well, she's doing half the work for you (in the meeting-attractive-people department, not the getting-shit-done department). Come here on a weekend morning though, the place is filled up with boisterously hung-over people craving Sunburst's popular breakfast. Definitely a different vibe than the average afternoon.

P.S. If you aren't down with Sade, you probably hate sex too.

Woorijip
12 W. 32nd @ 5th Ave.

In the center of Manhattan's would-be Koreatown (see Los Angeles for an example of Koreatown), this popular spot slangs hot Korean food, lunch buffet style ($6.95 a pound) as well as pre-made packaged goodies. Personally, I hate the smell of kimchi, but otherwise, this place rocks. Domestic beers here go for $2, and even though it's located to be a lunchtime spot, it's still crackin' after 8pm. That being said, this place must be insane at lunch during the week. At least they play traditional Korean music like the Gipsy Kings.

Yatra

32 W. 31st St. btw 5th Ave. & Broadway

A simple Indian food place that has a $9.95 all-you-can-eat-lunch buffet every day of the week, except for Sunday when they are closed. I always eat until I make myself sick and then spend the rest of the day whimpering and farting.

Bars

There are a ton of bars in the Murray Hill. The only problem is that 99 percent of them are fucking depression inducing. So I've done the best I could. Truth be told, I hate going out around here.

Barfly
244 3rd Ave. btw 27th & 28th Aves.

Not a place I would normally hang out unless pressed to do so for research purposes. You see what I do for you? (Sorry, that's the 5,000 years of inherited Jewish mothering coming out.) This place has a sports bar feel and Miller Lite is $3.50 a pint; hey that's not too bad.

Black Bear Lodge
274 3rd Ave. btw E. 22nd & 23rd Sts.

Although it's just as douche-baggy on the weekends as the rest of the neighborhood, it can be an okay place to hang during the week and is at least interesting looking. The theme here is log-cabin–in-the-woods-esque, and because of this, there are snowshoes and a buck's head on the wall. I don't remember if the head is hanging over the two Big Buck Hunter games, but it really should be. There's also a fireplace and a picnic table just in case you still weren't sure what the theme was here. You can buy PBR for $3, which I guess makes this place the lesser of all evils, but just barely.

Bravest
700 2nd Ave. @ E. 38th St.

Photo by Tobias Womack

Seeing that Bravest is a fireman's bar, it makes sense that the entire place is a memorial to 9/11 and beer. They've really got it figured out here; the bartenders and servers are all friendly and accommodating, and more importantly you can buy Budweiser, Bud Select, and PBR for $2.50 all the time. It used to be called Wanda's, but after 9/11 they changed it to Bravest. Basically, it's a place to drink cheap beer, watch a game, and eat cheap wings. Remember when I said that the staff was accommodating? I talked our cute waitress into giving us a basket of wings for free. I mean, I had to try them to write about them right? They were pretty good.

The Bull's Head Tavern
295 3rd Ave. @ E. 23rd St.

This place has a $4 beer of the month. That's their cheap drink. I don't even know why I'm putting this in here … ugh.

Copper Door Tavern
272 3rd Ave. btw E. 21st & 22nd

I am putting this in here begrudgingly. They have great specials every night of the week, but the latest the specials go to is 10pm and that's only Mon–Wed. It's like they're faking the funk. Even the "cheap" bars in this area aren't really that cheap. I fucking hate it over here.

Hook and Ladder Pub
611 2nd Ave btw 33rd & 34th Sts.

During football season, Hook and Ladder puts out free pizza and wings at halftime. Although the beer is generally $4, there is a different beer special every day that puts beers at $2–$3. It makes dealing with the beer-pong crowd a little easier.

Grand Saloon
158 E. 23rd St. btw Lexington & 3rd Aves.

A big place with red walls and lots of B&W photos of old New York; the Grand Saloon has been around since the 1880s. It's been through many owners and incarnations in that time and today is just an average sports bar that gets a fair amount of after-work customers who are craving a $3 PBR and a burger. I've been here on nights when it was fucking *dead*. In fact all the times I was there it was dead, and since it's such a big place, it feels even emptier. But if you want a place to bring a lot of people, this could be your spot. I have a feeling it was a lot more interesting back when it was one of the city's best brothels.

Whiskey River
575 2nd Ave. btw E. 31st & 32nd Sts.

Just like the rest of this area, the customers here are generally chodes and the attractive and vapid girls who tend to accompany them. They do sell $3 PBRs and $10 pitchers, but at the consequence of having a beer pong table (I swear that shit is like catnip for douchebags). What I always find interesting though is that the girls who work in places like this often dig me because I'm different than the cats who usually come in. This generally means free shots for me. Hooray for free shots! Unfortunately, the bouncers at these places generally feel the complete opposite way about me and tend to use any excuse to kick me out. But really dude, how about the chick with her shoes off over by the beer pong table? What the fuck does she think this is, a school dance? Maybe a Bar Mitzvah party? I'm so glad that this is the last bar in Murray Hill that I have to write about. Could you tell I was getting bored?

Shopping

H & M

1328 Broadway @ W. 34th St.

See p. 211 (Midtown East)

Jack's 99 Cent Store

13 E. 40th St. @ Madison

This place is like Trader Joe's for broke mo-fo's. It's got tons of shit you don't need and even a few things you do, all for around the price of 99 cents. Frozen cocktail weenies? Check. Cold Arizona ice tea? Check. Hangers, toys and nylons? Check, check and check! And the place is huge; they probably have to sell *so* many boxes of frozen mozzarella sticks to pay rent (note: I have no idea if eating the food will kill you or not. I haven't actually purchased any of those lovely delicacies yet).

Jack's 99 Cent Store

110 W. 32nd St. @ 6th Ave.

See above.

Kara New York

1052 6th Ave. @ W. 40th St.

Kara's sells really cheap women's clothing. It honestly seems like nothing here is over $30 and, while the styles are fairly generic, the clothes aren't half bad considering the prices. But then again I'm a guy. You can get blouses here for $15, and jeans and dresses are around $30, like I mentioned two sentences ago. Though this may or may not be the only Kara New York around, I know they have a chain of sister stores called Steps throughout the city, but I don't feel like talking about them really. If you wanna know the locations, go to *www.stepsnewyork.com*

Steve and Barry's
901 6th Ave. @ W. 33rd St. (in the Manhattan Mall)

A chain I'd apparently never heard of, Steve and Barry's carries clothing lines licensed by people and things that no one wants to buy from like Ford, Stephan Marbury, Shawn Michaels, and the US Marine Corps. That being said, this spot is *stupid* cheap. The day I happened to be there was a President's Day sale or something and *everything* was $8.98! Even the shoes and leather jackets were that price. Yes I know this is a super corporate spot, but I feel like I'd be remiss in my duty to all you fine people if I didn't clue you into it. It's basically a ridiculously cheap place for people who don't mind mediocrity. I couldn't find a single thing I wanted in the place, which pissed me off because it was like, "Finally I can afford anything in a store, but all the clothes are designed for blind people in the middle of America."

Vintage Thrift Shop
292 3rd Ave. @ E. 23rd St.

While not exactly having the most original name, I had to put something in this section that wasn't a chain. I mean, just look at the rest of the stuff under "Shopping" for this neighborhood. Vintage Thrift Shop sells all kinds of glasses, frames, bars, wall decorations, lamps and other odds and ends, and all the proceeds go to some charity organization or another. I don't remember which one though. I do remember though that I got a fantastic blue, olive and grey blazer here for $16. It looked really sweet, until I accidentally split the armpit area open, which makes me wish I'd done more research about tailors. Dammit.

Sights & Entertainment

The Complete Traveller Antiquarian Bookstore

199 Madison Ave. @ W. 35th St.

By the name of this store, I was expecting (more like praying for) the place to be run by a crusty old English dude smoking a pipe who still called Zimbabwe "Rhodesia" and Sri Lanka "Ceylon", and talked about the waning glory of the British Empire. Unfortunately, there were just a couple of regular guys and lots of cool, rare books, mostly about travel and history. Many of the books are from the late 1800s and the turn of the century, but there's also a grip of other shit here like an editor's copy of John Irving's *Cider House Rules,* and a signed copy of Quincy Jones' autobiography. So, while it's not as cool as I was hoping it would be, it's still pretty awesome for us nerdy, book-ish, history folks out there.

Morgan Library and Museum

29 E. 36th St. @ Madison

It's pretty safe to say that you're a serious collector when you've ac-quired an autographed journal entry of Henry David Thoreau, but when you also have multiple Gutenberg bibles, autographed sheet music by Mozart and Beethoven, and an amulet worn by King fucking Nebuchadnezzar II, that just means you have more money than God. I mean what else can you say about J.P. Morgan, a guy who bailed out the *United States Government* when it ran out of gold in 1895? After his death, J.P. Morgan's son donated his father's art collection and library so that it could be used as a public institution. Since then, the houses of both the father and son (both adjacent to the library) have been added to the museum as well as a garden court and a performance hall. Think it sounds swanky? Then you should really come and check it out for yourself on Friday evenings when it's free from 7–9pm (ad-mission is usually $12). You will be floored by the magnificence of this place. It's just slightly nicer than my Bushwick apartment.

Rodeo Bar
375 3rd Ave. @ 27th St.

While this is technically both a bar and a restaurant, I'm listing it as entertainment because you get to see live Americana and alt-country music for free every night of the week. It's decorated like a Texas honky tonk with a giant bus or trailer in the middle of the place. To make things easier for you though I've broken down Rodeo Bar into a list of pros and cons:

Pros:
- There's decent free music every night.
- It's a pretty ethnically diverse crowd, which is uncommon for the area.
- They've got troughs of free peanuts for you to eat and then throw the shells on the floor.
- If you aren't dressed like a tool, the cute waitresses and bartenders will flirt with you and give you special treatment.
- Once again, you get to throw shit on the floor, which is a guilty pleasure for people like me who never litter.

Cons:
- PBRs are $4. I politely asked the bartender not to ever tell anyone I paid $4 for a PBR.
- The crowd is mostly full of wankers, but then again so is the whole neighborhood.
- Once again PBRs are $4.

So now you weigh the pros and cons and what do you come up with?

Sniffen Court
a little spot on E. 36th St. btw 3rd & Lexington Aves.

Sniffen Court might be the tiniest gated community in the world. It was originally built as a collection of carriage houses around the time of the Civil War, but ever since the 1920s, the buildings have been used as places of residence. While it's not likely that you'll be able to actually get inside this cute little gem, you can peer through the gates and tell people that walk by, "Hey this is where they shot the cover of the Doors' *Strange Days* album".

Teddy Roosevelt's Birthplace
28 E. 20th btw Park & Broadway

While the actual house that old Teddy was born in was torn down, this recreated brownstone was erected in 1919 by the Women's Roosevelt Memorial Association. Did dude really have a women's association that went around building memorials for him after he died? That's some seriously gangster-ass shit! How do I get one? I'll call it Sweet Stuart's Brokeasssss Broads and have them roll around in Cadillacs, bumping Curtis Mayfield and umm, well, I haven't thought it out much more than that, but it's a good start. Visit Teddy's birthplace though, and see what a typical well-to-do family's house looked like in mid-19th century New York. It's only $3 to get in.

P.S. You knew that the Teddy Bear was named for Roosevelt right?

Sniffen Court sounds more like a place where junkies congregate than a cute little place like this.

GRAMERCY PARK and MURRAY HILL

Grub-a-dub-dub
1 Carl's Steaks
2 Curry & Curry India Restaurant
3 Curry Dream
4 The Famous Chicken Place
5 Joe Jr. Restaurant
6 The Kati Roll Company
7 Katsuri
8 Mark Cafe
9 Minar's Taj
10 Spade's Noodles, Rice & More
11 Sunburst Espresso Bar
12 Woorijip
13 Yatra

DRINKS DRINKS DRINKS
14 Barfly
15 Black Bear Lodge
16 Bravest
17 The Bull's Head Tavern
18 Cooper Door Tavern
19 Grand Saloon
20 Plug Uglies
21 Whiskey River

Shopping
22 H&M
23 Jack's 99 Cent Store
24 Kara New York
25 Steve and Barry's
26 Vintage Thrift Shop

Stuffis to See and Do
27 The Complete Traveller Antiquarian Bookstore
28 Gramercy Park
29 Morgan Library and Museum
30 Sniffen Court
31 Teddy Roosevelt's Birthplace

Free Food Bitches!!
32 Hook and Ladder Pub
33 McCormacks Pub
34 Rodeo Bar
35 Rolf's
36 Tracy J's Watering Hole

Herbivore Friendly
37 Chennai Garden
38 Franchia Teahouse & Restaurant
39 Saravana Bhavan Dosa Hut
40 Tiffin Wallah

Douchebags

Hot girls who like douchebags

The sweet smell of Indian curry houses

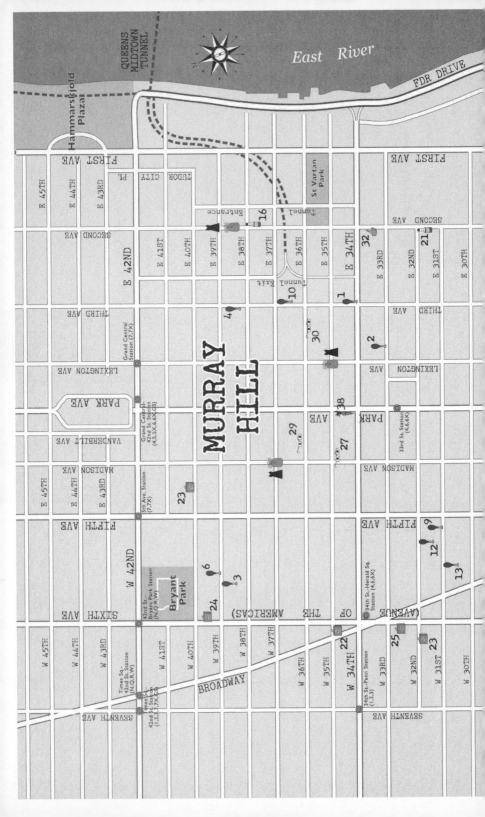

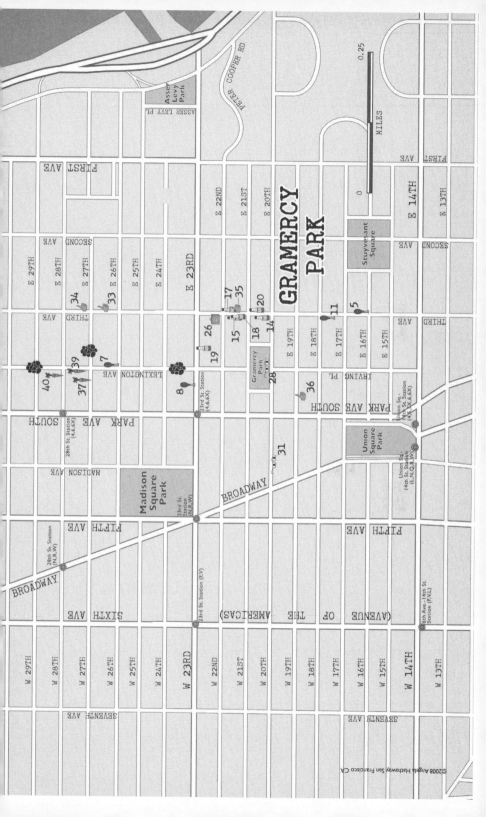

Midtown East

Midtown East is the Manhattan of movies; it's where ghosts get busted, children trapped in adult bodies play huge pianos with their feet, and awkward, neurotic, Jewish, clarinet playing comedians lament *everything*. It's also the Manhattan of landmarks: the Chrysler Building reaches for the heavens in all its art deco glory, while the huddled masses steam off the subway into Grand Central Terminal, and the future of the planet is deliberated at the United Nations. People travel from the ends of the earth to visit this part of New York, and they come to take photos of it so they can brag to their friends that they've been here. Whether they realize it or not, people have Midtown East in mind when they put New York on the top of their list of things to see before they die.

But this part of Manhattan is more than just a foil for motion pictures and a backdrop for still ones. It's also a place where millions of people work everyday in industries ranging from banking to television and from jewelry to advertising. Serious money is made here, and it's spent just as seriously, too. Just stroll up 5th Ave. towards Central Park and you'll be inundated by hundreds of the world's biggest and most expensive clothing brands, all vying for the opportunity to convince you that buying their products will make your life better (trust me, they won't).

Anyplace that sees this much money change hands is always gonna be expensive. On the other hand, anywhere this densely packed with storefronts, restaurants, and bars is bound to have some great deals if you just know where to look. A good place to start is **Little Korea,** which runs roughly from 31st to 36th Sts. between Broadway and 5th Ave. You can find great food here at inexpensive prices. Little Brazil, running the length of 46th St between 5th and 6th Aves., is another option that, while not being all that cheap, sounds great just because Americans go cuckoo for anything remotely Brazilian (Come on, don't front like that. Didn't get you all excited?).

The boundaries of **Midtown East** are approximately 59th St. in the north, 40th St. in the south, 6th Ave. to the west and the East River to the … well you can tell by the name it's in the east.

Food

99-cent Fresh Pizza

151 E. 43rd St. btw 3rd & Lexington Aves.

Well the name says it all. It's 99 cents and actually pretty good. $2.75 gets you two slices and a soda or water. Simple enough.

Buttercup Bake Shop

973 2nd Ave. btw 51st & 52nd Sts.

With all these cupcake shops, I wonder if in the future NY will be known for cupcakes instead of pizza and bagels, like someone will be all, "You know I really love living out here in Portland, but for fucks sake, can't a man just get a decent pink frosted cupcake for once?" Most people get bulk orders here, so the girl was surprised that I only wanted one of their tasty $2 cupcakes. I should really be fatter than I am with all this crap I eat, but luckily I walk around so much that it counters all the eating (either that or it's this healthy adderall habit). Do you chew on the cupcake paper? I love it!

Café Zaiya

18 E. 41st St. btw 5th & Madison Aves.

This is Café Zaiya seen through the eyes of the woman standing behind me: *This is Midtown kid. I've got shit to do and I don't have time for weirdos like you, with a camera and a notebook, asking tons of questions about the average price of food here. Don't you get it? This is my lunch hour, (well lunch 45 minutes really) and I just need to get my cheap pre-made bento box, and scarf down one of those little seaweed triangles stuffed with rice and shrimp, and get back to my cubicle. I'm an important person goddamnit! I'm the administrative assistant to ... oh shit, I didn't know they had Beard*

Papa up in here. I need to get me some of those yummy little cream puffs. Those things are fucking delicious. Now what was I grumbling to myself about? Ah, crap. I gotta get back to work already. Fingerless-glove-wearing motherfucker slowing up the line ....

Gourmet 53

875 3rd Ave. @ E. 53rd St. (in the basement)

In the basement of 875 3rd Ave. there is a failed attempt at a food court (let's just call it a food basement). In this food basement is Gourmet 53. There is no doubt in my mind that "gourmet" is a very flexible term here, but everything (burgers, burritos, heros, salads, etc.) is $6.75 and a soda is included in the price. Have I told you about my horrendous Coca-Cola addiction? I just can't kick that shit. Every time I try, I just come crawling back.

John's Coffee Shop

823 2nd Ave. @ 44th St.

John's is a classic Greek diner one avenue from the UN, where food costs regular people prices and coffee abounds. The staff is friendly, the food comes out quickly and, most importantly, a burger and fries is $4.95. I know this doesn't sound very special to you if you haven't been here for too long, but listen to me very carefully; fries don't usually come with burgers in New York. I know that's crazy right? You have to buy them separately. How un-American is that? How many diners are in this book so far? I bet by now you're wondering what my obsession with diners is and if I was conceived in one or something. I'm starting to wonder the same thing.

Morning Star Café

949 2nd Ave. btw E. 50th & 51st Sts.

Just another moderately priced 24-hour diner with a giant menu.

Scott's Food Court

28 W. 48th St. btw 5th & 6th Aves.

This is the type of busy-ass lunch place where they hardly look you in the eye before they say, "Hey boss, hurry up. There's hungry people behind you." There's nothing over $7 here, which is good, because I'd feel ripped off if I paid any more.

Taam-Tov

41 W 47th St. btw 5th & 6th Aves. 3rd floor

While not the absolute cheapest place in the world, I was so intrigued by the fact that it's Glatt Kosher Jewish-Uzbek food that I couldn't say no. Only in New York (well maybe Uzbekistan, too). I got a meat pie for $1.99 and a shish kebab for $4, and to be completely honest with you, they were fucking delectable. Their specialties here are all around $8 and it's stuff like Uzbek pilaf, which sounds a lot like Edith Piaf to me. The strange part though was that amongst the photo of the Rebbe and the signs that say, "We do Shabbas Catering", were a fair amount of Japanese decorations. I'd love to see Hasidic Jews rolling sushi. Doesn't that sound like something from a Mel Brooks movie?

Bars

Ashton's Bar & Restaurant
208 E. 50ᵗʰ St. @ 3ʳᵈ Ave.

Ashton's is a nice looking place with after work business people and at least one drunk other than myself. Although the cheapest beer is $5 Bud, they put out free food Monday–Friday from 5–7pm. The food is different each night; my night was pasta with chicken and sausage. It was really greasy, but it was free. The local drunk sitting next to me kept giving me the "This is certainly quite some place isn't it buddy?" look each time I got up to get some more food, until I finally started asking him a few questions about other free grub in the area. Then he did what they all do, start talking crazy fucking nonsense about his old lady, and how she left him for the guy who nails shit into his face at the Coney Island Sideshow. Going solo to as many bars as I do (for research, of course), I've heard thousands of drunk sob stories. You'd be amazed at how many of them end up tied to the Coney Island Sideshow.

Blarney Stone
710 3ʳᵈ Ave. btw 44ᵗʰ & 45ᵗʰ Sts.

This is what I'm fucking talking about! The Overlook up the street wanted $4 for a PBR and here you can get a 22oz. glass of Sam Adams for $4. Shame on you Overlook, shame, shame (yes, I'm wagging my finger). Blarney Stone also has way affordable food, like a chicken cutlet with two sides for $7, daily specials for $5–$6, and a half pound burger for $4. It's the type of place where OTB races play on the TVs in the afternoon and the patrons are a mix between after work business people, and local drunks who don't have all their teeth. There was a super friendly Irish bartender, who seemed to know everyone's name, and he and I spent most of the time cracking jokes about the Jews, the Irish and the fantastic dead writer Peter McCarthy. Fuck the dumb shit, this is what a bar in Midtown should be like. If I had a rating system, this place would get a lot of stars.

Channel 4

58 W. 48ᵗʰ St. btw 5ᵗʰ & 6ᵗʰ Aves.

The beers here are $5, which is shitty, but there is free food during happy hour, which is the opposite of shitty. When I was here a little bit ago, there was this strange and delicious stuffed potato skin/possibly quiche hybrid thingy, that I consumed quite a bit of. Other than for the free food, though, I would never go here.

Jimmy's Corner

140 W. 44ᵗʰ St. btw 6ᵗʰ Ave. & Broadway

What's this? A fantastic dive bar in crawling distance from Times Square? The hell you say! Jimmy's Corner is a relic of old school New York; it never got the memo that someone was cleaning up the city and anything that didn't glimmer or shimmy wasn't in the game plan. But who needs to do that when you can bob and weave? For many years, Jimmy Glenn was a well regarded trainer and cut man for world-class fighters like Floyd Patterson. In 1971 he opened Jimmy's Corner to help pay rent on his gym uptown. I doubt if anything has changed in this bar since then. The entirety of this tiny, skinny, place

See the Paul Robeson poster? He was so much cooler than you or I will ever be. You should google him right now.

is covered in boxing memorabilia, like old school yellow fight posters and enough Muhammad Ali pictures to make anyone worth a shit get a little choked up. The drinks are cheap, cute girls work here, Jimmy holds court by the jukebox that plays mostly soul music, and they give out free bar munchies. If this isn't your type of place, we can't be friends anymore.

Overlook Lounge
225 E. 44th St. btw 2nd & 3rd Aves.

The Overlook has a good happy hour which is two for one from 2–6pm, but otherwise PBRs are $4 and Bud is $5 ... lame! It has a dive bar feel but at almost fancy pants prices. The only reason I'm putting it in here is to benefit you happy hour drunks. Otherwise don't bother.

Muldoon's
692 3rd Ave. btw E. 43rd & 44th Sts.

Like most typical NY Irish pubs, Muldoon's has $4 pints of Bud, moderately priced to mildly expensive food, framed photos of various Irish writers, and is full of Irish people. If that's your sort of thing, then welcome home. It tends to be dead on weekends, but it can get pretty busy on Wednesday and Thursday nights when many people's post-work happy hour bleeds into 10:30pm's "drunk, slurring and finally banging that redhead from Human Resources" hour. Wednesday nights also see a guy who plays Irish songs as accompaniment for the aforementioned depravity. Not too much else about this place to speak of really.

Shopping

Bookoff
12 E. 41st St. btw 5th & Madison Aves.

You ever have someone go overseas and bring you back all kinds of DVDs that only cost them 50 cents, only to realize that your stupid American DVD player can't read them? If so, stop into this location of Japan's largest used-bookstore chain, and pick up one of the DVD players that play both American and Japanese discs. Bookoff has three floors of cheap media including $1 books, $7 DVDs, Japanese novels translated into English, and an entire top floor dedicated to comics and Manga. Plus, if you've got Asian Fever, this is probably a great pickup spot for you because *everyone* here is Japanese!

H & M
505 5th Ave. @ E. 42nd St., 640 5th Ave. @ E. 51st St., 731 Lexington Ave. btw E. 58th & 59th Sts.

A big chain store that sells reasonably priced, fashionable clothes. Should this even be in here? I guess so because it's cheap but ... well ... you know how you try to shop ethically, supporting independent business and not buying sweatshop-made clothing, but at the same time you are totally broke and also want to look good? I guess H&M fully encompasses that dilemma.

Laila Rowe
1375 6th Ave. @ W. 56th St.

It's really hard to find good, cheap, independent stores in Midtown Manhattan, so I had to settle with just cheap and include Laila Rowe. While it's primarily a jewelry store, Laila Rowe also sells other things like rain boots, bags, and cute shit to attach to your cell phone. You can get trendy looking jewelry for $20, $12 and less here, if you want to. I kinda hate places like this, but they serve a purpose. There are eight other locations in the city, so if you really want to check them out go to *www.lailarowe.com*

Sights & Entertainment

American Folk Art Museum
45 W. 53rd St. btw 5th & 6th Aves.

Folk art is the art of the people. It's not art made with high concepts or pop sensibilities; it's art that comes from a specific time and place and it directly reflects that time and place. It can be anything from paintings to needle work to pottery. An ornate quilt made by the wife of an 1850s farmer can be folk art; so can the paintings your grand-mother does at the Senior Center. While it's often not as sophisticated as the art we're used to seeing at sleek museums like the Met and the MOMA, it's this exact quality that makes it special. Wanna know what the fuck I'm talking about? Then come here on Fridays after 5:30pm when admission is free. Otherwise your curiosity will cost you $9.

Brigandi Coin Co.
60 W. 44th St. btw 5th & 6th Aves.

Attention all history geeks: Brigandi Coin Co. is awesome! Not only do they have coins from as far back as Rome in the first century BC, but they also have mad sports memorabilia, like a baseball signed by Babe Ruth. For some reason, they wouldn't let me touch anything in here.

Bryant Park
6th Ave. btw E. 40th & E. 42nd Sts.

While it has a history of being a potter's field (burial spot for poor or unknown people), the location of the Crystal Palace exhibition during New York's first World's Fair, and a haven for junkies during its days nicknamed, ahem, "Needle Park", Bryant Park is currently muy tranqilo. The lovely landscaping here reminds me of some park I went to in Paris when I was 20, and the genteel nature of the area lends itself to free ice skating in the winter and free movies at 5pm on Monday nights in the summer. They also have a free concert se-ries that gets huge acts like Counting Crows and Ashanti on Friday nights at 7pm during the summer, and free Wi-Fi year round. Let's just hope that all those poor and unknown people buried under the park don't rise up as zombies and start fucking shit up. Or if it does happen, let's hope it's during fashion week (they put up a big tent here for that crap).

FAO Schwartz
767 5th Ave. @ E. 59th St.

I had a friend visiting from Spain, and since FAO Schwartz is the biggest toy store I've ever seen, I figured that I had to take her so she could see it for herself. It only took about 20 minutes before they threatened to 86 me from the store. It's just that I got so excited about all the cool toys everywhere, that when I saw a humongous pile of stuffed puppies, I knew that I *needed* to lay down in it. Apparently the employees at FAO Schwartz thought I was disturbing the other holiday shoppers. What's so disturbing about a grown man getting so excited about a pile of stuffed puppies that he wants to belly flop into it? They didn't say shit when Tom Hanks commandeered that giant piano.

Lehman Brothers Park
Runs up the middle of the block between 6th and 7th Aves. from W. 48th St. to W. 50th St. Southern half runs just west of 1221 Avenue of the Americas. Northern half runs just east of Lehman Brothers.

This random little park area is super busy during lunch time because everyone is set free from their cubicles in an orgy of trying to get fed. There are a few little fountains throughout the park, but the money shot here is the tube that allows you to walk through a wall of water. It's pretty rad. The chemicals for water treatment though make the place smell like all the weird indoor water stuff in Vegas. Not that that's a bad thing, it just reminds me of too much blow, too much booze, and that whatever happens in Vegas, stays in Vegas, unless you bring home the clap.

Main NYC Public Library
5th Ave. @ E. 42nd St.

Apparently called the Humanities and Social Science Library, this brilliant piece of architecture is as much a place to visit as it is a place to borrow CDs that you plan to rip to your computer. It's hard not to be impressed by the beautiful entry hall full of marble and arches and the lovely inlay on the library's ceiling, but my friends, the best has yet to come. With its ornately carved reliefs and intricately carved ceiling, the map room is absolutely gorgeous and a must see (I'm like a Hobbit–I love old maps). Unfortunately, though, I wasn't allowed to photograph the map room. Bummer. This library also has a big gallery that displays great free exhibits throughout the year like one about Jack Kerouac's *On the Road* and another one I saw where there were all these amazing photos of New York in betweern the '50s and the '70s. Stop in and take one of the free tours they give throughout the day.

MoMA

11 W. 53rd St. between 5th & 6th Ave.

www.moma.org

What can I say about the Museum of Modern Art that hasn't already been said by every other guidebook on NYC? I don't have any crazy stories about knife wielding peyote fiends or losing all my clothing in a craps game in the cellar; that was a different MoMA in a different city. I guess I should just tell you that it's free from 4–8pm on Fridays.

Paley Park

3 E. 53rd St. @ 5th Ave.

I first heard about Paley Park one morning while having breakfast with my friends Alaina and Matt. They were visiting from Oregon, where Alaina goes to architecture school, and were doing the tourist thing. When we were talking about things that should be seen and things that should be skipped, she told me about Paley Park. Apparently this place is like porn for design people; it's mad famous in the world of urban planning. Paley Park is a tucked-away, little square park within three walls, where there are a bunch of chairs, tables and a 20-foot waterfall. If you get close to the falls, you can't hear the rest of Manhattan at all, and the water, the foliage and the drink you bought at the refreshment stand make the city melt away. It's totally refreshing and makes me have to pee.

Piece of the Berlin Wall

520 Madison Ave. btw E. 53rd & 54th Sts.
(in the courtyard)

I remember being in elementary school when the Berlin Wall came down. I was like seven or eight, so I didn't quite catch the significance, but I remember it was around the time that my school was having a bake sale fundraiser. I guess there was an award for the best looking cake design, and I remember the kid who won it had decorated his cake with sugar cubes, making it look like the Berlin Wall being taken apart. All the parents thought it was so brilliant, and I was just pissed off because I wanted the prize. Anyway, if you never saw the Berlin Wall in person, or bought a cake bearing its resemblance during a bake sale, you can come here and check out this five-slab piece of it that's still wearing its same graffiti.

Rainbow Room

30 Rockefeller Plaza @ W. 49th St.

I thought that I'd outsmarted the folks that run the Top of the Rock. The Top of the Rock is the observation deck at the top of Rockefeller Center, and to get up there to see the view costs $20 a ticket. Since I knew that the Rainbow Room was only like two floors below, I figured that I could just go buy a beer at the bar and take in the exact same view. How much could a beer really cost, $8? That's still saving a grip of money. So I got in line and waited (they open up around 5pm, I think), and when I got upstairs they made me check my coat, hat and bag, even though it said that men were required to wear jackets (I guess mine had too many holes in it). After unsuccessfully trying to weasel my way out of checking my belongings, I sat down at the bar next to a beautiful German tourist, and ordered a Budweiser; it was the cheapest thing they had. Guess how much it cost? Come on, guess … it was $12!!! When the barkeep told me how much it cost, I laughed and beer came out my nose. German chicks must dig that sort of thing because she later invited me out with her, which I of course declined because I have a girlfriend. But what I did do was take a photo of the beer for posterity and so I could show people what a $12 Bud looked like (it looks the same as a $3 one). I also made sure to eat as many bar nuts as possible. All the shenanigans aside, you should know that the view from the Rainbow Room is heartbreakingly amazing, and I found a way to rationalize the expenditure. I told myself that I spent $12 to see one of the best views of New York, and they threw in a free beer. Doesn't that sound much better?

Sony Wonder Technology Lab
550 Madison Ave. @ E. 56th St.

A free, hands-on, technology and entertainment museum for all ages made by Sony. Sounds sweet right? Wrong. This shit is wack; I've seen Brendan Fraser movies more entertaining than this place. Maybe if I was really high I'd like it. Apparently though they are in the process of redoing it, so maybe by the time you get your grubby little hands on this book it will be cool. I mean, all they would have to do is put a whole bunch of PS3s in there and it would be awesome. As a word of advice, go late so you don't have to deal with millions of kids who have no concept of what it means to wait in line.

Tram to Roosevelt Island
59th St. @ 2nd Ave.

This is a totally slept upon little way to have some cheap fun and it's a great thing to do as part of a date. There's no real reason to spend any time on Roosevelt Island unless you live there, but you can take the tram (kinda like a gondola in the sky) there and back to catch the fantastic views, and it only costs the same as a subway ride. You can even use your monthly metrocard. It closes at 2am, so it's a good way to see the city lit up at night.

Grand Central is always full of people doing stuff and things.

Grand Central Terminal

E. 42nd St. @ Park Ave.

A cat named Wade dropped some info on me about some of the strange and unknown things in New York. One of them was that there are seven secrets about Grand Central Station. He had seen a TV program about them, but couldn't remember what all of them were. Of course this set off my curiosity meter and I've spent countless hours trying to figure out what all of these secrets are. Here is what I've learned so far; there's more than seven things listed, but some are not as secret as others:

• The name is technically Grand Central Terminal. Grand Central Station is the name of the nearby post office and the name of a station that used to be on this site.

• Grand Central has an amazingly successful lost and found department. Over ¾ of the things lost here are reunited with their owners. Do you think they've got my sense of dignity somewhere in there?

• All four faces of the clock on top of the information booth in the main concourse are made of opal. Because of this, it's so valuable that no one has been able to properly appraise it. It's been valued as high as $20 million. That's a lot of million dollars.

• Grand Central has the most train platforms in the world. Take that Trainsylvania!

• The constellations painted on the ceiling were painted backwards. The artist said that he did it on purpose to show what it would look like if you were a celestial looking down on them. That's almost as weak of an excuse as when Pete Townsend got caught with kiddie porn and said that he was just looking at it for research. The ceiling also used to be so covered in soot and grime that you could barely see the painting. When they cleaned it up, they realized it was mostly from indoor smoking and left one square dirty just to show how much restoration was done. They also didn't fix the hole made by a giant rocket display in the '50s.

• There's a secret basement like 10 floors down called M-42. During WWII those who guarded it had shoot to kill orders because the generators there powered all the trains used to move soldiers around the Eastern seaboard. These days they just rent it out to be used in German snuff films.

• There is a special tunnel that goes directly to the Waldorf-Astoria. This was used by FDR so that he could come in from DC and go directly and safely to his hotel suite, while not having to navigate through the madness of Manhattan. It's a tough city if your legs don't work so good.

• The stairs of the east staircase are one inch shorter than the ones of the West Staircase. Me thinks this was just a way to fuck with OCD people.

• The Biltmore Room used to be called the Kissing Room because the famous 20th Century Limited train would drop off rich and famous people there who would then commence smooching their loved ones. Today rich and famous people just leak sex tapes.

Whispering dirty talk over an expanse of a few dozen feet is more exhilerating than it looks.

• My buddy Ben Wise told me about this one, and it might be the coolest of them all. Right outside the Grand Central Oyster Bar is the Whispering Wall. Because of something having to do with the curvature of the vaulted ceiling and the Gustavo tile, two people can face into diagonally opposite corners, and whisper things to one another over a distance of a couple dozen feet. No matter how crowded the terminal is, this works; you should seriously go do it today. It's much cooler than whatever you're doing right now (aside from reading this book).

MIDTOWN EAST

Grub-a-dub-dub
1 99-Cent Fresh Pizza
2 Buttercup Bake Shop
3 Cafe Zaiya
4 Gourmet 53
5 John's Coffee Shop
6 Morning Star Cafe
7 Scott's Food Court
8 Taam-Tov

DRINKS DRINKS DRINKS
9 Blarney Stone
10 Jimmy's Corner
11 Muldoon's
12 Overlook Lounge

Shopping
13 Bookoff
14 H&M
15 Laila Rowe

Stuffis to See and Do
16 American Folk Art Museum
17 Brigandi Coin Co
18 Bryant Park
19 FAO Schwartz
20 Grand Central Terminal
21 Lehman Brothers Park
22 Main NYC Public Library
23 MOMA

Stuffis to See and Do (ctn'd)
24 Paley Park
25 Piece of the Berlin Wall
26 Rainbow Room
27 Sony Wonder Technology Lab
28 Tram to Roosevelt Island

Free Food Bitches!!
29 Ashton's Bar & Restaurant
30 Channel 4
31 Keen's Steak House
32 Pig n Whistle
33 T.G. Whitney's

Herbivore Friendly
34 Zen Burger

Street Meat
35 53rd & 6th Halal
36 Biriyani Cart
37 Hallo Berlin
38 Kwik Meal

Good writer who works for awful magazines like US Weekly

Cubical jockey on a very short lunch break

Europeans taking advantage of the pitiful state of the U.S. dollar

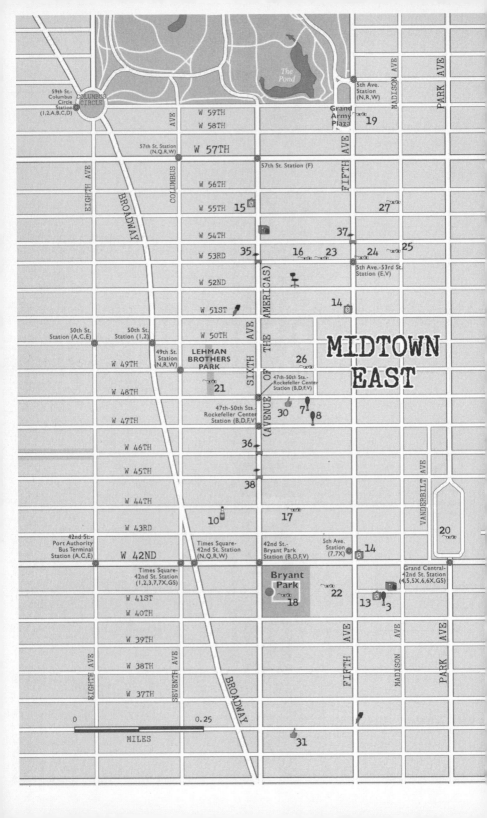

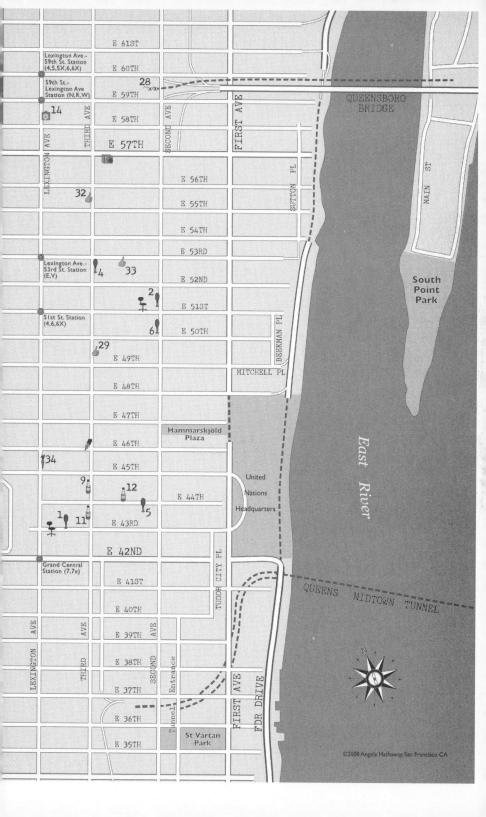

Hell's Kitchen & The Theatre District

I t's never nighttime in Times Square. The blinking, beaming, luminous glow from the billboards and marquees illuminates the theatres and stores below like a light left on to help a scared child get to sleep. And while Times Square has always been brilliant, these days it seems like it's overcompensating, almost smiling too hard, in hopes that its dark past never comes back. I personally miss the old New York City, the one that existed before Giuliani started cleaning it up by busting homeless guys with squeegees. I used to visit all the time as I was growing up, and while it was, without a doubt, a more dangerous place to be, you were at least getting a genuine experience in a real city with real people, instead of the dandified and declawed version that's passing itself off as Manhattan today.

That's why I like walking around Hells Kitchen out past 10th Ave.; it feels a little like the New York I remember visiting when I was a kid. It's still got some grit left to it. But even that is slowly drifting away. Besides the fact that Hell's Kitchen is probably the best name for any place in the history of the world, it also used to be an area that warranted such a name. For a long period of New York's history it was a primarily Irish neighborhood full of tenements and gangs which eventually became a haven for junkies, prostitutes, porn stores, and dirty movie theatres. It wasn't until the end of the 1990s that the area began to pull itself up by its bootstraps. While it's definitely much safer now, Hell's Kitchen has had to trade some of it's authenticity and soul to get that higher ground.

The Theatre District, on the other hand, is something that continues to amaze me. I'm so blown away that a medium, basically considered archaic or dead in the rest of the developed world (sorry theater junkies, but it's true), has such a huge culture surrounding it, that people deliberately travel across the earth to view it. That's like traveling to Japan just because they still have actual video arcades. Fucking brilliant!

Proximity to the Theatre District, and the dollars spilling over from it, is actually what helped Hell's Kitchen turn itself into what it is today: a fairly gay neighborhood with trendy bars and restaurants populated by many of the actors who work on nearby Broadway. But if cheap is what you're looking for, make sure to check out all the Garment District discount stores in the high 30s and low 40s west of 7th Ave.

The boundaries of the **Theatre District** are W. 34th in the south, W. 59th St. (Central Park South) in the north, 6th Ave. to the east and 9th Ave. to the west. Hell's Kitchen has the same north/south boundaries, but runs from 9th Ave. in the east to the Hudson River in the west.

Food

99-cent Fresh Pizza
569 9th Ave. @ 41st St.

See p. 205 (Midtown East)

Andrew's Coffee Shoppe
246 W. 38th St. btw 7th & 8th Aves.

Andrew's is just a typical diner, but it's a very big typical diner, which is why I like it. Everything is $7.25 or under and the vinyl booths (there's lots of them) have a cheesy floral pattern that only exists in cheap diners. Could you imagine seeing that pattern anywhere else in the world? I'd like my coffin to be lined with the same cheesy vinyl. There's also two big half-moon lunch counters in the middle of the restaurant, kinda like the Grand Central Oyster Bar, but infinitely divier and without the oysters. And breakfast here is mad cheap; two eggs, home fries and toast for $2.95. I might as well start saving up for open-heart surgery now.

Azuki Japanese Restaurant
520 8th Ave. @ W. 36th St.

Spend $15 and get a free bottle of sake. Can you say Antidisestablishmentarianism? Can you say it after a bottle of sake?

Cosmic Coffee Shop
132 W. 31st St. btw 6th & 7th Aves.

I saw a fat cop on the street one day over by Macy's, and just by looking at the fucker, I deduced that if anyone knew of a good cheap place to eat in the area, it would be him. He directed me to the Cosmic Coffee Shop, and I'm glad he did, because that was the day I was introduced to the pizza burger. How had I never heard of this delicacy before? A burger with melted mozzarella and pizza sauce on it? Brilliant! Once I had left though, and made it all the way back to Brooklyn, I realized that I'd forgotten my Molskine back at the restaurant.

That just meant I had to go back the next day and get another pizza burger. God bless the NYPD.

P.S. The term "cop" is a shortened version of "copper" which is what the bad guys (think James Cagney) used to call police officers because of their copper badges ... I think.

Desi Deli
742 10ᵗʰ Ave. btw 49ᵗʰ & 50ᵗʰ Sts.

Whoever Desi* is, he's a busy guy. There's a smattering of places named after him all over town. Luckily for us Desi is down with the Broke-Ass Revolution and slangs good cheap Indian food 24/7. Plus, if you need a phone card or need to wire money back to your wife and kids in Calcutta, Desi's your man once again. Never worry cousin, with Desi in your corner, you're gonna be just fine.

Desi Junction
688 10ᵗʰ Ave. @ W. 48ᵗʰ St.

This tiny, hole in the wall place has just a handful of tables and is a cabbie hot spot (which is generally a good sign). You can get two awesome samosas for $2 and most other things are $7.50. I have nothing snarky to say about this place. Do you know how hard it is to sit at a computer for hours thinking of new ways to say snarky things?

Djerdan
221 W. 38ᵗʰ St. btw 7ᵗʰ & 8ᵗʰ Aves.

I wish that I were fat, like really fat. I wanna be the 600 pounds kind of fat where I'm just like, "You know what? Fuck it. This dieting thing just ain't gonna work. I'm gonna just eat anything I want, *all* the time." Anyone who knows me knows I'm far too vain for that, but a boy can dream can't he? I guess what I'm trying to get at here is that I love food. I'm just as comfortable eating at Le Cirque (actually happened once) as I am eating at White Castle (actually happened a lot more than once). And I love trying food from regions whose cuisine I've never had before. So when I walked by Djerdan and saw the sign saying "Authentic Balkan Food" I thought to myself, "What the fuck kind of food do they eat in the Balkans? I should investigate!" And so should you. Stop in and get a burek. They're like slices of pie made from stuffed phyllo dough and blessed by God. They are $4 and will

---

*"Desi" is actually a blanket term meaning someone from the Indian subcontinent. It's like how Jews say, "Is she a member of the Tribe?" and Mexicans say "La Raza".

blow your mind (which is the only thing you can have blown for $4 these days anyways).

Empanada Mama
763 9th Ave. btw 51st & 52nd Sts.

Paul and I ate here part way through a night of bar research. One of us had said that it would be a good idea to put food in our bellies so as not to get too drunk, but we both knew we were too far along the booze trail for that. Any intelligent human being knows that a couple of empanadas isn't enough to soak up all the hooch we'd been drinking (and planned to drink). It was simply a precautionary measure to make sure we had enough stamina to make it back to Brooklyn at the end of the night. And in that capacity Empanada Mama really came through like the fine, upstanding dame she is. The empanadas here range from $2.25–$3 and are delicious (try the Cuban).

Hallo Berlin
626 10th Ave. btw W. 44th & 45th Sts.

A haiku for Hallo Berlin:

> Sausages and beer
> Indoor-outdoor beer garden
> Beer and sausages

Hallo Berlin Express
744 9th Ave. btw 50th & 51st Sts.

Same concept as above, but cheaper prices and not nearly as much seating. Both locations do have some veggie options if you're into that sort of thing.

H&H Bagel
639 46th St. @ 12th Ave.

H & H makes yummy, doughy bagels, but since they mostly sell bulk, they won't toast your shit. That's jacked up, right? It's like selling someone a pair of shoes but not giving them shoelaces. I'm the type of motherfucker who likes his bagel toasted with butter, but oh well, it's still $1.20 of deliciousness and you can buy a little package of cream cheese for 65 cents. This assuages your frustration for a moment until you realize that they won't even slice the bagel for you either. God-dammit! It's like dealing with fucking Rain Man! They're really, really good at one thing and fuck up the rest of it. Needless to say there are a number of ways this place can be improved upon, but the first thing would be to turn off that shitty light rock station they had on. What kind of world is this where Richard Marx still gets airplay?

International Food House Restaurant & Buffet

240 W. 35th St. btw 7th & 8th Aves.

They should change the name of this $8.95, all you can eat spot, to the Pan Latin Food House because that's really what it is. Radio Romanatica plays in the background while you fill your plate up with things like oxtail soup, rice, pork, beans, chicken and platanos (my spell check is so uncultured, it doesn't even know what platanos are). So many choices and only one stomach. I've actually been thinking about getting a colostomy bag. Why not? People get fake tits, fake asses, and even fake calf muscles, why not get an extra stomach? It's not like gluttony is one of the seven deadly sins. Oh, right it is.

Kashmir Express

8th Ave. btw W. 39th & 40th Sts.

Kashmir Express is a 24-hour Indian/Pakistani buffet where food is $4.99 a pound and snackers like samosas go for a buck each. Can't go wrong with shit like this yaddadamean (that's Bay Area talk for "You know what I mean?")? They also have a 24-hour sit down restaurant downstairs. Where the fuck is Kashmir again? Oh yeah, that disputed region shared by India, Pakistan and China. Sounds contentious.

Lunch Box Buffet

257 W. 34th St. btw 7th & 8th Aves.

An extremely long steam plate Chinese buffet where you can get five items for $5. It's not an all-you-can-eat buffet, but honestly, at this price it's pretty damn close. The buffet is probably more than 30 yards long. They also have a large pastry section and those delicious drinks with the tapioca pearls in them. For some reason someone who didn't speak Chinese was trying out their language skills last time I was in here, and it didn't seem to be working out too well.

Minar Indian Restaurant

138 W. 46th St. btw Broadway & 6th Ave.

Same menu as Minar Taj. See p. 187 (Grammercy/Murray)

Papaya Dog

400 W. 42nd St. @ 9th Ave.

Not nearly as awe inspiring as the one on p. 124 (west village)

Piece of Chicken

362 W. 45th Sts. btw 8th & 9th Aves.

It's kinda crazy to think that there's a place in New York where everything on the menu is really great and only costs $1 or $2. Sounds like I'm shitting you, right? Well I'm not. I think they just keep their costs down by being really tiny and not having any seats. This soul food menu has it all: chicken wings, chicken legs, collard greens, you name it. The only problem is that, since Piece of Chicken only does take out, and they only use Styrofoam, it becomes one of those things where you have to weigh your wallet and stomach against your ecological conscience. My suggestion is to bring your own container.

Tehuitzingo Deli

695 10th Ave. btw W. 47th & 48th Sts.

Though I can't pronounce the name of the place, I can tell you that it's an actual authentic taqueria, in the back of a tiendita, that's surprisingly good. All tacos are $2 and the ladies who make them are extra sweet; they give you a little wink after they take your order. Tons of articles line the wall talking about how dope the restaurant is, and all kinds of hot sauces line the counter so you can spice up your edibles. My faves are Tapatio and Valentina. Combine all this with the Telemundo on the TV and the Mariachi on the jukebox, and ah ... it feels like home.

Bars

Ninth Avenue Bistro

693 9th Ave. btw W. 47th & 48th Sts.

Occasionally you stumble into a bar on what happens to be the right night; completely irrational events unfold in front of you, and you wonder if this type of magic happens on a regular basis. When I first staggered into Ninth Avenue Bistro, I lurched into a barstool just as an older-looking version of John Waters screamed out "Bingo!" In my condition, I wasn't quite sure what had transpired; I thought he was so excited to see some fresh, young meat in the joint that he jumped up and screamed with glee. I started to mumble something about being flattered and that I'd take a vodka tonic if he was buying, when a loud voice said, "Alright, it's Jim again, folks! He's on fire tonight! Come on up for your copy of the new *Ass Cruisin'* DVD!" It was then I noticed everyone in the bar had a Bingo card in front of them, and that, while I was the youngest person by 40 years, nobody had noticed me stumble in, let alone jumped for joy. Nobody that is, except for the hiccupping drag queen with the four-day beard and disheveled wig, who sat on the next stool over. She managed to squeeze out a "Welcome to Porno Bingo, sweetie" between hiccups before pinching my ass so hard I bruised. I didn't stay around much longer, but I did manage to ask Miss Pinchie Fingers how often this type of thing happened. Apparently it's every Wednesday night.

Barrage

401 W. 47th St. @ 9th Ave.

Barrage is great because it doesn't try to be a dive and it doesn't try to be a diva; it's perfectly comfortable being a regular neighborhood bar with strong drinks and pretty boys. Medium in size and smartly decorated, Barrage might have been a garage at one point. I say this because it has two big glass garage doors that roll up when it's nice out. It's generally a laidback place, so if you're looking for a crazy night of partying, your best bet is to come here after midnight on the weekends. Word to the drink specials, too. I don't know what was in that shot, but it was good.

Dave's Tavern
574 9th Ave. btw W. 41st & 42nd Sts.

The single most impressive thing about Dave's Tavern is that every night one of the regulars gets 86'd. It must have been me and Paul's lucky night because we saw two of them get the boot. The first one was this guy who was obsessed with one of the female bartenders. She was off work, having a drink, and he was wasted and trying to get her to understand some point he was making. After a few minutes he yelled, "WHY WON'T YOU JUST TALK TO ME!?" at which point the massive bouncer (who looked like the Rock) came over and told him that if he didn't calm down, he'd have to leave. Drunk Guy apologized to both of them, and two minutes later started in again with, "I JUST WANT TO TALK TO YOU!". You could tell that Drunk Guy and the bouncer knew each other because the bouncer sighed loudly before asking him outside. They talked for a bit and when Drunk Guy finally calmed down, the bouncer let him go back in. Drunkie immediately bolted back to the barstool and began screaming at the girl, "WHAT THE FUCK IS WRONG WITH YOU, YOU COLD BITCH? WHY WOULD YOU TREAT ME LIKE TH..." At this, the bouncer snaps. He grabs Drunkie off the barstool, picks him up like he's his jailhouse bitch, lays drunkie down on his back on the sidewalk outside, while yelling at him to, "GO THE FUCK HOME!" (please note that Paul and I are absolutely dying of laughter from all this). When Roid-Rage finally lets Drunkie up, Drunkie starts mouthing off to him (we couldn't hear what he was saying), and Roid-Rage snaps again. He shoves Drunkie *really* hard and Drunkie's feet lift into the air, his back hits the ground, and his head knocks into a parked cab (we heard the thump from inside the bar). Drunkie gets up, rubs his head and slinks off (at this point the off-work bartender had already dismissed the incident completely and had absconded with a different guy into what appeared to be a janitor's closet. Seriously.).

By now the girl who was actually working had bought me and Paul each a beer because we were having such a good time. She was the one who told us that shit like this happens all the time here. Just then, the bouncer comes back in after letting himself cool off for a bit, and another regular had taken his shirt off and was waving it around his head to the beat of the music. The Bouncer was not in the mood for this shit: "OUT KYLE! GET OUT OF HERE! YOU'RE DONE TO-NIGHT! (Paul and I are clinking beers by this point, giving each other high fives, and claiming this to be the best bar ever). Then, as Kyle was walking out the door, still shirtless, we saw the original drunkie standing outside, looking into the bar through the window, and crying. True story.

Oh wait you probably wanna know some info about this place, huh? The clientele is a mixture of geezers and hipsters, you can play Ms. Pacman, drink $3 PBRs, and throw the shells of free peanuts on the floor (this makes me feel like a rebel).

Holland Bar

532 9th Ave. btw W. 39th & 40th Sts.

Holland Bar is a real dive bar where most people are regulars who aren't worried about how cool or attractive or sober or sane they come off. They come here because there's a decent jukebox with shit like Jim Croce, Sinatra, and the Stones, pints of Budweiser for $3, and you can sit around telling dirty jokes with a bartender named Dr. Bill (I have a feeling he's not a real doctor). Sure some of the regulars don't have all their teeth, but you don't plan on kissing them do you? Who needs all your teeth when you've got really fucked up stories to tell anyways? Holland Bar has been around since 1929, and has an old-man-bar ambience with a slight glaze of character: an American flag, a few collages of the regulars and a neon sign above the bar that doesn't work, so it's ringed with blue X-mas lights and lit that way. Basically this is the kind of bar where you get really drunk and spill your guts, telling your most awful dark secrets to the barkeep and he doesn't blink because he gets baby-eating crackheads from the Port Authority in here all the time. And it opens at 8am. And they sell gift certificates.

Port 41

355 W. 41st St. @ 9th Ave.

Yet another of New York's illustrious bikini bars, Port 41 distinguishes itself in my memory as having the biggest set of fake tits I think I've ever seen in person. There is a big fake hippo head on the wall that is almost as big as the girl's fake tits were, almost. Bless you plastic surgery, you strange and prickly beast. As expected this place was all dudes and most of them were Port Authority-ish. But hey, PBR tall boys were only $3! There's also a big back room that smells like smoked weed, where one can play pool and throw some darts. I

Everybody knows that any bar that has girls in bikinis selling tall boys of PBR has to have a big fake hippo head on the wall.

think they may have shows back there. Another added bonus is that there are free hot dogs and free popcorn here, but I feel like, with this crowd, there's a high chance of there being jizz in the popcorn machine. You can never be too safe. I will, on the other hand, eat the free wings given out on Fridays though. Everybody knows that buffalo sauce automatically cancels out jizz. It's part of String Theory, I think.

Rudy's Bar & Grill
627 9th Ave @ 44th St.

My good friend Anton plays violin for bands like Bright Eyes, Mates of State, and Judgment Day, so when he played Town Hall with Bright Eyes he got us some tickets. After the show, we all met up at Rudy's for a beer and then headed down to the after party at some bar in the Meatpacking District that the band had rented out. We ended up closing down the bar that night; we were the last ones standing. But this isn't about drinking for free in the Meatpacking all night, because I hate that place. This is about Rudy's being what is probably, the best bar above 14th Street. The booths at this fine establishment are all taped up with red duct tape, in fact, I think the entire place is actually held together with red duct tape. But as they say, if you can't duct it, fuck it. This isn't just another one of those dives filled with eye patch wearing old timers that your pal Broke-Ass usually sends you to, no ma'am (ok there's a few of them here); Rudy's is usually busy with attractive and cool people every night of the week, even Mondays (though weekends can get a little fratty). And if for some reason it feels too crowded inside, there's a huge backyard that's even open in the winter because they cover it with a tent and heat it. Plus Rudy's is mad cheap; pints of Rudy's beer ring in at $2.50 and pitchers are just $7. Oh WAIT! I almost forgot to tell you, *they have free hot dogs, too!!* I'm not even a hot dog man, but free is beautiful. I'd like to buy Rudy a drink, as long as it's at his bar.

Smith's Bar & Restaurant

701 8th Ave. btw W. 44th & 45th Sts.

This place is filled with tons of hot chicks, sober Irish guys, well-dressed tourists and really great, cheap food. It's also always opposite day here. Seriously though, it's not terrible considering its proximity to Times Square. And the neon sign is amazing. One time I was here and some weird Indian guy from London bought me and Krista drinks because it was *his* birthday and we were nice. Hey, I've always said that you attract bees with honey (or was it that you attract weird British Indian guys when you have a hot girlfriend?).

Shopping

B&Q
210 W. 38th St. btw 7th Ave. & 8th Ave.

One of the many stores in the garment district that sells DIY stuff for making clothes at discount prices, I just chose B & Q because my crafty friends (me = not crafty at all) said it was the cheapest and best. I guess that's for you to decide. They sell buttons, trimmings, feathers, sequins, patches, lace but no zippers or patterns. There's a sign on the door that specifically says so, twice. This is totally the place to go to if you wanna make a dope costume for Carnival.

H & M
435 7th Ave. @ W. 34th St.
See p. 211 (Midtown East)

Drama Book Shop
250 W. 40th St. btw 7th & 8th Aves.

A veritable gold mine for all the theater people in the city. Actually it's kinda like a porn store for them. You can buy plays, books about plays, plays about books, books about books about plays ... you get the picture. They also hold some auditions there. So basically if you're looking for a dramatic person to date, just hang out here for a little while. Also the store carries stuff about costume making, screenwriting, and being a stagehand. Not super cheap but it's an interesting specialty store, and I think theater girls are kinda hot.

Hell's Kitchen Flea Market
W. 39th St. btw 9th & 10th Aves.

Open from 9am–6pm every Saturday and Sunday, the Hell's Kitchen Flea Market has been an institution for over 60 years. While I'm sure the wares have changed a bit since that time, the concept is still the same; bargain your ass off motherfuckers. Just like any swapmeet, you get a wide range of quality and vendors here. Sure there's the cute elderly gay couples who sell shit like art deco coffee tables and vintage lamps, but there's also the crazy Vietnam Vets who sell army fatigues, bayonets, and switchblades, and can probably also get you live grenades if you know how to ask them. Then again, I might be thinking of the swapmeet I used to go to in the San Diego Sports Arena's parking lot. Most of the vendors there were just a half step away from being carnies.

Midtown Comics
200 W. 40th St. @ 7th Ave.

Midtown Comics is a big two story spot to get your geek on. Its corner location and big windows give you a nice view of all the madness down below so you can imagine the ways you'd squish those puny humans if only you had super powers. I'm actually a little bummed mine never came into effect. When I was younger I was convinced that once I hit puberty I'd start having mutant powers. Looking back I realize I was probably just watching too much of the X-Men cartoon. Speaking of X-Men (nice segue, Stu), Midtown Comics also sells shit like manga, graphic novels, DVDs, fantasy novels and sci-fi novels, as well as also carrying lots of cool back issues of rare comics. They carry back issues of adult stuff like *Playboy, Club* and *Bizarre* magazines, too, as well as cartoon porn like *Housewives at Play* and *Kiss Comix.* I didn't even know that shit existed. Silly me, I'd been looking at real naked girls on the Internet all this time (well, most of their body parts are real).

NY Men
34th St. @ 8th Ave.

I'm not sure of the address here, but I do know that they sell really cheap men's clothes. The clothes aren't really anything special, and there are a few too many shiny shirts, but they have crazy sales like two suits for $150.

Spandex World
228 W. 38th St. @ 7th Ave.

I couldn't not put this in here. I mean, it's an entire store of Spandex fabric that you can make your own clothing out of. I now know where the Fly Girls used to get their outfits from.

Sights & Entertinment

Columbus Circle
Southwest corner of Central Park

So yeah, I know that this could very well be in the Central Park part of the book, but considering that I don't have a whole lot in this section I figured I'd put it here. It's my book, I can do whatever I want. There are lots of cool buildings surrounding this rotunda but the neatest part is the statue of Columbus that sits on top of a 70-foot granite column. When people measure New York's distance to or from a place, this is the spot from which the measurements are taken. So why don't you just put that in your pipe and smoke it?

Museum of Arts and Design
2 Columbus Circle @ 8th Ave.

Formerly known as the American Craft Museum, this neat place displays artistic objects that have a functional use. Between you and me though, I never actually went to this museum, so I can't really tell you much more about it. Maybe they have really nice looking staplers, or some of those house phones that are made out of squishy foam and look like hamburgers. All I know is that they are moving into a new building in September 2008 and that Thursday nights are free here.

Port Authority Bus Terminal
625 8th Ave. @ 42nd St.

Bus terminals in any city are special places. They are crossroads for all the grifters, drifters, deviants, dead beats and drug addled zombies who circulate through this country, from city to city, doing whatever the fuck it is that they do. The Port Authority Bus Terminal (PABT) runs with this same concept, but just does it New York style: bigger, faster and more. I remember what Time Square used to be like before it became the monstrosity that it is today; it was populated by pimps, junkies, hustlers, strip clubs and camera stores. The camera stores are the only things that are left. I used to visit NY a lot as a kid and I learned what 24/7 meant when my dad, his friend and I were walking through Time Square once. I saw a neon sign advertising that what went on inside happened 24/7. When I asked my dad what this meant, he said, "It means you can see titties 24 hours a day, seven days a week." *That* Time Square is long gone (cleaning it up a bit may have been necessary, but they completely overshot their mark), but if you're curious as to what it was like, just set foot into the PABT for a toned down version (minus the strip clubs of course). Paul and I actually wanted to spend a night roaming the PABT and catalogue how many times we were offered crack or pussy, but we never got around to it. I also managed to check out the upstairs bowling alley once, hoping for a gem of a dive bar, only to be let down by the fact that it had just been remodeled and was now a decent attempt at a swanky bus terminal bowling alley (really). Who knows, maybe this place is heading towards the up and up like it's buddy Times Square. If so, you better drop in and observe this complete and utter fuck show while you can.

P.S. Make sure to check out the Ralph Kramden statue out front. Spousal abuse just hasn't been as funny since *Honeymooners* went off the air.

HELLS KITCHEN and THEATRE DISTRICT

Grub-a-dub-dub

1 99-Cent Pizza
2 Andrew's Coffee Shoppe
3 Azuki Japanese Restaurant
4 Cosmic Coffee Shop
5 Desi Deli
6 Djerdan
7 Empanada Mama
8 Internatonal Food House Restaurant & Buffet
9 H&H Bagel
10 Hallo Berlin
11 Hallo Berlin Express
12 Kashmir Express
13 Lunch Box Buffet
14 Minar Indian Restaurant
15 Papaya Dog
16 Piece of Chicken
17 Tehuitzingo Deli

DRINKS DRINKS DRINKS

18 Barrage
19 Dave's Tavern
20 Holland Bar
21 Ninth Avenue Bistro
22 Smith's Bar & Restaurant

Shopping

24 B&Q
25 Drama Book Shop
26 H&M
27 Hell's Kitchen Flea Market
28 Midtown Comics
29 Museum of Arts and Design
30 NY Men
31 Spandex World

Stuffis to See and Do

32 Columbus Circle
33 Port Authority Bus Terminal

Free Food Bitches!!

34 Ben Benson's
35 Kennedy's
36 Langan's
37 Pig n Whistle
38 Port 41
39 Rudy's Bar & Grill
40 Zanzibar

Street Meat

41 Bulgogi and Kimchi Street Cart
42 Daisy May's BBQ USA

Tourists

Theatre Junkies

Homeless who have managed to escape Guiliani's city clean-up

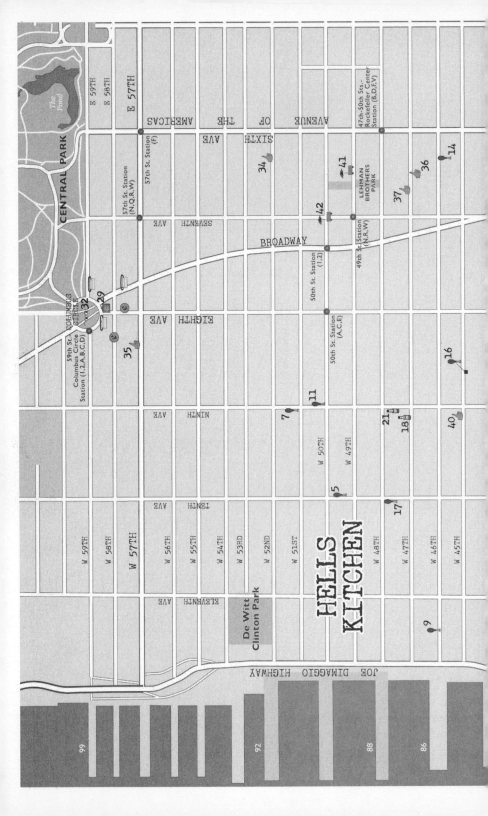

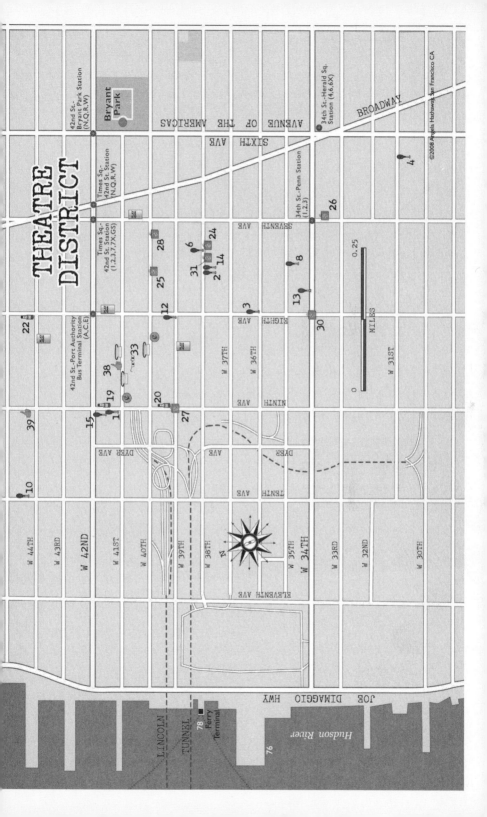

THEATRE DISTRICT

Bryant Park

42nd St.–Bryant Park Station (N,Q,R,W)

Times Sq.–42nd St. Station (N,Q,R,W)

Times Sq.–42nd St. Station (1,2,3,7,X,GS)

42nd St.–Port Authority Bus Terminal Station (A,C,E)

AVENUE OF THE AMERICAS

SIXTH AVE

34th St.–Herald Sq. Station (4,6,6X)

BROADWAY

34th St.–Penn Station (1,2,3)

SEVENTH AVE

EIGHTH AVE

NINTH AVE

TENTH AVE

DYER AVE

DYER AVE

ELEVENTH AVE

W 44TH
W 43RD
W 42ND
W 41ST
W 40TH
W 39TH
W 38TH
W 37TH
W 36TH
W 35TH
W 34TH
W 33RD
W 32ND
W 31ST
W 30TH

0   0.25
MILES

N

JOE DIMAGGIO HWY

LINCOLN TUNNEL

Ferry Terminal

Hudson River

76
78

©2008 Angela Hadwick, San Francisco CA

Upper West Side

O nce a pastoral landscape called Bloomingdale, where rich city folk had their country estates, the Upper West Side is today still stocked with the affluent class but now has a hell of a lot more buildings. Most of these buildings were built during the neighborhood's late-19th century boom period. So a good deal of them are architectural masterpieces worth staring at and imagining what it would be like to live in. But the Upper West Side isn't strictly a residential neighborhood. Just take a stroll up Broadway or Amsterdam and you'll see loads of bars, restaurants, and stores all catering to the neighborhood's rich clientele. As for the nightlife, the closer you get to Columbia and Morningside Heights, the frattier the crowd gets. But there are some decent neighborhood bars if you look for them.

The salient feature you're most likely to notice in this area during your wanderings is the sheer number of babies. The Upper West Side should really be called the Upper MILF Side, even though it's mostly Dominican nannies pushing around the baby strollers, not the kids' mothers. They generally have more important things to do like run businesses, plan fundraisers, or get mani-pedis.

Besides being sandwiched between beautiful Riverside and Central Parks, the Upper West Side is also home to many cultural institutions like Lincoln Center, the American Museum of Natural History, and a shit load of synagogues (Jews just love it up here). Apparently, of Manhattans two up-market neighborhoods, the Upper West and East Sides, the UWS is supposed to be considered the more liberal of the two. This is in part due to it being the home of many artists, actors and musicians throughout the 20th century. But as it stands today, the only two differences I see are that the UWS is on the west side of the park and has a whole lot of MILFS. The Upper East Side just has too many women who look like Cruella de Ville.

The boundaries of the **Upper West Side** are from W. 60th St. in the south to W. 116th St. in the north, and from the Hudson River in the west to Central Park West in the east.

Food

Big Nick's Burger Joint & Pizza Joint
2175 Broadway @ W. 77th St.

Having been around since 1962, Big Nick's has mad soul and feels like old NY. You know the kind of 24-hour place I'm talking about, where the walls are cluttered with autographed headshots, drawings, random posters, neon lights, and hand-drawn signs. It also has an absolutely tremendous 27-page menu that's full of more burgers than you knew existed. These juicy slabs of meat start as low as $5.95 and get up to $8.75. I got the "Bistro Burger" which had gruyere, fried mushrooms and tomato on challah. I added waffle fries, but made them take off the onions of course (onions are the devil). There are also veggie options like, getting the fuck out of Nick's ... just kidding, there are plenty of veggie options here, too. Considering that the menu is bigger than my first zine, you can find just about anything here. While I inhaled my food, a middle-aged German waitress saw a woman and three kids, possibly on a field trip and asked, "Are they all yours?" When the woman said, "No," the waitress replied, "Good because they all look so different, that if they were all yours, your husband wouldn't be very happy with you." She might be my favorite waitress ever.

Big Nick's Burger Joint & Pizza Joint Too
70 W. 71st St. @ Columbus Ave

See above.

Café Con Leche
424 Amsterdam Ave. btw W. 80th & 81st Sts.

Café Con Leche is a moderately priced Latin American restaurant with a nice interior. You see more and more of these the further you head uptown. I may or may not have come here really hungover once after an Aesop Rock show when I was 23.

Chirping Chicken
355 Amsterdam Ave. btw W. 76th & 77th Sts.

Reasonable prices and reasonable décor for a reasonable person. But are you reasonable? Ask yourself that.

The Cottage
360 Amsterdam Ave. @ W. 77th St.

As Americans, we aren't used to getting shit for free, so when we do, we often act completely inappropriately. It's not our fault really, the Capitalist system we grew up in has reared us towards an "I'm gonna get mine motherfucker!" mentality, and living in New York only exacerbates this. Just go to Costco on a really busy day, and watch as grown-ass men slyly try to cut in front of each other for their third sample of Annie's White Cheddar Macaroni & Cheese. So it's with this shirking of culpability in mind that I relate to you the Cottage's policy of giving out unlimited free wine with dinner. Just as inviting me to an open bar event is the surest way of getting me in trouble, offering me all the wine I can drink with dinner only assures my inevitable response: "None of this is my fault." Yes, I know that it was my choice to drink carafe after carafe of the Dionysian drink, and that this decision led to me eventually being cut off, arguing for more wine, getting kicked out, and ultimately puking dumplings and sweet and sour chicken all over 77th St., but it's not my fault. It's Capitalism's fault; I was never taught to say "no"... okay, maybe it was a little bit my fault.

Homer's World Famous Malt Shop
487 Amsterdam Ave. btw W. 83rd & 84th Sts.

When I first heard about Homer's, I was excited and hoped it was gonna be an old school authentic soda fountain in the same vein as the St. Francis Fountain in SF. I don't get paid enough to lie, so I'm gonna tell you I was a little disappointed. It's more like one of those things that starts off as a great idea, but ends up looking a little half-assed. But hey, at least they sell beer! What great soda shop doesn't? Another redeeming quality is that it's connected to a bar called the Blue Donkey, where $2 gets you either a PBR or a Schaefer. What the fuck is Schaefer beer? My guess is that the true idea here is that you can plop your kids down at Homer's in front of a big milkshake and the Disney Channel, while you mosey on over to the Blue Donkey and shotgun a couple Schaefers.

La Caridad
2199 Broadway Ave. @ W. 78th St.

La Caridad is a Chinese/Cuban restaurant. No, it's not the fusion of these two sublime cuisines, it's literally a spot with two different menus, where the dishes are written in Spanish with English translations. What's interesting though is that while the folks here are obviously of Chinese descent, their primary language is Spanish; they grew up in Cuba and speak English with a Cuban accent. The food here isn't super cheap (average price is $8.25), but it's pretty damn good. Plus, how often do you get to eat in such a place as this? I try to qualify my life by the amount of unique experiences I have. How about you?

Levain Bakery
W. 74th St. btw Amsterdam & Columbus Aves.

Look, I know the idea of paying $3.75 for a motherfucking chocolate chip cookie sounds completely ridiculous, but all that will change once you try one of these big and dense delights. Honestly, these things are huge and amazing. If you have a sweet tooth, you might cream your jeans, and if you're diabetic … well, I'd walk on the other side of the street if I were you. If you're trying to get laid, this cookie is better than a bouquet of flowers and a roofied drink combined.

Roti-Roll – Bombay Frankie
994 Amsterdam Ave. @ W. 109th St.

Open late and with a color scheme reminiscent of a 1970s Easter egg hunt, this tiny place serves up food so good that you'll probably end up licking off the sauce that dribbled onto the sleeve of your hoodie. I don't know much about Bombay Frankie, other than that he sounds like a character from a Dashiell Hammett book, but I know enough to want to hang out with him, if he even exists*. I mean wouldn't it be cool to have a guy in your group of friends named Bombay Frankie (I knew a kid in college named Memphis Dave. That's almost as cool)? The roti roll is griddled flat bread with all kinds of goodies rolled up into it, like a delicious Indian burrito. They start at $2.75 (two for $4.50) which is the spicy egg omelet one, but I got the Chicken Malai Frankie for $4.50 (two for $8) and it was amazing. Literally the first thing I wrote in my note book was "Holy Shit! So good and cheap!"

---

*He doesn't.

Sal & Carmine's Pizza

2671 Broadway btw W. 101st & 102nd Sts.

Sal and Carmine are these two old, ornery Italian guys who have probably been making pizza since back when the Upper West Side was known as the Bloomingdale District (the 19th century). But you know what? The pizza is absolutely perfect. Just don't ask for parmesan though, because they will yell at you. It's kinda like having an Italian grandfather who doesn't really like you very much.

Sido

267 Columbus Ave. btw W. 72nd & 73rd Sts.

Every neighborhood in New York has a good, cheap falafel place, and the Upper West Side's is Sido. I'm personally more of a shawarma guy (although I did have a short, obsessive love affair with those lovely fried balls of chickpea) and luckily Sido comes through solidly on that front as well. I actually used to have a whole rant about this one falafel guy in Santa Cruz, CA who had a tiny kiosk on Pacific Ave. and had no boss and no employees. His food was absolutely stellar, and you could tell that he truly got joy from selling people fantastic falafel. I looked at what he did as a model of contentment; he worked for himself, loved what he did, and made people happy. Then one day his kiosk closed down, and I just haven't been able to eat very much falafel since. I miss you falafel guy, wherever you are.

Super Tacos

W. 96th St. @ Broadway

A truck. A taco truck. An awesome taco truck. This Shangri-La on wheels pulls up to the corner at 6pm every night and is easily some of the best Mexican food I've come across in New York City. After months of searching I finally found what I was looking for (take that Bono). It was on St. Paddy's Day, which from now on will be St. Mexican's Day for me. This shit was like a holy epiphany.

Bars

Overall the bar scene up here is pretty wack.

Bourbon Street
407 Amsterdam Ave. @ W. 79th St.

The last time I was at this Mardi Gras–themed sports bar was on St. Paddy's day and it was full of drunk firemen. In fact, the whole city was full of drunk firemen. How pissed are you if you're one of the firemen who doesn't get to go out and drink that day? Generally speaking though, the clientele here is wasted frat boys (current and former) in pink polos with popped collars, calling each other "bro", and the attractive yet mentally deficient women who are into that sort of thing. Why bother coming here, right? Destructively cheap beers, that's why. Wednesday = Coors for 50 cents from 9–11pm, $1 from 11pm–2am. Thursday = 50 cent draughts from 9–11pm; $1 from 11pm–1am; $2 from 1am–close. Friday = Bud for 50 cents from 9–11pm. Yeah, I know, it's almost preposterous. They should just hand out condoms with every third beer. It's too bad that the thing that makes it worth going to Bourbon Street attracts the loathsome element that makes the place so unattractive.

Broadway Dive Bar
2662 Broadway btw W. 101st & 102nd Sts.

Solidly attended by a mixed crowd of older drunks, college kids, and locals, Broadway Dive is the sort of place where, when "Mr. Jones" by Counting Crows comes on, everyone sings along. Part of the "Dive Bar" chain, this location keeps true to form by having cheap drinks ($3 Bud light drafts), a fish tank and at least one slurringly sauced regular who wouldn't leave me the fuck alone. In this case, it was some guy who kept interrupting our conversation to see if we were rooting for the Celtics. When we finally got annoyed and rebuffed him he made fun of my fingerless gloves. I was a little disappointed that after 30 years of being alive, the best this guy could come up with was making fun of my gloves. At least call me a dirty Jew or something.

Candle Bar

309 Amsterdam Ave. btw W. 74th & 75th Sts.

Candle Bar is a gay neighborhood dive where locals who don't feel like dealing with the cruisy Chelsea or West Village scenes can unwind and have a cheap drink or three. While the clientele in this low lit spot is primarily men, I did get my ass handed to me in a game of pool by an incredibly friendly lesbian. In fact, everyone here is incredibly friendly, which is something you don't find enough of in this strange city we inhabit. I guess the most important thing to acknowledge about Candle Bar is that it's the only gay bar in the neighborhood, so if you're looking for something a bit more exciting you may just have to head south.

Ding Dong Lounge

929 Columbus Ave. btw W. 105th & 106th Sts.

When I asked the bartender, a guy named Chet who looked like a lost member of the Ramones, what the crowd was like he said, "intellectual punk rockers." But I think he may have just been talking about himself. When I asked him if there was a DJ every night, he said, "Yeah, if they show up". It was at this point that I knew I was falling in love with this bar. The Ding Dong Lounge is almost entirely lit by candles, making it really dark inside, and the only real decoration on the brick walls are old punk posters. For both Mateo and I, it was our first time in here, and I was glad that we found it considering how close this place is to his apartment and how shitty most of the rest of the bars around here are. He needs this place in his life. We spent a good amount of time completely befuddled by the big brick thing in the middle of the room that may or may not have once been a chimney. When asked, the sagely Chet responded, "I don't know what the fuck that thing is. All I know is that this place used to be a crack den." With our curiosity not satiated we did the only reasonable thing we could do: take lots of photos inside the thing. And you know what? The pictures came out pret-t-y damn cool.

Photo by Mateo Goldman

Dive Bar

732 Amsterdam btw W. 95th & 96th Sts.

Dive is a misnomer here. This place is not a dive at all, it's a fratty bar with pub grub. Some girl saw me eyeing her wings and gave me what she didn't finish. I'm kinda like a dog around food; I sniff around and whimper until someone feeds me leftovers. But hey, it's got a huge beer selection that includes the very fine $3 Bud Light and the crowd isn't overly obnoxious. It could be worse–you could be at Bourbon Street.

Dive 75

101 W. 75th St. @ Columbus Ave.

Dive 75 has a fish tank and board games like Boggle (apparently Boggle is a real word because my computer didn't do a red squiggly) and Connect Four. Are these considered board games since there aren't boards? The crowd is mostly local regulars during the week, and on weekends it becomes about as mixed as the UWS can get, which isn't a whole lot. The beer selection is a good one, but it gets more expensive outside the Budweiser range of course. The real highlight of the bar though is that there is always free candy like mini Kit-Kats and Tootsie Roll Pops sitting out.

Lion's Head Tavern

995 Amsterdam Ave. @ 109th St.

Decorated with strange ninja weapons and a Captain America shield, the Lion's Head is a good mix of what the neighborhood has to offer: older black guys and young college kids of every ethnicity you can think of. And I think it's the diversity that makes this bar great. Without it, the Lion's Head would just be another sports bar with an autographed Oscar De la Hoya photo and a *Dogma* poster signed by Kevin Smith. But that's not all that makes this place great: the $2 PBRs and stellar nightly drink specials definitely add to its allure, as do the 25 cent wings on Monday nights. To top it off, there are actually a fair amount of attractive people in here, too, which will hopefully lead to tons of beautiful ethnically mixed babies.

O'Connell's Pub

2794 Broadway @ W. 108th St.

Just an Irish pub/sports bar with $4 Buds and a giant deer head on the wall. It was probably killed playing the Big Buck Hunter in the corner. There are lots of TVs here and nothing else too special.

P&G Café

279 Amsterdam Ave. @ W. 73rd St.

Having been around and owned by the same family since 1942, P&G has the oldest neon light in NYC and it's fucking amazing. I'm so pissed at myself for not charging my camera and therefore not getting a photo of it. That shit would be like porn for me. During the day, OTB plays on two of the four TVs and old guys sit around checking to see if their pony is winning. Come nighttime, the regulars who haven't drunk themselves to sleep yet mix in with a crowd of slightly more highfalutin' UWS denizens ... very slightly. This keeps the vibe of this medium-sized place pretty cheerful and friendly. I will admit that the $4.50 Buds are a little more expensive than you'd expect to pay here, but hell, $1 of that is probably paying for electricity for that beautiful, sexy sign.

Yogi's

2156 Broadway @ W. 76th St.

Owned by the same people who own the Patriot Saloon way downtown, Yogi's sole mission is to get you really fucked up. Cans of PBR here are $2, while pitchers are $6 and the most expensive beer they serve is $4. These libations are dished out by hot and flirty female bartenders to a crowd that's a mix of blue collar construction workers and over privileged college kids; it's more blue collar in the day and more collegiate at night. The jukebox at this trailer trash–themed bar plays only country music, which for some reason inspires many drunk ladies to dance on the bar and leave their brassiere as a souvenir. As for decoration, you can count on a giant wooden carved bear and some taxidermy. My favorite is the big dead turkey, but the deer and bear heads are pretty thoughtful as well. If getting your hard earned cash siphoned out of your wallet by deceptively flirty bartenders and listening to Waylon Jennings isn't enough entertainment for you, you can always watch whatever is on the 50-plus-inch TV from the late 80s that's almost as deep as it is wide. It's hard to miss considering that it's hoisted up by strong metal chains.

Shopping

Essentials Plus
2259 Broadway @ W. 81st St.

A discount store where they sell anything you could ever possibly need. Advil, deodorant, hair products, and even hand puppets. The difference between this and other discount stores throughout the city is that it's in the Upper West Side, so it's like totally organized and well maintained. Also, there is a big focus on the babies. They fucking run the Upper West Side like a fucking crime syndicate. I'm worried about a baby revolt.

Knitty City
208 W. 79th St. @ Amsterdam Ave.

Fucking Christ! I can't believe I'm putting a knitting store in this book. What's wrong with me? Look, my friends who reside in this neighborhood basically have to make their own clothes to afford to live here, so this is one of the places where they buy their goods.

Super Magic Fingers
173 W. 81st St. btw Columbus & Amsterdam Aves.

The name alone piqued my curiosity immensely; it reminded me of this one girl I dated in college. And $48 for a one hour massage is a pretty damn good deal, even if the only thing separating me from the other people getting massaged in the room was a hanging bed sheet.

Robot Village
252 W. 81st St. @ Broadway

This robot store is such an awesome place to nerd out; it even makes an R2D2 sound when you walk in instead of a door chime! While it's not super cheap, how much is it worth to you to have your own robot to do your bidding? If I had a robot, I'd teach it to write travel books for me so I wouldn't be trapped inside with my eyes bleeding from months of consecutive 10 hour days in front of the computer. Either that or I'd dress it up like Natalie Portman and snuggle with it.

The Sidewalk Bookseller
Broadway & W. 71ˢᵗ St.

How could you not wanna buy a book from this man?

Antonio the Sidewalk Bookseller is there every day if the weather permits. The nicer the day, the more books he has on display. Books start at $3. He seems like good people to me, so buy a book and support independent entrepreneurship. You gotta respect this type of hustle.

Westsider Rare and Used Books Corporation
2246 Broadway @ W. 81ˢᵗ St.

A solid used bookstore where one can buy or sell books, and very easily lose track of time. It's not terribly big but that doesn't stop them from cramming mad books in here. Make sure to peep the second story that is much smaller but has more of the old and rare books. I have no idea why there are a couple of random gold records on the wall.

Sights & Entertainment

American Museum of Natural History
Central Park West & 79th St.

If you took all the taxidermy mentioned in this book (and there's *a lot* of it) and put it in a museum, it wouldn't come close to having as many dead animals as the Natural History Museum. What are you looking for? Caribou? They got it. Bears? Yup, that too. They've even got a fucking huge collection of complete dinosaur skeletons. They got that Diplodocus holding it down. But honestly, you already know about all this shit, so why am I bothering to tell you? All I know is that this spot is totally worth the $15 suggested donation, but luckily, since it is suggested, you can really pay what you want. Some of the special exhibits like the planetarium cost extra though. Last time I was here, the thing that stood out to me the most was the statue in front of the museum. The statue is of Teddy Roosevelt on a horse with a black guy on one side of him and a Native American on the other ... really? That is some seriously pandering shit. Who wants to bet that old Teddy used to drop the N-bomb like nobody's business? Back then being a racist was part of the job description.

Humphrey Bogart's Birthplace
245 W. 103rd St. @ Broadway

Ah Bogey, so quintessentially cool. Why'd you have to smoke so many damn cigs and go and get yourself esophagus cancer? You even started the Rat Pack and didn't live long enough to see it become a benchmark of cool that still hasn't been surpassed. Oh well kid, at least we'll always have the Upper West Side.

NY Historical Society

170 Central Park West @ W. 77th St.

There are so many historical texts and items at this library and museum that it can be a bit overwhelming. Luckily for you it's free on Friday nights from 6–8pm, which means that if you go for two hours every Friday for the rest of your life, you still won't see a fifth of what they got here. That's kind of a let down, huh?

Pomander Walk

Between W. 94th & 95th Sts. Near Broadway

Built in 1922, this random, little gated street looks as if somebody imported a tiny European village and plopped it down on the Upper West Side. Although they were originally supposed to be temporary, the cottages on this street now sell for millions of dollars. Even though it is gated, someone let me in as they were leaving and I got to snap a couple pictures. I guess you gotta look like a real pussy for someone to just let you into their UWS gated community. Apparently, that's me.

Riverside Park

along the Hudson River from W. 72nd St. to W. 158th St.

A big four mile stretch of green along the Hudson, Riverside Park is exactly what it's name says it is. That's refreshing isn't it? If you can't figure out what to do in this lovely area, then maybe you should have your park-visiting privileges revoked.

Wandering around:

If you want a good free activity I suggest wandering around the Upper West Side and checking out all the great architecture. To make it a little more interesting, eat some psychedelics and if things get too weird, you can always just duck into the park. Some of these buildings include: the Dorilton, Dakota, Ansonia, Lucerne, Kenilworth, and San Remo. A lot of the amazing architecture is centered around Verdi Square (W. 72nd & Broadway). Too bad my camera's damn battery died the day I was researching this, which is coincidental because it was on St. Paddy's Day. The same thing happened when I was checking out the Cliffs of Mohr in Ireland. Is it the curse of the Irish?

UPPER WEST SIDE

♀ Grub-a-dub-dub
1 Big Nick's Burger Joint & Pizza Joint
2 Café Con Leche
3 La Caridad
4 Chirping Chicken
5 The Cottage
6 Homer's World Famous Malt Shop
7 Levain Bakery
8 Roti-Roll - Bombay Frankie
9 Sal & Carmine's Pizza
10 Sido

🍾 DRINKS DRINKS DRINKS
11 Bourbon Street
12 Broadway Dive Bar
13 Candle Bar
14 Ding Dong Lounge
15 Dive 75
16 Dive Bar
17 Lion's Head Tavern
18 O'Connell's Pub
19 P&G Cafe
20 Yogi's

🛍 Shopping
21 Essentials Plus
22 Knitty City
23 Robot Village
24 The Sidewalk Bookseller
25 Super Magic Fingers
26 Westsider Rare and Used Book Corporation

🐛 Stuffis to See and Do
27 American Museum of Natural History
28 Humphrey Bogart's Birthplace
29 NY Historical Society
30 Pomander Walk
31 Riverside Park

👍 Free Food Bitches!!
32 Peter's

🚚 Street Meat
33 Super Tacos

🌱 Herbivore Friendly
34 Café Viva
35 Hummus Place

🏇 Dominican Nannies

💋 Milfs on their way to a mani/pedi

🎥 An episode of Law & Order being shot

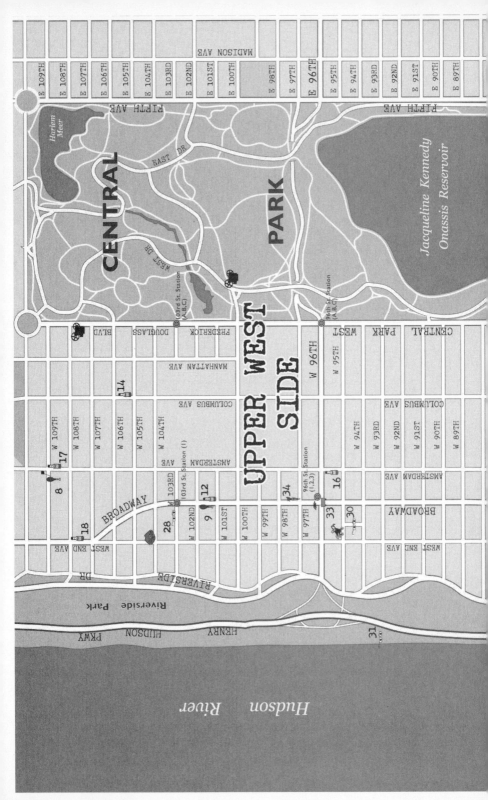

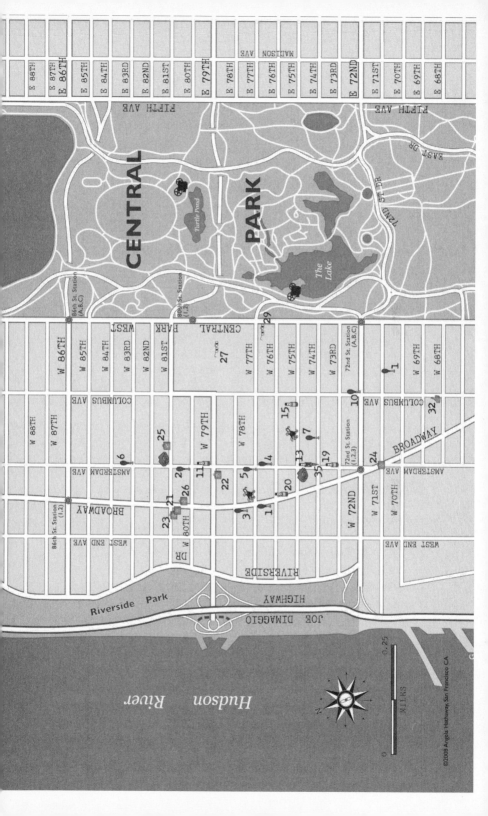

I'm always afraid that I'm gonna fall ice-skating and someone is gonna run over my finger and slice it off. Is that a weird fear?

Central Park

Designed by Fredrick Law Olmstead and Calvert Vaux, Central Park is 843 acres of a good time. And guess what? Most of it is free. Feel like smoking a bowl and playing frisbee? Head to the park. Wanna go for a jog and not have to dodge Dodges (or to be honest, cabbies)? Central Park is your place. Your old lady kick you out and you can't afford a hotel room? Nobody has to pay to sleep in the park! If you can't figure out what to do with wide open green spaces, big boulders, lots of trees and free time, I'm not gonna spell it out for you. But what I am gonna do is list off some of the attractions and make snarky comments about them to give you some ideas. These are for when you're tired of laughing at 17-year-old kids on mushrooms who are rolling around in the foliage and yelling that they've made some profound discoveries about the universe. Some are free and some cost money; it's up to you to decide which ones you want to try. I can only take you so far.

The Great Lawn

Sunbathing, free concerts, sports, and more sunbathing. At least skin cancer is free!

Belvedere Castle

While it's not a real castle (there aren't any real castles in the U.S.) and Mr. Belvedere doesn't work here, it's a great place to get a view of the surrounding area and try to figure out which sunbather you're gonna stalk. You are so creepy, you know that?

Alice in Wonderland Statue

Linda McCartney took some rad photos of Jimi Hendrix and the rest of the Experience on this statue in the '60s, so when I was 18 and had driven out here with some buddies after high school, I wandered the park in search of it. I found it. It's pretty cool.

Jacqueline Kennedy Onassis Reservoir

People like to run circles around this thing ... fuck that! I hate running.

Central Park Zoo

I've seen better, but you can't knock the location. Also, my mom got stung by a bee once when we were here. How the fuck that bee escaped from its cage is my question.

Strawberry Fields

Dedicated to John Lennon, by Yoko Ono, in 1985. Bring your tourist friends here so they can take photos. I'm gonna be so disappointed if

photo by Krista Vendetti

it's a deranged fan who kills me and not somebody that I've managed to piss off in my lifetime.

Statues throughout the Park

Why don't people make statues of motherfuckers anymore? That's not too much to ask for is it? If the aforementioned deranged killer gets me, I'm putting it in your hands to get a statue made of me. If for some reason Central Park doesn't want it, see if they'll take it at the Russian & Turkish Bathhouse in the East Village ... wow, I just managed to creep myself out with that mental image, and I don't even know why.

Sheep Meadow

No sheep here, just good looking people sun-baaaaaa-thing ... ugh, I hate myself for that one. Somebody please cue the deranged fan.

Wollman Skating Rink

Just like ice skating in Bryant Park, but not free. Donald Trump re-built this thing and now operates it—what the fuck does he need our money for? He should donate the proceeds to the city.

Shakespeare in the Park

While this summer festival at Delacorte Theater is free, it would probably be easier to get Donald Trump to donate his profits from the Wollman Skating Rink than it is to get tickets.

Rollerbladers Dancing to Disco near the Bandshell

This always makes me wish I was gay.

Summer Stage

One of the best places to see really good, free live music. For some reason, I just can't think of any smart-ass comment for this one.

Tavern on the Green

If you can actually afford to eat here, would you like to take me out to dinner? I'm a great conversationalist and generally put out on the first date.

The Lake

Where else in New York could you take your sweetie out for a row-boat ride? You can procure one of these boats at the Loeb Boathouse which unfortunately isn't where you will find Lisa Loeb...I asked. Where oh where has the patron saint of cute girls in glasses gone to?

Bethesda Terrace

You didn't know that that place with the fountain overlooking the lake had a name did you? Me neither until I looked it up at: www.centralpark.com.

The Dairy

Once a place where cows were milked and inseminated, The Dairy now serves as Central Park's official gift store. Now you know where to buy a stupid fucking Central Park coffee mug should you ever need to.

Swedish Cottage

Apparently the Swedish would like to be known for more than just their bikini team, candy fishes, and Ikea. They'd like you to know that they are very fond of marionettes too, because that's what happens here, marionettes.

The Obelisk

Also know as Cleopatra's Needle, this thing has been in existence for longer than your god has. Seriously, it was erected in 1500 BC in Heliopolis and wasn't brought to New York until 1879.

God damn! This photo makes Central Park awfully alluring.

Upper East Side

The Upper East Side reeks of old money. Elderly rich women walk down the street in fur coats and ridiculously big diamond earrings, clutching spoiled, shitty little dogs, while chauffeured Rolls Royces idle in front of high-rise co-ops, waiting for the boss ... seriously. The UES was literally founded by the wealthiest families in the history of the world, families like the Rockefellers, Astors, Carnegies, and Vanderbilts. To put in perspective how wealthy these people were, it's estimated that John D. Rockefeller's net worth, at its peak, was three times more than what Bill Gates is worth. That's fucking crazy! It was in this neighborhood that these American aristocrats built some of the most incredible mansions and townhouses in the country. They also donated millions of dollars to seed many of the Upper East Side's most famous institutions: the museums.

Museum Mile stretches mostly along 5th Ave. north of 60th St. and includes some of the most well-known museums in the world, like the Whitney Museum of American Art, the Frick Collection, and the Metropolitan Museum of Art. The most surprising thing about the Upper East Side, though, is that it has a large amount of affordable places to eat and drink, despite being such a fancy pants area. I was totally floored by how many places in this neighborhood actually made it in the book. My guess is that it has something to do with the fact that Hunter College is in the UES, and everyone knows that college students don't have shit.

Traditionally speaking, the Upper East Side was more conservative than its West Side equivalent, but these days many of the old distinctions no longer hold true. Then again, what do I know, I try to stay out of both those neighborhoods as much as possible.

The boundaries of the **Upper East Side** are E. 60th St. in the south to E. 96th St. in the north, and 5th Ave. in the west to the East River in the east.

Food

3 Decker Restaurant

1746 2nd Ave. @ E 91st St.

A sizable corner diner with cheap prices and a big menu. It's a simple place, therefore, only needing a simple description. Amen.

Aprovecho

1229 1st Ave. btw E 66th & 67th Sts.

The interior of Aprovecho is almost as colorful as its owner Elie, a middle aged Moroccan man who served in the Israeli army and now sings along with the loud Spanish and French music that plays in his UES Mexican restaurant. He's also been known to sit in and play spoons with the three piece band that plays here on Thursday nights. Yeah, basically he's awesome. Aprovecho is also called 879-TACO because that's the number people ring for delivery, which they do often, because it's moderately priced, and surprisingly tasty. I got a taco, quesadilla and a soda for under $10, and while it wasn't California good, it was still pretty good.

Beyoglu

200 E 81st St. @ 3rd Ave.

I honestly wasn't gonna put this in here but then I saw that it was Michelin rated and thought, "most people that read this shit aren't really gonna be eating at Michelin rated places often, and this is probably the best priced Michelin spot ever. Might as well hook my broke-ass brethren up." It's pretty cheap for how nice it looks; all the small plates are pretty affordable, topping out at $7, and the bigger platters average out at $15. The interior here is beautifully and brightly painted with pseudo mosaic tile tables. Like I said, it is a little splurgy and it's seems like the type of place where UES women go with each other when Panchita is watching the kids and they want to eat healthy and talk about different styles of strollers. Also, if for some reason you have to pay for someone's nice food (like a date or your significant other's parents) it's a solid bet.

Buddha BBeeQ

1750 2nd Ave. btw E 91st & E 92nd Sts.

While they don't have a bathroom (which is annoying), and aren't very good at spelling bbq, this is a nice, upscale looking, small place where you can get solid Korean bbq for under $10. The girls who work here are sweet and friendly and, more than anything else, it's a good place for a cheap date. Hey we all pay for sex in our own way. It's worth it, right?

Chicken Kitchen

1177 2nd Ave. @ E 62nd St.

Smokey with the smell of poultry, this small restaurant has only 3 tables and not a whole lot else except a Dominican guy working the grill who probably can't wash the smell of chicken off his skin. At Chicken Kitchen, $3.75 gets you ¼ chicken's worth of dark meat, while white meat is more expensive. You can also get a whole chicken breast for $6. All I know is that dogs must fucking love this guy whenever he walks down the street.

First Avenue Coffee Shop

1433 1st Ave. @ E 75th St.

I was standing outside of this cheap diner with a long lunch counter, and taking a photo of the place, when the owner came out to see what I was doing. I said that I liked the look of his place and wanted a photo of it. When I walked around the corner to write, he waited and then followed me to pester me about why I was taking photos. Impressed and a little bugged out by his persistence (I really don't think anyone is trying to steal your idea dude), I told him the real deal, and he told me to come back and he'd buy me some coffee. If I drank coffee, I would have taken him up on that.

H&H Midtown Bagels

1551 2nd Ave. btw E 80th & 81st Sts.

Open 24 hours this place slings amazing bagels *and* they cut, toast and butter them at your request, which is a lot more than you can say for the other H&H Bagels out on 12th Ave. (they aren't related despite having the same name). And if for some reason you're concerned, don't worry, these bagels are kosher. As for me, my dietary restrictions are monetarily defined (except for onions…oooh how I hate them).

Le Gourmet

1267 1st Ave. @ E 68th St.

Le Gourmet is like one of those midtown steam plate, pay by the pound places, but instead of being poopy, it's actually really good. Beyond the steam plates, they also make fresh, cheap Mexican food (made by real Mexicans!), pizza and kebabs. Yup, they've pretty much got everything, including all you can eat of their delicious bread. They also appeal to the hood by doing things like having hamentashens during Purim. Quite clever these Le Gourmet people are; they have Haman spinning in his grave (and I have all of you running to wikipedia to see what the fuck I'm talking about).

Papaya King

179 E 86th St. @ 3rd Ave.

You have to earn the name "King". They don't just give that shit out the day you're born (unless of course that's your last name, in which case they absolutely do), it takes something special. Elvis is the King of Rock 'n Roll because he was the first son of a bitch to steal that music and make it palatable for white people. Michael Jackson is the King of Pop because he's an amazing performer and he touches little kids (I hear he's writing a children's book called *Hop on the King of Pop*). The Papaya King (the business's original name was Hawaiian Tropical Drinks Inc.) is called such because back in 1932 the founder, Gus Poulos, was the first cat to pair up hot dogs with tropical fruit drinks. Yes dear reader, you can thank the Papaya King for all those late night drunken binges at Papaya Dog or Gray's Papaya, because this here spot on the corner of 86th and 3rd is the fucker that started it all. And if that's not enough for you, Anthony Bourdain eats here too.

Sassy's Sliders

1530 3rd Ave. btw 86th & 87th Sts.

A tad more expensive than White Castle, but made of far better quality products, Sassy's sells sliders made of beef, turkey, bbq chicken, veggie, or chicken parmesan. Your best bet might be a meal deal like four sliders of your choice + fries + soda for $7.29. The sliders, by nature are tiny, and the restaurant is only slightly bigger than its burgers, but I gotta tell you, tiny things like sliders make it a hell of a lot easier for me to taste more things on my research trips.

Taco City
1143 1st Ave. btw E 62nd & 63rd Sts.

Finally, Mexican food at California prices. The most expensive thing here is a $5.99 shrimp burrito, but the drawback is that it not only looks and smells like a cheap Chinese take-out place, it basically is. It just serves Tex-Mex instead of Chinese food. There aren't even any Mexicans working here and I know it's not like they couldn't find any. Don't be surprised if your taco tastes like wontons and your burrito has snow peas in it.

Totonno's
1544 2nd Ave. btw E 80th & 81st Sts.

Totonno's, out at Coney Island, is a Brooklyn institution that opened in 1924 and is the oldest continuously operating pizzeria in the US run by the same family. In recent decades, Totonno's has stretched its legs a little bit and set down some roots in Manhattan, meaning that all you folks don't have to go way the fuck to Coney Island to get some of this goodness. The pizza here is fantastic and it's cheap. You can get two slices of pizza and a soda for just $5. So what are you waiting for? Coal burning brick ovens bitches!

Wrap n Run
788 Lexington Ave. @ E 61st St.,
also 1125 Lexington Ave. @ E 78th St.

We all know that "Wrap" is Whitey's way of saying "Burrito", but at least Wrap n Run has the gumption to make their food interesting. I got the "Texas" which had chicken, mashed potatoes, corn, and bbq sauce. There are also ones with pasta in them and ones with turkey, cranberry sauce and stuffing. The wraps start at $5.85 and go to around $8. Hit this spot up yo! It's delicious.

Bars

Aces & Eights Saloon
1683 1st Ave @ 87th St.

In poker, a pair of aces and a pair of eights is known as "The Dead Man's Hand" because it's what Wild Bill Hickok was holding when he got shot in the back of his dome. It's a proper name for this sports bar because it honors the memory of Wild Bill by looking kinda like a saloon, and because it makes me feel like I'd rather be a dead man than hang out here again. As I've mentioned before, any bar with beer-pong attracts chaunceys like cocaine attracts underage models. But Aces & Eights does have one thing up its sleeve that keeps people coming back: really cheap drinks. From Sunday to Thursday, Bud and Bud light pints are $2.50, pitchers are always $10, and on Friday and Saturday from 9-12pm, $10 gets you all you can drink draft beer. With this many drunk frat boys, there's bound to be violence; it's one of the laws of physics.

American Trash
1471 1st Ave. btw E 76th & 77th Sts.

American Trash has been holding it down as one of the Upper East Side's better pseudo dive bars for over 20 years. Just to prove this to me, the bartender pointed out a woman and told me that she had met her husband here and that they now had two kids together. That's pretty cool. So is the free Wi-Fi and all the stuff hanging from the ceiling and walls like a gas tank from a motorcycle, a red guitar with the Soviet hammer & sickle painted on it, and a snowboard. If you're wondering, the cheapo beer here is cans of Northern Lights for $3. Previously the only Northern Lights I'd heard of, other than the aurora borealis, was the kind you smoked. You learn something new every day. While I was here, I had to drop a deuce and was amazed at how clean the bathroom was. Seriously, wow. That's why I said it was a pseudo dive bar. Taking shits in dive bar bathrooms are generally scarring experiences that leave you feeling used, cheap, and degraded. Not at American Trash my friends; not at all.

The Big Easy
1768 2nd Ave. @ E 92nd St.

Why can't New Orleans themed bars be about cool shit like Louis Armstrong, Dr. John, po' boys, the Neville Brothers, beignets or Lil Wayne? Why must they always be full of cheese dicks and girls begging for attention? I'm tired of this shit! Get it together people. Just because they have retardedly cheap drink specials, doesn't mean you have to act retardedly yourself. I understand why locals call the place "Big Sleazy", but unfortunately that name gives this bar too much credit.

Brandy's Piano Bar
235 E 84th St. btw 2nd & 3rd Aves.

It's almost impossible to have a bad time at this 30+ year old UES treasure. Maybe it's because Brandy's manages to have a sense of humor about itself; it comes off as simultaneously bawdy and classy, but maintains both postures with a knowing wink. Hanging out at Brandy's is like being in a Tom Waits song, except gayer and with show tunes. If that's not compelling you to rush over there tonight, I don't know what else I can say.

Brother Jimmy's BBQ
1485 2nd Ave. @ E 77th St.

While it's not exactly my first choice (or second, third...or seventh) as a place to go out, Brother Jimmy's is an Upper East Side mainstay and something that can't be overlooked. My publisher brought me here so I could really get the feeling of what the bars in this neighborhood are like, and he was right, this yuppie bar is a good indicator of what I was to see for the rest of the night. The crowd is slightly post-college with lots of older dudes and pretty girls drinking to get fucked up. I honestly think I saw a couple girls in little black dresses shotgunning $3 PBR tall boys like they were worried the bar would sell out of them. They also serve ribs here and everyone knows that little black dresses and ribs go together perfectly. Brother Jimmy's is actually part of a chain throughout the city (there's like 5 of them), but this is the original one and has a way bigger bar scene than the rest of them. They also have tons of TVs playing sports, so if you can't handle watching girls who normally starve themselves hoss down mac & cheese and collard greens, you can watch the Knicks blow another close game.

Phil Hughes Bar & Restaurant
1682 1st Ave. btw E 87th & 88th Sts.

A sports bar/dive bar/place where old drunks go to die, Phil Hughes sells pints of Bud for $3 and has a surprising amount of TV's given the space. If you stop in here, chances are you'll hear Irish music on the jukebox and find an Irish bartender mixing some strong drinks (just keep the drinks simple). It also opens really early just in case you wake up with a bad case of the shakes (most of the patrons do). Just one more note of advice, if an old guy with a white beard asks you to pull his finger, don't. He actually just ends up shitting himself (I can't believe he didn't foresee that happening).

Rathbones
1702 2nd Ave. @ E 88th St.

Rathbones has different specials every night of the week, but by the time I got here, I had too much to drink and was too lazy to write them down. I know they exist though. In fact, now that I think of it, I do remember something about 25 cent wings on Wednesdays nights, but that's just because I didn't have to pay for them; my publisher bank rolled me all night (I wish that happened every time I did research). Otherwise the place isn't terribly impressive. It's mostly the type of place for people in their mid to late 30s, who wear collared shirts, all the time. Regardless, I had a good time because I was eating and drinking for free, and Mr. Falls Media and I had a deep conversation about the importance of marriage. I might marry these chicken wings though because they were damn good.

Reif's Tavern

302 E 92ⁿᵈ St. btw 1ˢᵗ & 2ⁿᵈ Aves.

Reif's is a neighborhood spot where beers are $3 and you're encouraged to bring some food to cook up on their backyard grill. If you like the idea of your beers being cute, you can buy a bucket of little 7oz bottles for $10, but really, who wants little beers? That's just teasing yourself. While the average age here is late 20's to early 30's, there is no shortage of old guys sitting at the bar staring into their drinks (or at girls asses), or at the TVs playing sports or *Law & Order*. To get the true Reif's Tavern experience though, make sure to come on a nice day and hang out in their back patio; you'll hear cuss words you never knew existed before.

Subway Inn

143 E 60ᵗʰ St. @ Lexington Ave.

Neon beer signs and red lighting reflect off a black and white checkered floor, while people trade strange stories at little tables, each individually lit by it's own pinkish colored lamp. You scan the crowd and see a couple of old drunks, tall, hot model-looking girls, guys in jackets from a local union, and even some random foreigners who might be tourists. Yes, this is the Subway Inn, a classic spot which, if there were a dive bar hall of fame, would be part of the first group of inductees. I first came here with my publisher and a friend of his, who spent most of the night telling us about banging girls from J-Date and how he had had a threesome earlier that week (That lucky bastard. I've still never had a threesome; I weep about it nightly ☹.). He also went on to tell us an amazing story about how for someone's bachelor's party he answered an ad on craigslist by a middle-aged woman who was looking for a gang-bang. He invited her to the bachelor party hinting that she'd get a train run on her, but she ended up getting talked into cocktail waitressing the whole night instead, and never even got her ass grabbed, let alone a clusterfuck. There's just something about the Subway Inn that makes these stories come out.

Tin Lizzy

1647 2nd Ave. btw E 85th & 86th Sts.

The bartender here was so drunk that I'm honestly not sure what the real prices are. All I know is that I drank for cheap and that he apparently thought I was cool (he kept telling me so). While Tin Lizzy gets busy with a young, dumb-lookin'-for-some crowd on weekends, it's all locals during the week. Even if you're not a regular here, try to come off as one by chatting up the bartender; they give regulars special prices (or that's what I gleaned from the barkeep's slurring and swerving). When I was last here, it was just me, my publisher, four old drunks, one girl, a wasted bartender and lots of Led Zeppelin. Without a doubt, the best part of this bar is its name. It's funny because one of Ireland's most famous bands ever is Thin Lizzy, but since most Irish pronounce the "th" sound as a "t" sound, this Irish bar is making fun of the Irish accent. I'm such a nerd for word play... and making fun of people.

Shopping

I really just couldn't find much cheap shopping up here in the UES, so it looks like you'll just have to settle for what I've got below.

Shakespeare & Co.
939 Lexington Ave. btw E 68th & 69th Sts.

When I asked the girl working at this independent bookstore if it was related to the famous Shakespeare & Co. in Paris, she replied, "No. They just stole the name." And you know what? I can appreciate that. This was originally supposed to be *Broke-Ass Spencer's Guide to Living Cheaply in New York* but I stole the manuscript and buried Spencer somewhere in the desert 45 minutes outside of Marfa, Texas. The shitty part is that my partner in crime was a guy named Dan Brown, and though we both got to take one of Spencer's two unpublished books, Dan got something called *The Da Vinci Code* while I got stuck with this piece of crap. See what happens when you try to determine all your important life decisions by playing Rock, Paper, Scissors? Apparently there are a few of these book stores throughout the city and because of this particular location, they focus on books for old rich women and students, but mostly old rich women. Fabio sells tons of his romance novels here.

Sights & Entertainment

A lot of these sights are located along a stretch called Museum Mile. If you can't figure out why it's called that, you should buy another copy of this book. I swear the answer will be in there.

Asia Society
725 Park Ave. btw E 70th & 71st Sts.

If the Upper East Side just isn't far east enough for you, come to the Asia Society on Fridays from 6-9pm when it's free. Whether you come for the art, lectures, or events, you'll walk away feeling like your life is a little more enriched. Maybe if this place started selling five dumplings for a buck, I might actually come in one day instead of getting my fix of Asian society in Chinatown.

Biscuits & Bath
1535 1st Ave. @ E 81st St.

Hoy shit! A giant room full of dogs running around and playing with each other, and a big window for us to look in and watch. This is the best (and cutest) free entertainment I've ever seen. It's like watching Animal Planet but you can bang on the glass and cheer the animals on when they start humping each other. The best part is when a human walks in to do something, all 35 of the dogs crowd around, begging for attention, and looking up at the person. That must be what it feels like to be God, or at least Britney Spears.

Carl Schurz Park
East End Ave. @ E 86th St.

This beautifully land-scaped park along the East River sits across the street from a super cool, small block of houses that look like they belong in London, not New York. They remind me of that old UK show *The Young Ones* but instead of being inhabited by a punk, a hippie, an anarchist and a hipster, each residence probably houses people rich enough to lend money to God. The park itself has a view of Roosevelt Island, a cute little lighthouse, and one of Queens' lovely housing projects (is that Mobb Deep I hear?). It actually looks like someone lopped off a bit of Central Park and pushed it over to the water, just so they could try to make the cutest park in NYC. Just ask any mayor since 1942 how handsome this park is; the dope ass Gracie Mansion (the mayor's house), built in 1799, sits within Carl Schurz Park. Actually don't ask Bloomberg though, he's so rich he doesn't even live in the mansion.

The Frick Collection
1 E 70th St. @ 5th Ave.

Children under the age of 10 not allowed in the Frick Collection! I wish I could say the same for all the restaurants I've worked in. Let me tell you something about servers, we hate your children. Outside I find them cute and adorable and even want a couple of my own, but the second they step inside a restaurant, they just become shitty little people who squeal and throw tantrums when they don't get what they want. Plus, kids don't eat anything that costs real money, and what they do eat comes with TONS of special requests (which the kitchen guys curse at me in Spanish about) and mostly ends up all over the floor and table. Then the parents don't clean any of it up and often don't tip any extra for me putting up with their demon spawn and scraping up the mashed cheerios that their child decided to wing across the room. And we don't even serve cheerios God dammit! This is a seafood place! Sorry, I just had to get that off my chest (I had that exact table yesterday. They tipped like 12%). But yes, the Frick Collection is wonderful. When Henry Clay Frick died, he donated his mansion and his considerable art collection so that it could be used as a public museum. Everything in here is exquisite and most of the art was created by all those old, dead European masters who you learned about in your intro to Art History class. The best time to peep this shit is Sundays when admission is pay what you wish.

Goldberger's Pharmacy
1200 1st Ave. @ E 65th St.

I'm only putting it in here for its amazing neon sign. I think it's one of the best I've ever seen.

The Guggenheim Museum
1071 5th Ave. @ E 88th St.

Rumor is, before Frank Lloyd Wright designed this masterpiece, he gave the concept a practice run at the V.C. Morris Gift Shop on San Francisco's Maiden Lane. While that building is pretty impressive, it's quaint and meager compared to the ingenious piece of architecture that is the Guggenheim Museum. Holy crap is this place amazing. The one time I actually got to visit here was on a day when they were changing exhibits, so I didn't get to see too much of the museum's famous contemporary and modern art collection. But what I did see was sweet. I also wanted to include a photo of the building in these pages, but I figured every guide book probably has one and I wanted my book to be different.* While this entire complex is worth seeing, admission is $18, so I just recommend coming on Friday nights from 5:45-7:45 when it's pay what you wish.

Jewish Museum
1109 5th Ave. @ E 92nd St.

I'll give you one guess what this museum is about. If you've ever seen a Woody Allen or Mel Brooks movie and missed half the jokes, come visit this place and watch them again. It's free on Saturdays, which is funny because, shouldn't they be closed on Saturdays?

---

*Editor's note: Stuart is lying and is just trying to sound cool. He couldn't photograph it because there was scaffolding up.

Metropolitan Museum of Art (the Met)
1000 5th Ave. @ 82nd St.

Do you know how much easier it is to write about shitty greasy spoon diners that nobody knows exists than it is to write about a vastly important cultural landmark with over 2 million pieces of art in its permanent collection? I mean really, what kind of wise cracks can I make about the Met? Shit like, "Dude, I totally had sex with a sarcophagus when no one was looking"? No, that sounds retarded and it cheapens both of us (well actually just me). The Met is one of the biggest and most famous museums in the world. You know this. You could literally spend days in there without seeing everything. You know this too. But did you know that admittance is a suggested donation of $20, meaning that you can really pay whatever you want? Sure the vendor will give you the stink eye, but hell, you're used to that right? Oh you knew all that too? Well go fuck a sarcophagus or something, I'm tired of your shit.

New York Doll Hospital
787 Lexington Ave. Ste 2 btw E 61st & 62nd Sts.

Is this not one of the creepiest things you've ever seen?

Word! Inside the New York Doll Hospital, doll parts are strewn all over like some type of porcelain and plastic horror movie or a goddamn Toys R Us concentration camp. Third generation owner, operator and,

This is where the non-mutilated dolls live.

um...operator, Irving Chaise putters around doing what he does best, fixing sick and dismembered dollies with surgical techniques passed down from his grandfather, who opened the place in 1900. Irving himself has been at it for 68 years, and the man can fix just about any doll or toy you bring in, but he draws the line when it comes to anything that's battery operated. When I was there I saw all kinds of old, rare and antique dolls, including a Howdy Doody toy and a doll with 3 faces (take that two faced kid in India!). I highly recommend stopping in here and checking the place out even if you don't have anything that needs to be fixed, it's pretty damn interesting. Just be warned that Irving can be a little ornery, so give him some time to warm up to you.

The Whitney Museum of American Art
945 Madison Ave. @ E 75th St.

Being a museum located in New York that focuses on 20th century American art, is kind of like being a pedophile sex tourist visiting Thailand; it's just too easy. Why not try being located in Kabul and focusing on 20th century American art? We'll see how strong your convictions are then, won't we? Krista and I went to the Whitney for the Summer of Love exhibit that focused on all the amazing artistic revolutions that were happening in the late 1960s. Unfortunately we got there an hour before it closed, so we didn't get to see any of the permanent collection. But all the 60's shit was awesome, especially the rock posters and photographs. For some reason I get the feeling that being a 1960's rock star was a lot cooler than being a 2000's travel writer who fills his book with poop jokes. But hey I'm trying right? And you should try to get your ass down to the Whiney on Fridays from 6-9pm when it's pay what you wish.

UPPER EAST SIDE

Grub-a-dub-dub
1 3 Decker Restaurant
2 Aprovecho
3 Beyoglu
4 Buddha BBeeQ
5 Chicken Kitchen
6 First Avenue Coffee Shop
7 H&H Midtown Bagels
8 Le Gourmet
9 Papaya King
10 Sassy's Sliders
11 Taco City
12 Totonno's
13 Wrap n Run

DRINKS DRINKS DRINKS
14 Aces & Eights Saloon
15 American Trash
16 The Big Easy
17 Brandy's Piano Bar
18 Brother Jimmy's BBQ
19 Phil Hughes Bar & Restaurant
20 Rathbones
21 Reif's Tavern
22 Subway Inn
23 Tin Lizzy

Shopping
24 Shakespeare & Co.

Stuffis to See and Do
25 Asia Society
26 Biscuits & Bath
27 Carl Schurz Park
28 The Frick Collection
29 Goldberger's Pharmacy
30 Guggenheim
31 Jewish Museum
32 Metropolitan Museum of Art (the Met)
33 New York Doll Hospital
34 Whitney Museum of American Art

Free Food Bitches!!
35 Iggy's
36 Vudu Lounge

Herbivore Friendly
37 Gobo

Chauffer picking up the boss

Old mean woman who's rich enough to buy and sell your ass a thousand times over

Private school kids whose parents spend ungodly amounts of money on their educations, repaying their parents by loitering and smoking cigarettes on street corners

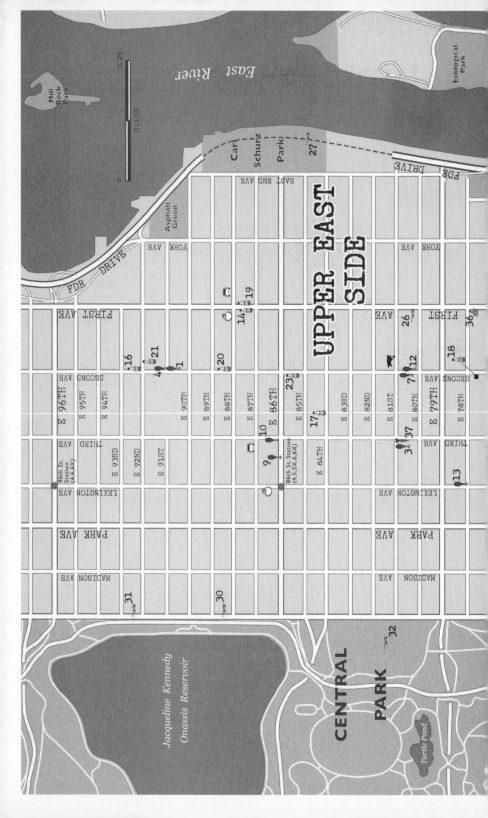

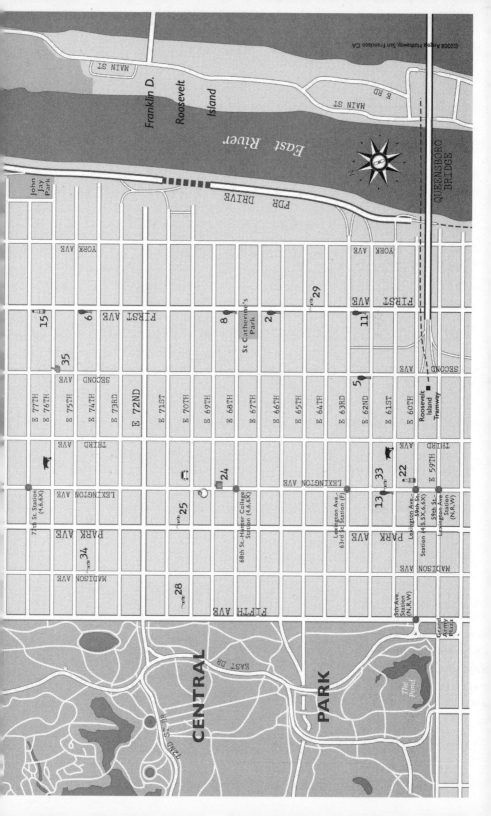

©2008 Amiga Hathaway San Francisco CA

Morningside Heights & Harlem

Maybe I'm just the most recent in a long line of liberal Jews to extol the Harlem experience, but I have to say I fucking love this place. There is so much going on and such a true blend of cultures and ethnicities that anyone who really loves living in a city should be able to appreciate this neighborhood. At the moment Harlem stands at the perfect juncture; urban redevelopment has made it safer than it was in the awful '70s and '80s, but it hasn't been over gentrified (yet) to the point where it's lost the authenticity of being the historic capitol of Black America.

Mix this in with a growing population of Mexicans, Salvadorians, Colombians and the other Latin American ethnicities now occupying the west 130s, and you have a neighborhood with an amazing diversity of entertainment, restaurants and cultural activities. You can have breakfast and read the paper at an artsy, bohemian café, grab excellent tacos for lunch at a taqueria, shop at discount stores in the afternoon, consume the gastronomic equivalent of heaven at a soul food restaurant for dinner, and see world class jazz in a dingy dive bar at night. Forces are colliding right now causing Harlem to once again be one of the most interesting neighborhoods in the entire United States. They even have a tiny section called Le Petite Senegal (116th St. west of St. Nicholas Ave.), that's adding West African shops and eateries to the mix. Hell, I'd even seriously consider moving to Harlem if all my friends didn't live in Brooklyn.

My personal favorite anecdote from my time in Harlem was when I was walking up Lenox Ave. and was stopped by a black lady in her early 60s who said, "Hey you smoke weed don't you? Here take my card, I deliver." And she was already walking away from me before I could answer her. When I looked at her business card it said, "Auntie Sonia. Herbalist" and listed her phone number.

Morningside Heights is the neighborhood directly south of Harlem and has been home to Columbia University since the 19th century. Considering that it's an expensive, private, Ivy League school, it spent most of its history educating an elite class of primarily white students, which obviously caused it to seem like a strange little bubble in the shadow of Harlem. But in the past 40 or so years, that bubble has been steadily increasing in size, to the point where Morningside Heights is now more or less an extension of the Upper West Side, just with a younger crowd.

To help you get better oriented with these interesting neighborhoods, you should know that 125th St. is the main commercial street in Harlem, and that some of the numbered avenues have been renamed in honor of famous black leaders. Above 110th St., 8th Ave./Central Park West becomes Fredrick Douglas Blvd. and 7th Ave. becomes Adam Clayton Powell, Jr. Blvd. Lenox Ave, which begins at 110th St. alternates between that name and Malcolm X Blvd. This shit can be confusing if you don't expect it.

The boundaries of **Morningside Heights** are W. 110th St. in the south to about W. 125th St. in the north, and from the Hudson River in the West to Manhattan Ave. in the East. The borders of Harlem are W. 125th St. in the south to W 155th St. in the north and Manhattan Ave. in the West to Lenox/Malcolm X Ave. in the east. The neighborhood east of Lenox/Malcolm X is considered East Harlem and El Barrio.

Food

Amir's Falafel
2911 Broadway @ W. 114th St.

College kids love falafel. It's a proven fact. Just look at them, they love the shit.

El Toro Partido
3431 Broadway btw W. 139th & 140th Sts.

I think that my entire time in New York, I was actually looking for this place and I didn't even know it. The huaraches, which cost $5, are seriously some of the best cheap eats you can find in this city. Holy shit, I feel good just telling you about it. If I lived nearby, all of the cats who work here would be like, "Look at that *pinche* gringo. He comes in here every single day and eats a huarache. I think he's going to turn into one. I've seen it happen before. It's really fucking weird man."

The Famous Jimbo's Hamburger Palace
1345 Amsterdam @ W. 125th St

See page 311 (Spanish Harlem)

The Hungarian Pastry Shop
1030 Amsterdam @ W. 111th St.

The Hungarian Pastry Shop has long been the haunt of the intellectual radical students from Columbia and Barnard. The old world, Parisian feel of the café's interior helps to foster that bohemian sentiment that so many college kids are searching for, and the bottomless cup of coffee gives them something to do while they read Henry Miller and discuss how Communism might still be a viable alternative to the system we have now. And, when I say bottomless, I mean that you can really just hangout there all day long. If you're as sharp as I hope you are, you've probably picked up on the fact that they sell pastries here, too. Whenever I go to the Hungarian Pastry Shop it reminds me of how much I miss being in college.

The Interchurch Center Café
475 Riverside Dr. suite 241 @ W. 119th St.

Nicknamed the God Box because it's a big boxy building full of various religions (actually just Christian denominations) working together blah blah blah ... I don't really care what happens in the rest of the building. Cheap food is my religion dammit! I'm just here for the cafeteria at which you can gorge yourself for like $6. A friend of mine who went to Columbia took me here one morning after I slept on his floor, and it was like a ray of light beaming down from heaven. Who doesn't like paying $3 for a heap of mac and cheese to be slopped onto their plate? The weird thing, and granted I was hung over with a blistering headache, was that I think the wall sconces illuminated as if they were glowing crosses.

Koronet Pizza
2848 Broadway @ W. 111th St.

While it might not be the best pizza in New York, it's probably the biggest slice I've ever had. I mean just look at that bugger next to my iPod, you seriously can't beat it for $3. It's the length of my torso for fuck's sake. Be aware about ordering toppings, though, because they literally pile them on. It's almost inhumane. If you order pepperoni, you better love that shit since that's what you're gonna be burping for the next two days.

La Nueva Flor de Broadway
3401 Broadway @ 138th St.

As I've been your guide for a grip of chapters now, I hope that we're at the point where our rapport has been built up enough for you to trust me on my word (I should hope so for your sake considering you bought this fucker). Listen to me when I say that it's imperative for you to follow these instructions step by step: go to La Nueva Flor, pull $3.50 from your pocket, order the Cuban sandwich, answer "yes" when they ask if you want garlic sauce and pickles, pay them your $3.50, go stand at the counter by the window, and eat that big flavorful sonofabitch you've been salivating over. This shit is the bomb, son!

Plus, if you're a diehard capitalist, I've heard that Fidel sheds a tear every time an American eats a Cuban sandwich.

Max Café

1262 Amsterdam Ave. @ W. 123rd St.

A groovy café with thrift store furniture and tons of art on the walls, Max Café is a great place to get some Italian food and espresso drinks while reading the paper or studying. If paninis are your thing (they are mine), you can obtain one here for the fair sum of six dollars in American cash tender. But really the nicest part about this place is that it attracts a hip and diverse clientele that perfectly represents the neighborhood. Sit at one of the outside tables on a nice day and it's only a matter of time before you end up talking to a stranger about the size of Nina Simone's catalogue and what project Dan the Automator is currently working on.

Mama's Fried Chicken

2158 Fredrick Douglas Blvd. @ W. 117th St.

Everything at Mama's is fried, greasy, yummy and super cheap. You can get a nine-piece nuggets for $3 … okay, I have something to confess to you. I sometimes get insatiable urges for McNuggets from Mickey D's and during one of these lapses in self control, I noticed that while old Ronald sells a 10-piece McNuggets for $4, you can get three four-piece McNuggets for $1 each. For all you non-mathematically inclined folks, that means, while 10 nuggets is $4, you can get 12 nuggets for $3. Does McDonald's really think their customers are so stupid that they can't figure this out? While I do feel like my intelligence has been insulted, I do appreciate this loophole in their system (so does my future cardiologist).

Saga

1268 Amsterdam Ave btw W. 122nd & 123rd Sts.

Cheap, no frills sushi and Vietnamese food. Really? Can you think of a better combo than that?

Sunshine Kitchen
695 St. Nicholas Ave. @ W. 145th St.

There are two schools of thought when it comes to eateries where the employee stands behind bulletproof glass and you receive your food through a small exchange area built into it. The first school says, "What the fuck is your pale-ass doing way the fuck up there in Harlem?" while the second school says, "Aww, hell yeah! I bet that shit is so good. I'mma go on Saturday." I, of course, am a strong proponent of the latter. With patties and roti this good, I'd be afraid of someone trying to rob me of my recipes at gun point, too.

Texas Star
741 St. Nicholas btw W. 147th & 148th Sts

A tiny place with just six stools and a couple guys from Puebla on the grill, Texas Star is incredibly cheap. An egg and cheese sandwich costs just $1.75 and a burger and fries is only $4.25. There's not a damn thing else I can really say about the place.

Tom's Restaurant
2880 Broadway @ 112th St.

Yup that's right, the exterior of Tom's Restaurant, with the great neon sign, is the one they always used in Seinfeld (not the interior though). Considering that it probably gets a decent amount of tourists because of this, I'm amazed that the prices aren't higher. You can get a burger for $4.50 here. That's pretty awesome, right? Hey, remember when Michael Richards (Kramer) went crazy and was throwing around the N-bomb like he was George Wallace or something? What a fucking idiot.

Bars

1020 Bar

1020 Amsterdam @ W. 111th St.

Decent-sized and with a history that includes being both a barber-shop and a funeral home, 1020 is a perfect neighborhood spot to catch up with your old friends Brooklyn Lager, Rolling Rock and Yuengling (all of which cost just $3). The checkered floor is a hard evidence reminder that this place has lived different lives, while awesome sepia-toned murals of 1930s trains and planes cover the wall, implying antiquity. But still this is a modern bar in every sense; besides a couple regular-sized TVs, there's also a big projector screen in the back for sports or movies. Plus if you're one of those obnoxious Boston fans, this place might be your new home; a photo of Babe Ruth in the Red Sox uniform hangs above the bar. Personally, I don't care who you root for, I'm a Padres fan, when I'm a fan at all.

A Touch of Dee

657 Malcolm X Blvd. btw W. 142nd &143rd Sts.

A Touch of Dee is an old black folks bar where I got a few strange looks when I came in, just as much for being young as for being white. Once I sat down though, everyone was sweet as could be. In fact, since it was the day before Memorial Day, they were having a cookout on the sidewalk (they do it for most holidays) and offered me some free food. But believe it or not, I actually turned it down; I had just eaten a sandwich from La Nueva Flor de Broadway and I was full. There was one old cat dressed to the nines, which made me realize that I've actually been trying to dress like an old black guy for all these years without knowing it. I've been doing a pretty shitty job of it though. Somebody was also running a numbers game here, which caught me off guard because I didn't know people still ran numbers. What's awesome is that I think it was an old lady running the game. And if you strike it big and wanna gamble some more, Dee's also charters buses to Atlantic City. Hell, I'd go; these old folks were cooler than half my friends.

Radio Perfecto

1187 Amsterdam Ave. @ W. 119th St.

A restaurant with a decent bar scene, Radio Perfecto manages to be right near Columbia without attracting an overly douchey crowd. Part of this is because it is technically a restaurant, but also because there is no beer pong. Yes! $3 PBRs and vintage radios abound, while smart and cute young things noodle and canoodle in the great back-garden patio. I just wish I knew what noodling and canoodling meant. Sometimes these things just pop out of my head and both you and I have to deal with it.

Soundz Lounge

3155 Broadway btw La Salle & W. 125th Sts.

I was bordering on blacked out when I was here, so my memory of the place is basically lots of red velvet, but I'm not sure if it was on the ceiling or the seats (you know what I mean?). I remember there being a downstairs with music, possibly a DJ, and a pool table that they wouldn't let me sleep under. All I managed to scribble in my notepad was: "$4 Coors Light. No more taking pills from strangers." Except the spelling was worse.

Shopping

Big Apple Jazz/EZ's Woodshed

2236 Adam Clayton Powell Jr. Blvd. @ W 132nd St.

A jazz record store, with unbelievable live music everyday from 2–8pm, Big Apple Jazz is dedicated to honoring and preserving Harlem's one of a kind musical history. It does this by being a gallery, a gift store and a restaurant, and by selling books and magazines, almost all of which are jazz related (except the food; there's no such thing as jazz food). My favorite thing about this place is that it kinda acts as a hang out for everyone in the neighborhood who gives a fuck about the past, present, and uncertain future of Harlem. I ended up getting into this crazy 25 minute conversation with a lady about the politics of gentrification in New York. It's strange to be in Harlem right now and watch the neighborhood change right in front of your eyes. Hopefully there will always be space for places like Big Apple Jazz.

H & M

125 W. 125th St. btw 7th Ave. & Malcolm X Blvd.

See p. 211 (Midtown East)

Hamilton Palace

3560 Broadway btw W. 145th & 146th Sts.

Originally a theater named the RKO Hamilton Theater, this ornately designed building now houses a three-story compound of cheap stuff. Oh, how the mighty have fallen, wouldn't you agree Mr. Hamilton Theatre? This gigantic discount store has *everything* from clothes to bathroom products to home furnishings, and it's all priced to fly out the door. It's like Kmart, but shittier.

Hue-Man Bookstore & Café

2319 Fredrick Douglas Blvd. @ 125th St.

The sizeable Hue-Man Bookstore & Café comes off looking strangely corporate, as if Barnes and Noble were gonna open up a branch called Mahogany and try to specifically sell books targeting black people. This is weird because Hue-Man is not corporate at all; it's independently owned, which makes me wonder why the store seems to lack character. Regardless, this black-focused bookstore has a great selection of books spanning all genres, including my favorite, the used-books-for-$1 genre. It also hosts some of the illest events and author readings by such luminaries as Cornell West, Tavis Smiley, Marvin Van Peebles, Bill Clinton, and ahem ... Kimora Lee Simmons.

Kim's Mediapolis
2906 Broadway btw W. 113th & 114th Sts.
See Kim's Videos on p. 111 (East Village)

Morningside Bookshop
2915 Broadway @ W. 114th St.
Any place that has a huge Bukowski quote that says, "Nobody who could ever write worth a damn ever writes in peace" above the entrance is my type of establishment. Sure, I maybe would've chosen, "The nine-to-five is one of the greatest atrocities sprung upon mankind. You give your life away to a function that doesn't interest you. This situation so repelled me that I was driven to drink, starvation, and mad females, simply as an alternative", but I would've chosen that one for my own purposes. Morningside Bookshop is one of the better independent bookstores in the city, hands down. It's full of used and new pieces of insightful and progressive literature, as well as all the classic shit that you're supposed to read to make you a more well-rounded person. Too bad people don't seem to be reading very much these days. There's also a store downstairs called George's Underground Bazaar which sells strange antiques like Greek jewelry and Ottoman embroidery, as well as older used books.

Sights & Entertainment

449 LA (aka SCAT)

449 Lenox Ave. btw W. 132nd & 133rd Sts.

SCAT is one of those things that I'm always worried about sharing because I don't wanna blow it up and ruin it. But shit, you gotta give love to places that deserve it, and SCAT definitely deserves all your love. Nestled in an unassuming part of Lenox Ave., this underground spot showcases all the talented jazz players, spoken-word poets, singers and rappers who are coming up in modern day Harlem. Being part of this place is special because you know much of what's happening here isn't gonna be found anywhere else. Free live music happens every night from Thursday–Sunday, but if you wanna get a chance to see someone before they blow up, come on the last Friday of the month for the open mic. It's off the hook.

Apollo Theater

253 W. 125th St. @ Manhattan Ave.

The Apollo is probably one of the best known music venues in the world. It's one of those spots where, when you're in a hostel in a foreign country and you mention living in New York, invariably a German kid says, "Yes, I vould very much like to see zee Apollo Theater in Harlem. I love Negro music!" And then you have to explain to him why it's not cool to call it Negro music. The list of people who've played here is like the line-up for a music festival in heaven. Also, *James Brown Live at the Apollo*, which might be the best live album of all time, was recorded here (when he died they brought the Godfather of Soul's casket here for a memorial service attended by thousands). While it doesn't get the same amount of shows these days as it did in Ella Fitzgerald's time, there is still one major cultural happening which you absolutely must attend: Amateur Night at the Apollo. There is nothing more enthralling/heartbreaking/amazing than watching someone pour their whole lives into a performance and get booed off the stage. Watching the crowd yell shit at the performers is almost better than the performances themselves.

Bill's Place

148 W. 133rd St. btw Lenox & 7th Aves.

When I stopped into Big Apple Jazz to check it out, I asked the guy who runs it for some suggestions about other great places in Harlem for the book. Without even blinking he said "Bill's Place. It's the hottest place in the city to see straight-ahead jazz. It's like an old school speakeasy, except that you can bring your own drinks." The best jazz in the city and it's BYOB? Can't say no to that. Bill's Place is owned by Harlem's legendary saxophonist Bill Saxton who plays two sets on Friday nights with his band. It only costs you $15 to see the show, which is *way* less than it would cost just for drinks at any other venue in the city. If anybody ever says your boy Stuart doesn't hook you up with the illist shit in New York, pop 'em in the mouth for me.

Cathedral of St. John the Divine

1047 Amsterdam Ave. btw W. 111th & 112th Sts.

For anyone who's a fan of the underdog, this should be your favorite cathedral in the city. While being one of the biggest Christian churches in the world, St. John the Divine (aka St. John the Unfinished), has still yet to be completed, despite being commenced in 1892. Construction was well underway on the building when the outbreak of WWI, followed by the Great Depression, halted work on the cathedral. Construction finally began again and the cathedral was officially opened in 1941, only to have Pearl Harbor happen a day later. The church's head honcho at the time decided that the money allocated for the building would be better used for charity and thus the construction stopped again. It's been steadily worked on since the '70s, but they still haven't gotten their shit together to finish it yet. Maybe it's better that way; besides, no one goes to church anymore anyways. Make sure to check out the lovely courtyard at 111th St. for a nice place to chill out and ignore the more important shit you have to do that day.

City College
W. 136th St. @ Amsterdam Ave.

I found this place unintentionally during my wanderings one day. It's totally beautiful and looks like a college from England, not the States. Who the fuck designed this? Kudos to you, old chap!

Grant's Tomb
Riverside Dr. & 122nd St.

Ulysses S. Grant was one of the United States' best generals (see: the US Civil War) and also one of its more disappointing presidents (see: graft, corruption, alcoholism), but as true then as it is now, Americans love a celebrity, which is something that Grant undeniably was in his time. Motherfuckers loved him so much that 90,000 of them donated money to build this enormous tomb (the largest in the US), which was opened in 1897. And the best part is, it's totally free to visit.

Madame Alexander Doll Company
615 W. 131 St. @ Broadway

Housed in this old Studebaker factory (which were great looking cars by the way), the Madame Alexander Doll Company has been delighting little children and crotchety old ladies with its creations since the 1920s. I'm not really too much of a doll man myself, but for those of you who are, you can stop by the factory here and take the free tour. It's pretty interesting because you get to see the whole history of the company illustrated through dolls ... if that's your sort of thing.

Morningside Park
W. 110th to 123rd Sts. and Manhattan Ave.
to Morningside Dr.

Built because the City of New York was too lazy to deal with extending the street grid down this steep slope, Morningside Park is a beautifully landscaped area that includes a lovely waterfall, and a bitch of a walk to get back up to Morningside Dr.

Shrine
2271 Adam Clayton Powell Jr. Blvd.
btw W. 133rd & 134th Sts.

The drinks aren't super cheap at Shrine, but there's free world music every night and it's actually really good. Decorated awesomely with

record covers and a huge blown up photo of Fela Kuti, this hot Harlem spot lures lots of the neighborhood's ill dressing, good looking young people. It's the type of place where most of the cats wear Kangols and soul patches. You know what I mean? It's that type of ill. I hear the food's pretty good too, but I just come for the live music and DJs.

St. Nick's Pub

773 St. Nicholas Ave. btw W. 148th & 149th Sts.

St. Nick's is one of the true gems you'll find in this book and one of the best underground places in NY (possibly the world) to see live jazz. It takes jazz back to where it came from: small dingy dive bars with real drinkers and working class people, not the bourgeois shit it is today. Ya'll motherfuckers can have the Lincoln Center, I'll take St. Nick's any day. The crowd here is a mix of older black folks from the neighbor-hood, and young jazz heads from all over the world who all come together to hear the hottest sessions you can possibly imagine. You will be blown away ... and it's free! If you decide to sit at a table, there is a $3 charge and a two drink minimum, but you can stand or sit at the bar and only pay the cost of your drinks. St. Nick's Pub is almost as special as the first time you got laid; meaning it's hard to go back to just fooling around once you've experienced the real thing. It's also a great place to hang out in the daytime when it's just a bunch of regu-lars sitting around and clowning each other, like the two guys who argued playfully about which one of them made the best mac and cheese and collard greens. Or the other two guys who argued about the lady who brings the food at night and whether or not she charges (she does, but not everyone). There aren't many places in the world that allow you to tap into the soul and essence of a neighborhood simply by attending them. St. Nick's Pub is one of these few rare spots.

MORNINGSIDE HEIGHTS
and HARLEM

Grub-a-dub-dub
1. Amir's Falafel
2. El Toro Partido
3. The Famous Jimbo's Hamburger Palace
4. The Hungarian Pastry Shop
5. The Interchurch Center Café
6. Koronet Pizza
7. La Nueva Flor de Broadway
8. Mama's Fried Chicken
9. Max Café
10. Saga
11. Sunshine Kitchen
12. Texas Star
13. Tom's Restaurant

DRINKS DRINKS DRINKS
14. 1020 Bar
15. A Touch of Dee
16. Radio Perfecto
17. Soundz Lounge

Shopping
18. Big Apple Jazz/EZ's Woodshed
19. H&M
20. Hamilton Palace
21. Hue-Man Bookstore & Café
22. Kim's Mediapolis
23. Morningside Bookshop

Stuffis to See and Do
24. 449 LA aka SCAT
25. Apollo Theater
26. Bill's Place
27. Cathedral of St. John the Divine
28. City College
29. Grant's Tomb
30. Madame Alexander Doll Company
31. Morningside Park
32. Shrine
33. St. Nick's Pub

Herbivore Friendly
34. Strictly Roots

Old School jazz guy who still plays around town

Indecisive liberal arts major

People trying to sell weed to indecisive liberal arts majors

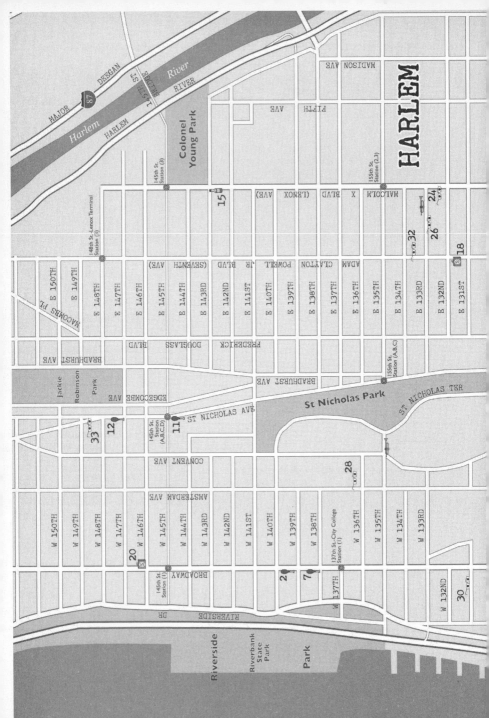

East Harlem & Spanish Harlem (El Barrio)

Despite the western part of Harlem's recent resurgence, East Harlem is still kinda shitty. It has been one of the poorest parts of Manhattan for decades and because of this, it can be a pretty dodgy place to be at night. On the other hand, it is also one of the largest Puerto Rican communities outside of Puerto Rico–hence the names "Spanish Harlem" or "El Barrio"–and has a wealth of eateries and activities that can only be found in this unique ethnic enclave.

Puerto Ricans started moving here en mass after WWII. But before then, Spanish Harlem was actually called "Italian Harlem" because of the large number of Southern Italian and Sicilian residents. During this time, the western part of this neighborhood, closer to Lenox Ave., was still heavily inhabited by black folks like the rest of Harlem. Today very little remains of the Italian history of Spanish Harlem, other than a few restaurants, but the area around Lenox is still primarily black, making East Harlem an interesting blend of cultures. But with the way the city is going, it will be interesting to see how long this neighborhood remains what it is before the gentrification train hits it full on. A few high-rises are already going up, so this change might come sooner than expected.

The main artery of Spanish Harlem is 116th St. It's the heart of El Barrio, where tons of shit is sold on the street and cheap eateries abound. In recent years this area has also become a destination for Mexican immigrants, and today you can find almost as many taquerias as you can Puerto Rican restaurants.

The boundaries for **Spanish Harlem** are Lenox Ave./Malcolm X Ave. to the west, the East River to the east, the Harlem River to the north, and E. 96th St. to the south.

Food

Cuchifritos Frituras

168 E. 116th St. btw Lexington & 3rd Aves.

Looking like a food stand from Coney Island, the name of this super cheap Spanish Harlem mainstay translates to "easily the healthiest eatery around". How could it not be healthy with this fried stuff? Want some fried pork skin? Got it. Looking for fried chicken? You can get a pound of it for $3. And if fried isn't your thing, you can always get $1.25 blood sausage or cow tongue.

P.S. Just in case you couldn't tell, I lied about the translation. It literally translates to "fried pork fried stuff (fritters)".

El Rincon Boricua

158 E. 119th St. @ Lexington Ave.

An inexpensive Puerto Rican place famous for its suckling pig. How famous? *New York Times* famous (just ask the owners, they'll gladly tell you all about it.) Get here in the early afternoon, though, because they close whenever the food runs out, which is mad early– like 3 or 4pm.

The Famous Jimbo's Hamburger Palace

52 E. 125th St. @ Madison Ave.; *also* at
284 Lenox @ W. 124th St.; 2027 Lexington Ave.
btw E. 123rd & 124th Sts.

A really cheap place with a lunch counter and some booths, you can get a burger and fries here for $4.75. Shit, you can get a whole breakfast for $3. Your boy Jimbo is hooking you up; he also gives out coupons for his angioplasty clinic that he runs out the back. How could you not trust a guy named Jimbo? Just ask the derelicts who've been chilling outside of Jimbo's for years. They might answer, "Who the fuck is Jimbo?" but that just means they love him, too.

Joy Burger Bar
1567 Lexington Ave. @ E. 100th St.

Where the fuck did this place come from? I've been wandering from fried food spot to pizza spot to greasy spoon diner, and all of a sudden Joy Burger Bar pops up looking like someone forgot to tell the owners where Union Square is. But hell, I don't mind a delectable burger at East Harlem prices. You can get a burger, some mozzarella sticks, and a drink, while still having a buck left over from your ten-er to give homeboy a tip. Or you could just save it and put it towards your gym pass.

L&T Donut Shop
2265 1st Ave. @ E. 116th St.

I love a greasy spoon diner in any language (this one seems to be in Spanish and without subtitles). $3.75 gets you two eggs, bacon, toast and potatoes until noon. And of course they sell yummy donuts. It's a good place to have a sit down with your hangover when you wake up on someone's floor and say to yourself, "How did I end up in Harlem?" Then you wonder how long this place has been here and then wonder how long you've been here, too. Whose house is this? I'm so confused.

Mannas Restaurant
51 E. 125th St. btw Madison & Park Aves.

I have two words for you: dope-ass soul food by the pound. Okay, that's more than two words, but if you can't dig that, then you can't dig shit. Go back to wherever the hell it is that haters come from–Hatersville or Haiti or something.

Mesa Mexicana
207 E. 117th St. @ 3rd Ave.

I heard from reliable sources (other Californians) that the food here might actually be good, so I decided to try it. And you know what? It's pretty fucking solid. There, I said it. But as I've also said before, just don't fuck with the burritos. New York just isn't a burrito friendly part of the world. Leave that to other states. Get yourself some tacos.

Patsy's Pizzeria

2287 1ˢᵗ Ave. btw E. 117ᵗʰ & 118ᵗʰ Sts.

This is the original Patsy's Pizza. Other ones have been built since and made all downtownish, but this is the OG spot. Believe it or not, East Harlem used to have a huge Italian population and this is a holdover from that time. Opened in 1933 and still using the original coal burning oven, Patsy's makes pizza that's so fucking good that Frank Sinatra used to come here and hang out on the late night. Thin crusted and delicious (fuck, I'm drooling now), you can get a slice for $1.75 and a whole big pie for $12. Do yourself a favor and stop in here. What, do you think you're better than Frank Sinatra or something? I didn't think so.

Sam's Famous Pizza

150 E. 116ᵗʰ St. @ Lexington Ave.

At Sam's, the employees wear red and white barber-shop-quartet-looking striped shirts and they deal out slices of pizza with aplomb. Is it good? Yeah definitely; it's not Patsy's, but it's damn good. Is it famous? Probably not, but people seem to like it. What's not to like about a place with $2 slices, $2.50 burgers, five garlic knots for a buck, and those sharp looking outfits? And by sharp I mean, not very.

Shrimp Box

62 W. 125ᵗʰ St. btw 5ᵗʰ Ave. & Malcolm X Blvd.

Why can't all soul food places be this cheap? I mean, I don't get it; soul food cuisine is based on taking the cheap food that no one wanted to eat and making it delicious. How did it get to the point where it's $20 a plate in some restaurants. Same goes for Jewish delis while I'm on it. That shit was the original ghetto food—why the fuck is a sandwich at Carnegie Deli $25? Places like Shrimp Box should be revered for making soul food available to the likes of us. Fried chicken starts at 75 cents, and you can get a catfish sandwich for $5. Sure there're no seats, but who needs seats when you've got cheap-ass food in your hands? Can I get an Amen?

Bars

Camarades el Barrio

2241 1ˢᵗ Ave. @ E. 115ᵗʰ St.

Last time I checked, this neighborhood was a pretty dodgy place to go out at night and therefore didn't really have much going on, except for Camarades el Barrio, that is. This joint serves up beer from around the world, and while it's not uber cheap ($5 for the cheapest beer), it is (as I just mentioned) the only hip thing around. Live music and DJs perform every night, Wednesday through Saturday, and attract a sexy looking crowd who's too lazy to take the train downtown. Basically, if this is your neighborhood, Camarades el Barrio should be your local spot; but you don't need me to tell that to you because, well, you already know it.

Shopping

Harlem Underground

20 E. 125 St. btw 5th & Madison Aves.

Angela Davis teaches at UC Santa Cruz, where I went to college, and as much as I love my alma mater, some of the students have a tendency to be so far left, they aren't in reality. Don't get me wrong, I'm about as left thinking as a motherfucker can get, but when people wanna get together and hold hands for peace, I think they're missing the point. This is why I LOVE the fact that Angela Davis is a professor there. I never personally had her, but I would have enjoyed being in her class while some stoned kid with nappy white boy dreads said some asinine shit and seen Angela Davis give a smile that says, "I dodged bullets and faced a murder rap for my convictions; how strong are yours?" But what can I say, all my heroes are revolutionaries, which is why I love this store. They sell some of the illest shirts I've ever seen, with folks like Malcolm X, Marvin Gaye, and Barrack Obama on them. They even have one with Angela Davis holding a bullhorn that says "Power to the People". Plus the shirts are all around the $20 range, which prices them a good $8 below corporate-type places. Hey listen up! Support local stores like this that actually believe in the products they are selling, instead of trying to dumb down and commodify things that were once subversive. That's about the best way you can prove your individuality.

Malcolm Shabazz Harlem Market

52 W. 115th St. btw 5th Ave. & Malcolm X Blvd.

Looking for a nice kufi to match the dashiki you got for Kwanza last year? Well look no further than the Malcolm Shabazz Harlem Market, an open air bazaar specializing in all things African. Walk down the aisles here and check out the stalls selling things like woodwork, clothing, and tapestries, as well as places that do food or hair braiding. Much of the stuff here is negotiable, and it's a good place to stretch your legs on a nice day. Plus there's usually all kinds of cute little kids running around, and who doesn't like that?

Xukuma

11 E. 125th St. btw 5th & Madison Aves.

This great store sells excellent men's and women's clothes and accessories that are really well priced. T-shirts start at like $15 and have really cool uptown-centric designs that play into the '70s soul brotha/sista vibe. Naturals are hot and Black is beautiful up in this motherfucker, or at least they are on the t-shirts. I've always wanted to buy one of those shirts that say, "I © Black People" and see if I could pull it off. I honestly don't know how people would respond to seeing my pale Jewish ass wearing it. Who wants to bet it makes hipsters really uncomfortable because they wouldn't be able to tell if I was being ironic or not. I'm not being ironic by the way, I'm over irony ... mostly.

Sights & Entertainment

El Museo Del Barrio

1230 5th Ave. btw E. 104th & 105th Sts.

While the galleries are currently under renovation and set to reopen in Fall '09, El Museo is still doing tons of great events like concerts, dance performances, and walking tours. Dedicated to Puerto Rican, Caribbean, and Latin American art, El Museo is the only one of its kind in New York City and has been doing its thing for over 30 years. Besides the fantastic permanent collection that includes ancient artifacts from pre-Columbian times, El Museo also gets great exhibitions by masters like Frida Kahlo and Diego Rivera. How's that sound, considering I never saw the museum due to it being closed? Passable, right?

Graffiti Hall of Fame

E. 106th St. & Park Ave.

I remember leaving a party one time in San Francisco and seeing some kids tagging the liquor store across the street. It really pissed me off. Look, if you wanna go around writing your name on shit all over town, be my guest; but if you're gonna hit up private property,

Oh I get it! Ghost Writers is a play on words.

hit up big corporations like Blockbuster, McDonald's, or H&M. The guy who owns the liquor store those kids were tagging is most likely an immigrant who works 15 hour days with the hope of eventually putting his kids through college. He can't afford to be cleaning your shitty-ass tag off his marquee every other week. Which brings me to my next point. If you are gonna bomb shit, be good at it, dammit. Little children draw on walls all the time, but we don't call this art because they are really shitty at drawing. If you wanna go around throwing things up, practice on some sketch pads and canvases first. The cats who're real graffiti artists have been practicing that shit for years. Just come down to 106 and Park and see for yourself what these cats are capable of. The entire wall surrounding this schoolyard is covered in some of the most amazing street art you will ever see, but all it takes is one punk ass kid with a spray paint can to come and write their name over the art to fuck it up. Anyway, if you do come check it out, make sure to go into the school yard too, so you can see all of the pieces.

Malcolm Shabazz Mosque
102 W. 116th St. @ Malcolm X Blvd.

Formerly the Lenox Casino, this building was redesigned by Sabbath Brown in 1965, and reappropriated by the Nation of Islam following the assassination of Malcolm X. For many years it was the official Nation of Islam Headquarters in NYC, and the center of Muslim life in Harlem. While it still is a mosque, the Nation moved its headquarters to another part of Harlem. I find it interesting that the Nation of Islam had the balls to name this mosque after Brother Malcolm, considering that they're the ones who wacked him. Unless of course you believe the CIA did it. Regardless, I think it's pretty telling about the current state of Harlem that right next to this mosque, a giant condo building is going up.

Marcus Garvey Memorial Park
Between Madison Ave. & Mt. Morris PK West and W. 120th & E. 124th Sts.

Originally called Mount Morris Park, the name was changed in 1973 while Mayor John Lindsay was trying to expand his uptown base. But a great park by any other name is still a great park, and this is *the* spot to be on any holiday where Americans traditionally BBQ, like Memorial Day, Labor Day and in this neighborhood, Saturday. Besides grass and hills, this lovely park also has an outdoor amphitheatre for free concerts and a large pool for hot days. Just make sure you wait 45 minutes after eating before you go swimming; the last thing I need is one less person willing to buy my shit.

Museum of the City of New York
1220 5th Ave. @ E. 103rd St.

Free Sundays from 10am-12pm, this is a great place to learn about the history of the city of Chicago.

Manhattan off the Map

The Cloisters
in Fort Tyron Park

Located *way* the fuck up there in Fort Tyron Park (like past 190th St.; way the fuck up there), the Cloisters houses the Metropolitan Museum of Art's collection of medieval European art. John D. Rockefeller, Jr. donated the land, a lot of the art and the impressive building itself, which is pieced together from five different actual French cloisters. He also purchased the land across the Hudson River in New Jersey so that the view from the Cloisters could remain pristine. I went here with my mom and her friends when they were visiting, and I was totally blown away by the art. The pamphlet thingy they give you highlights the "Unicorn Tapestries" which are pretty cool, but my favorite was a set of playing cards from the 15th century. It's actually the oldest complete set of illuminated playing cards in the world. The Cloisters also has a beautiful garden that grows herbs and other stuff that medieval monks and nuns might have needed, including a section of "magic plants" (i.e., hallucinogens). The Cloisters is well worth the trip, and just like many of New York's bigger museums, entrance costs whatever you feel like donating (even though they ask for $20).

Rucker Park
155th St. & Fredrick Douglas Blvd.

The people who play basketball here are better at that than I will ever be at anything in my life. I've come to accept this fact and coming up here to watch these games of street ball becomes easier and easier for me each time because I keep betting on the right team. If I can keep this shit up, I'll never have to worry about being good at stuff again. I'll just buy a Pulitzer.

Track and Field Hall of Fame
216 Fort Washington Ave. @ 168th St.

Do people really visit this place?

CENTRAL HARLEM and SPANISH HARLEM (EL BARRIO)

Grub-a-dub-dub

1 Cuchifritos Frituras

2 El Rincon Boricua

3 The Famous Jimbo's Hamburger Palace

4 Joy Burger Bar

5 L&T Donut Shop

6 Mannas Restaurant

7 Mesa Mexicana

8 Patsy's Pizzeria

9 Sam's Famous Pizza

10 Shrimp Box

DRINKS DRINKS DRINKS

11 Camarades el Barrio

Shopping

12 Harlem Underground

13 Xukuma

14 Malcolm Shabazz Harlem Market

Stuffis to See and Do

15 El Museo Del Barrio

16 Graffiti Hall of Fame

17 Malcolm Shabazz Mosque

18 Marcus Garvey Memorial Park

19 Museum of the City of New York

Gangster-ass fool in a ski mask who's part of the reason this place has no nightlife

Developer trying to figure out a way to flip this neighborhood

Member of the Nation of Islam

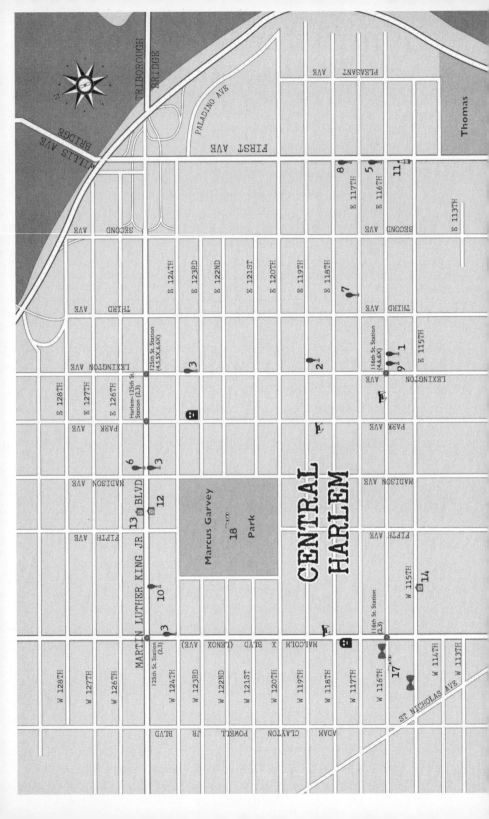

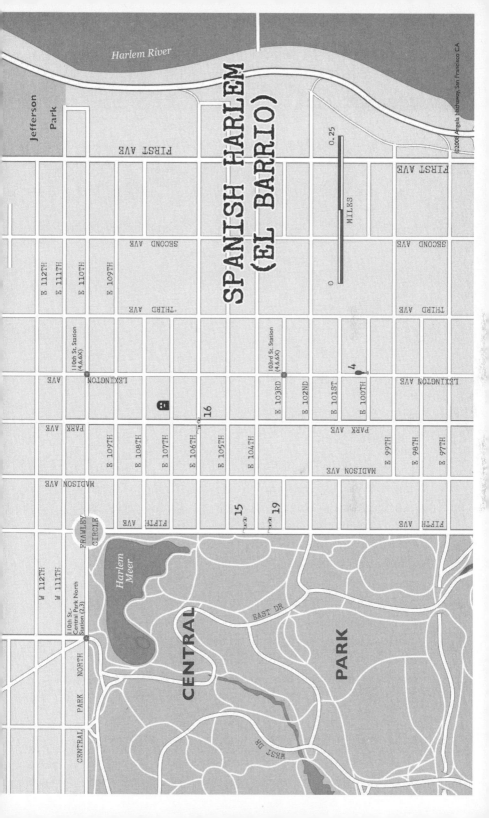

HOW TO PISS PEOPLE OFF

art by Mike Force

Let me tell you something important. The bars stay open in New York City until 4am. The bars in California stay open until 2am. Although two hours doesn't sound like a big difference, when it comes to putting your margarita where your mouth is, two hours can make all the difference. When drinking in California, the routine is generally, meet at someone's house around 9:30pm, pre-drink (which is still actually drinking) till around 10:30, head out to bars till around 2am, get buffalo wings at the place on Valencia and then more often than not, be in bed by 3 or 3:30am.

It's a simple ritual that works wonders in a land where the bars close at 2am, but I can honestly say I was not prepared for the caliber of shit required for 4am bar drinking. I instinctively tried to stick to my regular schedule. Needless to say I was three-sheets to the wind, shit talking drunk by the time 1am rolled around. It was around this time that Nolan and I walked up to a bar whose name and location is long forgotten, but whose staircase I am doomed to remember.

Nah man, the music's too loud in there. But what have I told you about trying to reason with bouncers in this city? Don't even try; most of them aren't even human.

They only have two modes of operation, 'Destroy' and 'Don't Destroy' and I have a feeling this guy is better at option number one."

Finally, the door opened.

I fucking hate waiting in lines for anything and I never did it back in San Francisco because I was always on the list or knew someone at the door. If I didn't, then I just didn't go to that particular spot.

But I figured that since it was New York, and Nolan said it was a dope spot, why the fuck not. But here my patience was getting thin and the line behind us was getting longer.

There's only two of us, me and my buddy here. Can we come in yet?

NO

I was drunk as fuck and I wanted another drink, and I wanted music, and I wanted to look at hot girls in skimpy Saturday night outfits made specifically for August in New York.

I didn't want to sit in some fetid, humid hallway with a bunch of other thirsty and depraved motherfuckers.

FUCK THIS GUY! I'M GONNA PISS ON HIS FUCKING DOOR!

At that moment four blonde girls, all dressed up for a night on the town, started walking up the left side of the stairs, passing all those in line. It was like a flash of cosmic consciousness, everyone in that hallway knew the exact same thing at the exact same moment;

these girls weren't gonna have to wait for shit, the bouncer would let them in. We were all suckers, every single one of us.

Eeewwwww! Is he peeing? Oh My God that is SO gross!

I hope those shoes are expensive, because I'm gonna get piss all over them.

And then it happened.

Clarity cold-cocked me like a creeper in a street fight. It dawned on me that I was about four seconds away from this chick telling Nature's Biggest Mistake about the guy pissing on the door

...most likely resulting in severe head injury and massive internal hemorrhaging that no amount of physical rehabilitation would be able to help.

Thankfully brain chemicals are stronger than booze chemicals, because fight or flight syndrome kicked in with a strong emphasis on flight.

We ran for another couple blocks, continually looking back to make sure the terminator wasn't behind us, before we decided we were in the clear. We then took the only natural course of action; we got a slice and another cold beer.

Apparently I blacked out after that, which is something I almost never do. In fact, I probably would never have known about blacking out if I hadn't called my girlfriend the next morning to tell her all about my night. When I began to get into the story she cut me off, "Yeah I know all about it. The bouncer was some minotaur or monster or some shit and you pissed on his door. Blah blah blah. Do you know how fucking mad I am at you?"

I was dumbstruck. How did she know about that goddamn bouncer? Was she in league with him? Did she not want me in the bar either? "I can tell by your silence that you obviously don't remember calling me last night, which means you also don't remember grilling me about what the fuck I was doing and who I was watching a movie with."

I sat that there trying to think. Am I really that fucking guy when I blackout? I would never trip on shit like that normally. I knew I should have paced myself better. I guess there's always tonight to try again.

If you can't find a place to live, you can always sleep under the Brooklyn Bridge. Look how nice your front yard will be.

Brooklyn

Long considered one of Manhattan's four ugly little stepchildren, Brooklyn's popularity has skyrocketed in the past few decades as Manhattan's real estate prices have done the same. Originally a separate city in its own right, Brooklyn became one of the five boroughs in 1898. It has a long history as an industrial and shipping center, as well as being home to many different ethnic enclaves. These days it's become a haven for all those who want to live in New York City but don't want to pay exorbitant prices to live in a shoebox. Its current most popular ethnicity is hipsters.

As a side note, I would have liked to include more areas of Brooklyn, but I neither had the time or the space. Have you seen how much stuff is already in this fucker?

Williamsburg & Greenpoint

While Williamsburg's history includes fairly substantial Italian, Puerto Rican, and Dominican communities, lately it's best known for its two largest populations, hipsters and Hasidim. While at first glance these two groups seem to have little in common other than occupying the same neighborhood, upon closer examination you'll be amazed at the similarities. Men from both communities tend to wear beards and lots of black clothing, both groups are fanatical about their beliefs, (Judaism for the Hasidim; indie-rock, irony, and bad haircuts for the hipsters), and both seem to think that if you're not as into what their doing as they are, you're a total fucking poser.

For the past 10-plus years, Williamsburg has been the reigning king of New York cool. Being that it's the first stop in Brooklyn on the L-train and that it's primarily made up of former industrial spaces perfect for converting into lofts and art studios, it makes sense that much of the East Village's artistic scene leapt over the river to find cheaper rents. Today Williamsburg's main drag, Bedford Ave., is awash with boutiques, restaurants, cafes, bars, and pretty young things intoxicated with city life. Other major thoroughfares include Grand and Metropolitan Aves. Sure the rents are rising steadily here now, too. But you can still find amazing prices all over this neighborhood for food, drinks and entertainment that would be two or three times as expensive in Manhattan. If you can't find something to do here, you must hate having fun.

Just north of Williamsburg sits Greenpoint, home of the second or third largest Polish population in the US. In recent years, it has also been flooded by the hipster diaspora and has seen an unbelievable amount of construction in the form of giant condominium buildings. As the prices and property values in Williamsburg continue to rise, more young artists are being pushed eastward into Bushwick and south into Bed-Stuy.

The borders in this area are tough to discern, but roughly speaking, **Williamsburg** is between Flushing Ave. to the south, Humboldt St. to the east, the East River to the west, and the northern point of McCarren Park in the north. East of Humboldt St. is considered by some to be East Williamsburg and by others just the western part of Bushwick. As for **Greenpoint**, the borders are the northern tip of McCarren Park in the south, the East River in the west and Newton's Creek in both the north and east.

Food

Acapulco

1116 Manhattan Ave. @ Clay St.

When I was a kid in San Diego we always used to go to a restaurant called Acapulco after my little league games. We must have been pretty young, because my little brother wasn't able to read yet, so when my mom would ask me to take him to the bathroom, I'd take advantage of his illiteracy and send him into the ladies' room. While I don't know what the policy of this particular Acapulco is regarding illiterate three-year-old boys in the women's restroom, I do know that people seem to love this place for it's cheap and tasty food. Yes, I did say "tasty". I didn't say "amazing", "superb", "stellar" or one of the other superlatives that I use over and over again; I said "tasty". That's because it's just that. In other parts of the world, this place would be a third stringer for me, but since New York is the land of shitty Mexican food, I'm bumping Acapulco toward the top of my list.

Grand Bakery

602 Grand St. btw Lorimer & Leonard Sts.

Have you ever been part way through a bagel and thought to yourself, "Where do these delicious, doughy bits of bliss come from?" No? Oh ... well this is awkward ... hmmm, I'm just gonna pretend you said "yes" and pick up from there ... Well guess what? They come from the Grand Bakery ... huh? What was that? Of course I know they don't *all* come from the Grand Bakery, I'm just using it as a stand-in for all the little bakeries in Brooklyn. Do you know how hard you're making this for me? I'm just trying to finish this fucking book. I'll continue now ... And you can get your bagels right from the source. Just walk by any-where from 9pm–2am (roughly) and look to see if they are loading up the truck. If so, and you ask nicely, they'll let you inside the bakery to pick out the bagels you want. And the best part is they're still warm and only cost $3 for a dozen. Enjoy ... wait, where did you go?

Big Apple Deli

671 Grand St. @ Graham Ave.

Everyone in this world is born with certain innate gifts; some people are great athletes, some people excel at math, I'm amazing at stepping in dog shit, and Ali at the Big Apple Deli is one of the best Philly cheesesteak makers the world has ever seen. I don't know what his secret is because, truthfully, I'm usually drunk when I'm there, but whatever it is, he has been blessed. If you wanna catch the master at work and get one of his $4 masterpieces, you have to stop in from 6pm–6am, because he spends his daytimes meditating on his craft and thanking Allah for his gift.

P.S. I actually stepped in shit again today. Can you believe it? I think I must have pissed off some warlock who put a curse on me or something. If that's the case, he must not be a very good at being a warlock because perpetually stepping in shit isn't exactly the worst spell you can cast on someone.

Christina's Polish Restaurant

853 Manhattan Ave. @ Milton St.

This is the only Polish restaurant where non-Poles are actually welcome inside, so it's worth eating here just so you can say that you're defying de facto segregation. Order the Polish platter, which consists of a large dong of kielbasa and some muscki on the side. The staff here is unbelievable. Your waitresses are all stripper quality from behind the iron curtain, which is to say that by the time these eastern bloc babes hit 30 they will turn into instant babushkas. Get them while you can!*

DuMont

432 Union Ave. btw Metropolitan Ave. & Devoe St.

This place is not too cheap, but it is excellent and is named after the short lived DuMont television network from the early '50s. DuMont was kind of like the Apple of television. You had to buy a DuMont television to watch the DuMont Television Network. Retarded, right? Well the owner saw a sign from a former DuMont store that still stood nearby and took the name as an homage to the days when there were no NFL sports packages. This is the kind of place to take mom and dad when they come visit and want you to take them to a nice dinner

---

Sent from the desk of Paul T. Alkaly, correspondent at large.

in the neighborhood. It's "New American" cuisine, which means dad can have a mouth-watering gourmet burger and mom can have a rosemary-scented meatloaf dinner and not complain. The backyard patio is so romantic it makes me sick. They also give out little beignets at the beginning of the meal as a nod to Café Du Monde in New Orleans ... at least I think that's why they do it.*

DuMont Burger
314 Bedford Ave. btw S. 1st St. and S. 2nd St.

In just a few short years, DuMont's burger got so popular that they were forced to open this outpost to keep up with the demand. It is already a nationally recognized burger. Los Angeles has the Father's Office burger. Idaho has the Huddy burger. But new kid on the block Williamsburg, Brooklyn has the best, the DuMont Burger. It comes with great fries or tempura-battered onion rings that are the size of donuts. Don't be stupid, get the rings. And get a side of the macaroni and cheese that you can have for breakfast in the morning. My favorite restaurant in the world.*

Egg
135 N. 5th btw Bedford Ave. and Berry St.

Although it's only been open a few years, Egg is really a historical tour through Williamsburg's culinary past. The menu features Steven Tanner's famous fried chicken, which he made everyday at the now defunct Pie's n Thighs. You can also order a burger reminiscent of the burger made by Sparky's, which used to be in the same location. (Every restaurant in Williamsburg goes under after about a year of good business except for the everlasting nuclear cockroach DuMont–I mean this in a good way). Egg is also a great place for brunch, and I love to brunch; even better, I love to brunch date. I am a master of the brunch date. It's just less hoopla. Less awkward, you know? She won't think that you are trying to get into her pants and you can bail out at anytime. Plus my broke-ass heart knows that brunch is cheaper than dinner. And, at Egg, you can draw on the tables!*

Foodswings
295 Grand Ave. @ Havemeyer St.

Cheap vegan fast food? What the fuck? I thought vegan food was all about lengthy meals involving earth tones, tea sipping, deep conver-

---

Sent from the desk of Paul T. Alkaly, correspondent at large.

sation, and hugs that last just a little too long for comfort. Oh wait, I forgot that it's not just hippies that are veganing out these days; somehow the hipsters got tangled up in this protein-deficient phenomenon, too. At least the hipsters got the price thing figured out; everything on the menu here is under $8 and there's tons of different fake meat options. Personally, I like real meat, just like I like real tits, but I'm not gonna hate on anyone who feels the opposite ... okay, to be completely honest, I have had some pretty good fake meat in my life, but I've never actually felt fake tits before. Is that weird? There's even a girl I dated briefly in college who's gotten them since then, but it's not like I can get fake boob reparations. I can't just walk up to her and say, "Hey J__, since you didn't have those when we were together, do you mind if I cop a quick feel? Come on, it's not like I haven't felt your tits before." The thing is, for once in my life I'm not being pervy; this is strictly for scientific purposes. So hey, if you're liberal with your fake tits and we run into each other, let me know if I can feel you up. Thanks in advance.

P.S. To all you vegans out there, don't forget to take your vitamins. Nobody wants to hang out with an anemic with rickets.

God Bless Deli

818 Manhattan Ave. @ Calyer St.

For a long time this place had a little sign by the cash register that read, "Accept the change as a fatal." I finally drummed up enough courage to ask the mean man behind the counter what it meant. He simply responded, "Sometimes there is change in the world and you have to accept it or else it is a fatal." The guys who run this place are from the Middle East. Needless to say, after 9/11 they changed the name of their establishment and added a big ole' US of A flag to their awning. I invented my own sandwich here; it's basically a chopped up cheeseburger on a roll. All you have to do is say "chop chop" to the guy behind the counter while doing a chopping motion with your hands. God bless that deli/grocery! *

Lady Octopus
495 Lorimer St. @ Powers St.

I was walking by this place on my way to Gimmie Coffee when my friend Dara popped his head inside to ask if they deliver. The woman behind the counter threw down her newspaper and asked him if he had read the menu. Dara responded that he had, and was interested in ordering for delivery. Lady Octopus told him that he obviously had "no read menu" and that he ought to take another look at it. Dara could not believe that the woman would not answer his straightfor-ward question and said, "Do you deliver? Yes or no? Simple question." I guess she just didn't like the look of him because all she did was glare back at him. Feeling, racially profiled, Dara gave her the finger and walked out of Lady Octopus to join me at Gimmie Coffee next door. Next thing I know, I see Lady Octopus chasing after Dara into Gimmie Coffee yelling at the top of her lungs, "YOU WHITE TRASH!" Which didn't make much sense to me because I always thought Dara was Persian. So everyone that is reading this book, call Lady Octopus right now and ask if they deliver. I hope you can still sleep at night; she scares the shit out of me (this still doesn't stop me from buying her cheap-as-hell fried seafood).*

Noodle Studio
116 N. 5th btw Bedford Ave. & Berry St.

A big and lovely Thai place with groovy lamps and cool art on the walls, Noodle Studio is a solid bet for a first date. The whole menu is $8.50 or under and for some reason the staff is exceptionally friendly. The best time to come here though is during the day for their lunch special. For $4.95 you get a soup, an entrée and some bean curd thingy. Kick ass!

Oasis
161 N. 7th @ Bedford Ave.

The best falafel in New York City is right off the Bedford L stop. Sometimes I walk in here without any intention of ordering just to hear the guy behind the counter say, "hot sauce." He says it really fast and nobody can quite understand what he is saying. Say "hot sauce"

Sent from the desk of Paul T. Alkaly, correspondent at large.

three times really fast and you might understand what I'm taking about.*

Palace Fried Chicken
Manhattan Ave. @ Nassau St.

Every time Paul walks into Palace Fried Chicken, Abdul, the guy behind the counter, says loudly in his Afghani accent, "MEEESTER CHEEEESE FRIES!". It happens to be an almost daily ritual since Paul eating here is an almost daily occurrence. This is quite understandable because a) it's incredibly cheap, b) it's pretty damn good and c) Paul lives virtually next door. But it might be more than that, too; Paul and Abdul seem to have a special relationship. For example when Abdul told Paul that it had been "seex months since I have push-push in de bush-bush", the two of them agreed that if Paul got Abdul laid, he'd get free Palace Fried Chicken for the rest of his life. So Paul spent the next month trying to pimp out his female roommate. He began slyly by asking questions like, "So, what do you think about Abdul over at Palace Fried Chicken? You know the guy with the mustache who always stares at you? He's pretty dreamy right?" And when that didn't work, he tried the direct approach: "Come on! Just fuck him once. We're talking about free Palace Fried Chicken for the rest of our lives!!" Needless to say, she moved out shortly afterwards.

Another time Abdul asked Paul to look at a website for him to help him figure out why he wasn't allowed to go back to Afghanistan to visit his family. So Paul took the information, went home, checked out the website, and entered the ID number Abdul had given him. Apparently Abdul wasn't allowed to leave the country because our government was concerned about his reasons for wanting to visit Afghanistan. Luckily though, Paul was able help Abdul get his trip home okayed by the State Department because everybody knows it's pretty hard to get some "push-push in the bush-bush" if the US government thinks you're a "threat". Girls just don't really dig that sort of thing.

Peter Lugar Steak House
178 Broadway @ Driggs Ave.

Okay, so $8 for a burger isn't exactly cheap, and considering that I've included Dumont in here, you'd think I'd hit my expensive burger quota for the book, right? Normally I'd have to agree with you. But

---

Sent from the desk of Paul T. Alkaly, correspondent at large.

this isn't normally, this is Peter Lugar, one of the most expensive restaurants in Brooklyn and a New York institution since 1887. As one would expect, the burgers here are phenomenal, but there are a couple of catches. The first is that they only serve them before 3pm and the second is that this place only takes cash. Only in Brooklyn could a restaurant this expensive get away with not accepting credit cards. I love it.

Peter Pan Bakery

727 Manhattan Ave. btw Meserole & Norman Aves.

This Greenpoint lunch counter offers a good mix of the old school Polish neighborhood and its new gentrifying inhabitants. Nobody can resist Peter Pan donuts. They have rad multilayered, cream-filled, glazed, twisty, powered sugar with cinnamon donuts. Mmmm ... "multi". They also have a great '50s lunch counter where you can get a light lunch and a cheap cup of coffee. Best of all, it's run by 16-year-old Polish girls who giggle and laugh when you order glazed, rainbow, swirly bear claws.*

Shachis Restaurant Arepas

197 Havemeyer St. @ S. 4th St.

On the walk over to Shachis, I encountered a Puerto Rican guy wearing a gold necklace that had a big three- or four-inch gold Mickey Mouse holding two AK-47s dangling from it. He wasn't wearing it ironically. As everybody knows, a golden Mickey wielding multiple fully automatic assault rifles can only mean two things: delicious arepas are ahead and that the guy wearing it hates getting laid. The inside of Shachis is painted the colors of the Venezuelan flag, which makes sense considering this is a Venezuelan restaurant. Empanadas go for $2 a pop here while the previously mentioned arepas range from $4–$6. Aye que bueno!

Warsaw Bakery

866 Lorimer St. btw Nassau & Driggs Aves.

Ah yes, the Polish hot loaf. This illusive Greenpoint special can only be had from roughly 10pm–2am and requires patience and adherence to the rules. You must wait until the roller door is half open and then knock three times, peek your little head under it, and ask for a loaf. A man who only speaks Polish will then open the side door and

---

*Sent from the desk of Paul T. Alkaly, correspondent at large.

billows of steam will flow out. At this point you are to present two dollars to him and say, "mushkie". He will then return with a whole loaf of bread directly from the oven. You then walk down to the nearst bodega, buy a stick of butter, and eat your famed Polish hot loaf. It is advised that you do this all while intoxicated. This is the best deal in town. Mushkie.*

Wombat
613 Grand St. btw Leonard & Lorimer Sts.

Of all the places I've eaten in New York, and there are a shit ton of them, I think I've probably eaten at Wombat the most. My lady and I lived right around the corner from it for awhile, so it became our go-to spot for the nights when we wanted to splurge a little. The staff is great. And I know at first the menu can look a little daunting if you're on the broke-ass tip, but let me tell you this—I don't think I ever shelled out for an entrée. I always just get one of their great burgers or sandwiches, which are all $8.50 or less. My shit is the chicken panini; hot damn is it good! But truthfully, we came here most often on Tuesdays for their awesome $13 lobster night. Hell of a deal, yes sir, but just make sure to get there early because they will sell out. The funniest thing about this place though is that even though it's an Australian restaurant, there isn't a single Aussie involved with the joint. But you know what? Who gives a fuck? I love this place.

Sent from the desk of Paul T. Alkaly, correspondent at large.

Bars

Alligator Lounge
600 Metropolitan Ave. btw Leonard and Lorimer Sts.

Almost everyone I tell in New York about my book says, "Hey do you know about the Alligator Lounge? Every time you buy a drink you get a pizza this big!" and they hold up their hands to approximate the size of a personal pizza. I just want to say thanks to all the strangers who were willing to try to help me out, so hold out your hands to about what size you think a personal pizza is. Your heart is bigger. Thanks.

Anytime
93 N. 6th St. btw Berry St. & Wythe Ave.

The first time I came here was a few years back when I was visiting New York for ten days. It was August and I ended up sleeping on someone's wood floor with no pillow and no air conditioning. While I came away from that night with a complete and utter hatred for that dude's apartment, I also ended up with a love of Anytime. How could you not love a place that looks this upscale, yet serves PBR for $1.50 and Bud for $2? This shit is amazing! They also have a solid food menu and will deliver it, along with beer and smokes, from 4pm–5am. Genius I say! But still, back to the cheap drinks. Last time I was here we got two PBRs and a vodka tonic for $5!! Is this paradise or a front for the Israeli mob? Some things are better left unknown.

Barcade
388 Union Ave. @ Powers St.

Paul took me here one night while we were making our research rounds and let me tell you that, despite being a little dead, (my fault for going out drinking on Mondays) this place satisfies roughly 5/8ths of my natural urges. Look at the name Barcade. What does it sound like? Arcade. Good, you got that one. Now look at the first three letters: B-A-R. What does that spell? BAR! That's right! You're very good at this. Put it all together and you have a cavernous bar that serves nothing but microbrews ($4) and has tons of old arcade games that you forgot existed like Toobin', Ghosts & Goblins, and Rampage (my inner nerd just squealed!). Inside are a few booths, candles for mood lighting (as if the glare off the Capcom screen wasn't enough) and what was either a jukebox or just another video game. And to cap it off (stupid fucking pun), outside is a beer cap mosaic that various local artists have helped, uh, mosaisize.

Bushwick Country Club

618 Grand St. @ Leonard St.

I like to stroll in here with my friends around midnight and order the Supersize: a shot of Old Crow and a tall boyeeeeee of Pabst for $6. They have an eight-hole miniature golf course in the back complete with a mini windmill. My friend Brian wasted away his life here and had to move back to Los Angeles. His days consisted of jerking off in the morning before walking around the corner to the BCC for his famed shot of Old Crow with a pickle back (a shot of pickle juice to chase the whiskey). At around 4am, he would stumble up the street to the Big Apple Deli for Ali's famed cheese steaks. We like to call this the triangle of death. You can reenact his dark days with me every night at what I prefer to call "The Club", with Big Buck Hunter in the front and a patio in the back.*

Capri Social Club

156 Calyer @ Lorimer St.

When Paul took me here, he prefaced it by saying, "I must have walked passed this place a 1,000 times before I realized it's not an abandoned crack den." While Paul tends to exaggerate, I will say the place did look like a locals-only dive bar for old drunks, which is exactly what it is. Part Polish, part Brooklyn, and 100 percent senior citizen passed out sitting up in the corner, the huge Capri Social Club is a hidden gem where you can smoke inside, hear some Fleetwood Mac and be the youngest person there by at least 20 years. But hell, if you're not concerned with getting laid (I shudder at the thought of bringing home someone from here), 10-ounce mugs of Bud are only $1.75. How long do you think it will be before this becomes the new hipster hang out?

---

*Sent from the desk of Paul T. Alkaly, correspondent at large.

Coco 66
66 Greenpoint Ave. btw Franklin & West Sts.

A big ass industrial chic* place housed in an old woodshop, Coco 66 has something to offer each one of it's attractive clientele. If you wanna play some pool or foosball, no worries, Coco has got you covered. How about a dance floor so you can boogie till you sweat through your mom jeans? Coco's got that too. They even have $3 beers. And while Coco doesn't actually supply blow, there's almost always someone chilling in the front loungy area who knows where to get some. Sounds perfect right? It is, and that must be why Paul hates it. He said it used to be much better when it was divier. Go figure.

Clem's
264 Grand St. @ Roebling St.

Clem's sells $2 PBRs and plays lots of Danzig every time I go in there. They also have two great beer specials for $5 each, the Patriot (PBR and a shot of Jim Beam) and the Federale (Tecate and a shot of Sauza). Speaking of Federales, here's a useful tip for if you ever make the unfortunate decision of going to Tijuana: Keep $40 in your wallet and the rest of your money in your sock. Also wear an undershirt. That way if you do something stupid and get shook down by the Federales, you can give them the $40 and tell them that it's all the money you have to give them. If they still want to take you to jail, you can be like, "Oh wait, I just remembered I have all this money in my sock. Here you go señor." So why the undershirt? Because sometimes they want your shirt as well as your money—seriously. Don't ever go to Tijuana. But hey, did I mention that Clem's plays lots of Danzig?

East River Bar
97 S 6th St. btw Bedford Ave. & Berry St.

While this huge bar was originally a paint factory, the only things currently being produced here are very drunk people. With the exception of me, that is. Every time I come here I'm already too drunk. In fact, the first time I was here was when my close friends, Nick and Laura, were visiting from Philly, and their friend Kalen brought us. The next day I had no idea where the bar was, nor its name, so I couldn't find it until months later when someone brought me here smashed once again. This time I made sure to write down the name

---

*I wish I was clever enough to think of something other than "industrial chic". I kinda hate anything that ends with chic. Why do I keep saying it?

of it on a bar napkin and stuff it in my pocket. So, East River Bar, you thought you could elude me, didn't you. Well you were wrong. You can't keep me away from a place this big, that has such a great juke-box, and allows me to grill my own food outside. You're mine now, bitch. I now know that if I ever lose you again, all I have to do is get shit faced, and I will stumble my way back to you. I feel like Dorothy after she figured out how to use her ruby red shoes.

Lazy Catfish

593 Lorimer St. @ Conselyea St.

Free beer on Tuesdays! If that doesn't appeal to you, then my question is this: how many pages did you make it through before you realized you were reading the wrong book? For those who are interested, just be warned that they stop giving it away for free at 11pm.

The Levee

212 Berry St. @ N. 3rd St.

I came here on my birthday last year wearing the full-length, fake fur coat I got at Atlantis Attic for $20. For some reason this really butch chick tried to pick a fight with me because she thought that I'd called her friend a bitch. Since I hadn't, I told her, "I've never even seen your friend before. It must have been another guy walking around in a full-length, fake fur coat." I think the sheer ridiculousness of my comment defused the situation. Luckily the incident didn't dampen my love for the Levee, one of my favorite bars in Williamsburg. Not only are the drinks cheap ($5 beer and shot specials), but they let you use a beer koozie to keep your bottled or canned beverage cold. It's a nice senti-ment that must stem from their sense of Southern hospitality, since the owner is from Texas (they even sell Lone Star Beer here). And if you get the munchies, you can always eat some of their weird bar food like the disturbingly delicious Frito pie (Fritos, chili, and nacho cheese). Paul told me that this spot used to be called Kokie's and they would slang yayo from the DJ booth. I gotta hand it to those people, naming your place Kokie's and then selling coke there is genius. It's like being a kiddie-toucher and driving around in big van with "ped-o-file!" painted in huge letters on the sides. It's so obvious, the cops will never catch you.

Metropolitan Bar

559 Lorimer St. @ Metropolitan Ave.

Williamsburg doesn't really have much of a gay bar scene, which is strange because there is not shortage of bars or gays. Luckily, though, if homo is your M.O., the Metropolitan is a really great dive full of artsy gay boys and a fair amount of androgynous lesbians. While the big indoor space (replete with couches and a couple fireplaces) is great for lounging or mingling all year long, this joint's back patio is what makes it really shimmer when the sun shines. Sundays are the best though because they serve up free BBQ to help wash down those cheap drinks.

Palace Café

206 Nassau Ave. @ Russell St.

Everybody calls this place the Heavy Metal Bar, so I thought that was it's actual name until recently when someone was describing the Palace Café as, "the weird medieval-looking place with the big horse-shoe bar that only plays metal and sells beers for like $1.50". Caught off guard and a little saddened, I was only able to respond with, "Oh … so you mean the Heavy Metal Bar isn't it's real name?" It was kinda one of those tough, earth shattering revelations, like finding out there is no Tooth Fairy or that your dad is gay. I came to realize, though, that the Heavy Metal Bar by any other name is still the Heavy Metal Bar, and that I should love it for what it is, not what I'd like it to be. The drinks are still dirt cheap, Judas Priest still blasts from the juke-box, and the hipsters and the heshers are still slowly becoming one and the same.

Radegast Hall and Biergarten

113 N. 3rd St. @ Berry St.

Ten years ago, if you had told a local that there would be a Bavar-ian-style beer garden in Williamsburg, they would have responded, "Vhut, are you meshuggenah? Vee moved to Brooklyn to escape ze fakakte Bavarians!" But lo and behold, today there's one sitting right on the corner of Berry and N. 3rd and it's fucking great!* Look I know that I constantly rail against kitsch, irony, and faking the funk, but considering that this place was opened by guys who used to run the 100-year-old Bohemian Hall and Beer Garden in Astoria, I'd have to

---

Publisher's note: Stuart is an insensitive prick who obviously can't tell the difference between a Bavarian beer garden and an Austro-Hungarian one. When confronted with this mix-up he responded, "All white people look the same to me."

say it's about as authentic as possible without being the real thing. As for the price, I'm not gonna lie and say it's über cheap, but every once in awhile a person wants to eat sausages and drink really good beer out of a giant glass brought to them by cute girls dressed like beer wenches. You feel me? They even have a retractable roof for fuck's sake! These guys thought of everything.

Rosemary's Greenpoint Tavern

188 Bedford Ave. @ N. 7th St.

Can you see the true glee on my face? A few giant beers does that to me.

If this bar were in any other location in the world, it would be filled with old man life-long losers and women with missing teeth and raspy cigarette voices. But given that it sits right in the heart of bloody fucking Williamsburg, the clientele is hip and good looking ... mostly. That's not the real reason people go there, though. The real reason is that a 32-ounce Styrofoam cup of beer is only $3.50. Yup, you read that right. Rosemary is doing a real service to the community; somebody should give her the key to the city (she already has the key to my heart).

Tommy's Tavern

1041 Manhattan Ave. @ Freeman St.

A strange place and a true dive, Tommy's is many things to many people. On week nights, it's a mostly local crowd (and by crowd I mean five people) who come to drown out their normal existence with cheap booze and the more than occasional cheap thrill of seeing other patrons kick the shit out of each other on the sidewalk outside. Come weekends though, the regulars give way to herds of hipsters who are here to see the live music in the back, and purchase $3 beers from a bartendress with equal helpings of tattoos and cleavage.

Trash Bar

256 Grand St. @ Roebling St.

Free tater-tots, $3 PBRs, grungy hipsters, weird shit on the walls, and a small venue for live music that I never bother to see; the only thing that makes this place even cooler is that I got checked out by Regina Spektor here. Alright!

Turkey's Nest

94 Bedford Ave. @ N. 12th St.

The Turkey's Nest is kinda like the United Nations of Williamsburg drunks. Hipsters, Hassids, Poles, and Puerto Ricans all gather here to watch sports, shoot some pool, play Big Buck Hunter and, more importantly, get fucked up. I mean, why else would you buy a 32-ounce styrofoam cup of beer for $3.50? To savor the taste of low-end American beer? Hell no, it's because you wanna get your swerve on. Same goes for those battery-acid-strength (and flavored) drinks dispensed from the margarita machine. I don't think anyone would actually drink them for the taste (at least I hope not); you order one because it's cheap as hell and they'll put a to go top on it so you can take it to McCarren Park across the street.

Union Pool

484 Union Ave. @ Meeker St.

Girls in granny glasses and bearded boys fill this former swimming pool supply shop on a nightly basis in the constant pursuit of libation, conversation and pleasures of the flesh. For better or worse, drinking at Union Pool is a quintessential Williamsburg experience; it's like an initiation rite that most people go through upon moving to this tight-pantsed part of the world. I can't quite put my finger on what it is that so powerfully draws people here. Maybe it's the layout, with the big booths, big bar, and big backyard, or maybe it's the single stall unisex bathrooms reminiscent of coed college dorms. It could also be that the DJ is always remarkably good and that bands play on nice nights in the wide-open outside area. Whatever the allure is, it seems to be a force of nature all on its own. Union Pool is the one bar where you can virtually guarantee that you'll run into someone you know. My favorite occurrence of this was when I was here for a going away party. I was walking up to the bar to grab another drink when I saw Krista and Paul in conversation with some guy. As I approached, Paul pointed to me and said, "This is him" at which point the guy said, "Holy shit, you're Broke-Ass Stuart? I'm a huge fan!" My immediate reaction was to accuse Paul and Krista of fucking with me, but when I realized they weren't, I was elated (what are the chances of being recognized in NY where no one has heard of me, considering it rarely even happens in SF?). The guy continued, "Wow, I'm so excited to meet you. I used to live in San Francisco and my stupid cunt of an ex-girlfriend gave me your book for Christmas. It saved my life. Seriously man, I met Chloe Sevigny earlier tonight and I'm more excited to meet you." Wow, what do you say to that? I responded in the most reasonable way I could: "Really? Buy me a drink." And he did, and continued to do so all night long.

Zablowskis

107 N. 6th St. btw Bedford Ave. & Berry St.

Big, homey, perfectly lit, and with lots of seating, this great bar is ideal for either a gaggle of your thirsty friends, or a weeknight date (as long as he or she knows how to drink). Because of its impeccable location, the people who frequent this spot are the typical young, broke and beautiful Billyburg crowd, but its pool table, dart boards, and wooden floors suggest that if it were in another part of the city it would just end up being another sports bar. I personally like it exactly the way it is now. Especially considering that cheap domestic beer is $2 and you can match one of those bad boys up with a shot for only $5. The only unfortunate thing about this place is that no one seems to know how to spell it.

Shopping

Artists & Fleas

129 N. 6th St. btw Bedford Ave. & Berry St.

This indoor indie market happens every Saturday and Sunday from 12–7pm. All kinds of cool vendors here sell screen printed shirts, used/vintage clothes, records, books, and even miniature cupcakes made by a cute cupcake girl. The whole scene reminds me of the weekend artisan bazaars that happen in the Palermo district of Buenos Aires. During those markets, indie designers set up shop and sell their ill gear in bars that are closed during the day. While this isn't Buenos Aires or a bar, it still rocks and I wholeheartedly advise you to stop in and support these local artists and designers.

Atlantis Attic

771 Metropolitan Ave.
btw Humboldt St. and Graham Ave.

A big used-clothing store way off the Bedford main drag, Atlantis Attic has a great selection and stellar prices. I got an amazing full-length, fake fur coat here for only $20! It was one of those things where once I saw it, I knew that I couldn't say "no". It's just so fucking fly! Now all I need is a Cadillac and some Curtis Mayfield and life will be perfect. While I'll admit my friends all make fun of me now, just wait and see who'll be laughing when in three years these coats are the hottest shit in hipsterville. I'm a visionary, goddammit.

Beacon's Closet

88 N. 11th St. btw Berry St. & Wythe Ave.

This juggernaut of a store is 5,500 square feet of used-clothing madness. While the prices here tend to be more on the vintage side of the used-clothing spectrum than the thrift store side, the sheer size of the collection makes it almost an attraction itself. Your best bet here is to try to go sometime during the week, because weekend afternoons are complete fuck shows and lead to frustration and possible fist fights with high school kids.

Brooklyn Industries Outlet

184 Broadway @ Driggs Ave.

Everybody loves Brooklyn Industries right? They've got a kick-ass logo and their gear is ill. The only problem is that a lot of times their products lie just out of my price range. Luckily for me (and for you, too), they also have an outlet store, making it so pauperized people like us can afford to look fly. They probably won't have the exact same shit that you saw in their retail stores earlier in the week, but what they do have is generally just as sweet and like one-third of the price.

Desert Island

540 Metropolitan btw Lorimer St. & Union Ave.

Desert Island is the type of place that you'd imagine Williamsburg to be full of, but strangely isn't. It sells comics, books, zines, prints and other neat stuff, both DIY and not. I started this whole Broke-Ass Stuart thing as a little 30-page zine, and because of this I always try to support any place that sells DIY products. So, I tip my hat to you Desert Island, especially since that cool old fanzine place in the East Village has been gone for a few years now. And best of all, I like the way you took the existing sign from the location's previous inhabitant and changed it to say, "Sparacino's Bakery Italian French Sicilian Bread And Comic Booklets." Fucking good show!

Eat Records

124 Meserole Ave. @ Leonard St.

For a very brief moment in college I had a dream of opening a record store/café/bar/bookstore/recording studio. Considering how fucked all of those industries are right now (excluding bars, they always do well), I'm really glad I decided not to chase that particular dream. But I'm glad the cats who run Eat Records decided to follow theirs. Not only does this record store sell great new and used vinyl and CDs, they also sell tasty food and great coffee. What more could you want in a hang-out spot? My homegirl Molly is the one who first took me here, and we discussed her shooting some photos for this book. Unfortunately, our schedules didn't coincide, so we weren't able to work together. Bummer.

Film Noir

10 Bedford Ave. @ Manhattan Ave.

I owed this guy about $400 dollars in late fees. I just never could bring myself to walk down the street and return the copy of Michelangelo Antonioni's *The Passenger* I had lying around my apartment for six months. I always had to avoid his store and walk all the way around the block when coming home for fear of him recognizing me and demanding his movie back. Sven, the owner is a great guy with an excellent taste in film and music. He turned me on to the films of Alejandro Jodorowsky and he has a good selection of kraut-rock and old psych records as well. It is the best video rental store in all of Williamsburg and Greenpoint, and he is always willing to talk film and music with you. Ask him for a recommendation and you will not be disappointed. He once recommended the Herzog film *Stroszek* with extreme caution since this film was found in Ian Curtis's VCR after he hung himself. Rad dude!*

The Thing

1001 Manhattan Ave. btw Huron & Green Sts.

In all my years of shopping, I've never seen anything quite like The Thing. It's everything you can think of in one store; it's where man's leftovers go to heaven. Basically a Goodwill, but without the clothes, The Thing just has tons of people's stuff that they no longer care for, like the 560 page book about Harry Truman I scored last week for only 55 cents! Go into the back of the store and down the stairs and you will find a basement full of records. It's the largest unsorted collection of records in New York City. DJs from all over the world travel here just to add to their massive collections; and no matter what you find, whether it be a rare Factory Records release or one of the thousands of copies of Fleetwood Mac's *Rumors* scattered amongst the bins, it's just three bucks a pop. Go and I'm sure you will find a Japanese tourist with a medical mask on digging through those dusty crates.*

Sent from the desk of Paul T. Alkaly, correspondent at large.

Sights & Entertainment

Brooklyn Brewery Tour
79 N. 11th St. btw Berry St. & Wythe Ave.

At first I was a little outraged that there was no free beer at the end of this tour. I mean, why else do you go on beer tours, right? But then I thought about the beer tours that I'd been on in the past, namely Heineken and Guinness (sweet Jesus the best beer I've ever had is a Guinness in Dublin) and I remembered that, although you do get a free beer at the end, you have to pay to go on the tour. The Heineken tour is currently like 11 euro ($17.50) and the Guinness tour is 15 euro ($23.86). Considering that the Brooklyn Brewery does free tours and lets you buy $4 pints at the end, I feel a little foolish for my previous outrage, and I'd like the good people of this establishment to know that I apologize for all the things I said about their mothers and those goats. I'd also like to say that every time I see euro to dollar conversions, I weep a little bit, and that when the Canadian dollar caught up with ours, a little piece of me died. I mean the Canadian one dollar coin is called the loonie and the two dollar coin is called the toonie, I shit you not. We're neck and neck with fucking Elmer Fudd.

City Reliquary
370 Metropolitan Ave. @ Havemeyer St.

Begun as a window display not far from this location, the City Reliquary is now an actual enterable museum displaying unusual relics from New York's past. Expect cool stuff like old subway tokens, brochures from past World's Fairs, and themed collections of black and white photos. While this great little museum is technically free to enter, they do ask for a little donation, so feel free to kick in a buck or two to help support this quirky little place.

East River State Park
East River btw N. 7th & 9th Sts.

Now that Grand St. Ferry Park is closed, the only place in Williamsburg where you can actually get down to the water is East River

State Park. The views of Manhattan are spectacular, but the problem is they close the park at dusk, which is too early to actually see the sunset. Oh well, maybe someday they will extend the hours; it would be my favorite place ever if they just move closing time to 11pm. For now, it's a great spot for a daytime picnic.*

Feast of St. Paulinus and Our Lady of Mount Carmel
Havemeyer St. btw Union Ave. & N. 7th St.
(one week in mid-July)

Once a year something magical happens on the streets of Williamsburg. All year former stool pigeons and goodfellas known as the Giglio Boys hang out in their social club on the corner of Lorimer and Devoe planning their signature event, the Dancing of the Giglio. The Giglio, a 50-foot-tall tower festooned with a statue of St. Paulinus himself is then lifted by those brave Giglios dressed in red or green with white hats (like little Marios and Luigis) and dance their way down Havemeyer St. There may be no Italians left in this section of Williamsburg, but it definitely strikes fear into many a gentrifying hipster. Ferris wheels and food stalls adorn the blocked off streets and families flock to the Feast. If Flava Flav was in attendance I have a feeling he would say, "Giglio, boyeeeeeeeeeeeeeeeeeeee"*

Leaving Brooklyn Oy Vey! Sign
Above Williamsburg Bridge, heading
toward Manhattan

The first time I saw this, I thought it was the best graffiti I'd ever seen, but then I found out that it was actually Marty Markowitz, Brooklyn Borough President, who had the sign placed there. All I have to say is that this man is a genius. I wish more public officials had senses of humor. If you wanna see the sign but not go over the bridge, you can see it pretty well from round S. 5th St. around Bedford Ave.

McCarren Park
Between Bayard St. & Nassau Ave. and N. 12th
& Lorimer Sts.

Sure there's soccer, kickball, baseball, basketball, a running track blah blah blah. Who cares? The shit you're interested in happens in

---

*Sent from the desk of Paul T. Alkaly, correspondent at large.

the emptied out pool. Some of the best free music all year long happens during the summer at McCarren Park Pool thanks to JellyNYC. Groups like The Hold Steady, Blonde Redhead, and Aesop Rock have been know to grace this stage. Unfortunately I heard a dirty rumor that this might be the last year it happens. I sure hope not because then I'll feel like a dumb-ass for putting this shit in my book.

Newton Creek Oil Spill
End of Manhattan Ave. in Greenpoint

This is already estimated to be the largest environmental catastrophe in the history of the environment. Something like 500 million times more oil than the Exxon Valdez spilled has seeped into the ground surrounding Newton Creek, the dividing line between Brooklyn and Queens. You can see wildlife covered in black goo dying on the banks of the creek right here in New York City. This is why I don't like environmentalists; they all move to the Pacific Northwest and live in trees ignoring the real tragedies taking place in large metropolitan areas. I don't give a shit if a forest I can't see nor hear gets bulldozed to the ground if the creek in my own backyard has a constant layer of goop floating on top of it. Meanwhile, I'll die of cancer while these tree huggers are smoking trees and giving natural birth. This is a message to all environmentalists: Move here and take care of this before I donate large sums of money to Halliburton. Actually don't, you smell and listen to bad music. I'd rather die of cancer.*

Pete's Candy Store
709 Lorimer St. @ Richardson St.

A dark barroom filled with PBR cans and unshaven hipsters greets you upon stepping inside Pete's Candy Store. $3 beers and $6 paninis flow freely through the room and the sound of music trickles in from somewhere in the rear. As you head toward the sound, you realize that there is actually a tiny-ass venue back there and some amazingly talented person is performing for a packed audience. The world needs more Pete's Candy Stores, a place where any night of the week you can see mind-blowing live music, poetry, author readings, or even spelling bees. The extreme intimacy in the back room of this former candy store and the caliber of performances makes Pete's truly one of the best things about Williamsburg.

Sent from the desk of Paul T. Alkaly, correspondent at large.

WILLIAMSBURG and GREENPOINT

Grub-a-dub-dub
1 Acapulco
2 Big Apple Deli
3 Christina's Polish Restaurant
4 Dumont
5 Egg
6 God Bless Deli
7 Grand Bakery
8 Lady Octopus
9 Palace Fried Chicken
10 Peter Luger Steak House
11 Peter Pan Bakery
12 Shachis Restaurant Arepas
13 Warsaw Bakery
14 Wombat

DRINKS DRINKS DRINKS
15 Anytime
16 Barcade
17 Bushwick Country Club
18 Capri Social Club
19 Clem's
20 Coco 66
21 East River Bar
22 Lazy Catfish
23 The Levee

DRINKS DRINKS DRINKS (ctn'd)
24 Palace Tavern
25 Radegast Hall and Biergarten
26 Rosemary's Greenpoint Tavern
27 Tommy's Tavern
28 Turkey's Nest
29 Union Pool
30 Zablowskis

Shopping
31 Artists & Fleas
32 Atlantis Attic
33 Beacon's Closet
34 Brooklyn Industries Outlet
35 Desert Island
36 Eat Records
37 Film Noir
38 The Thing

Stuffis to See and Do
39 Brooklyn Brewery Tour
40 City Reliquary
41 East River State Park
42 Good View of Leaving Brooklyn
   Oy Vey Sign

Stuffis to See and Do (ctn'd)
43 McCarren Park
44 Newton Creek Oil Spill
45 Pete's Candy Store

Free Food Bitches!!
46 Alligator Lounge
47 The Charleston
48 Metropolitan Bar
49 Sweet-Ups
50 Trash

Herbivore Friendly
51 Foodswings
52 The Lucky Cat
53 Wild Ginger
54 Williamsburg & Greenpoint
   Bliss Café

Hipsters

Hassids

Really hot 24 year old Polish girl
who will somehow turn into a frumpy
babushka, over night, at some point
in the next 2 years.
It's uncanny how this happens.

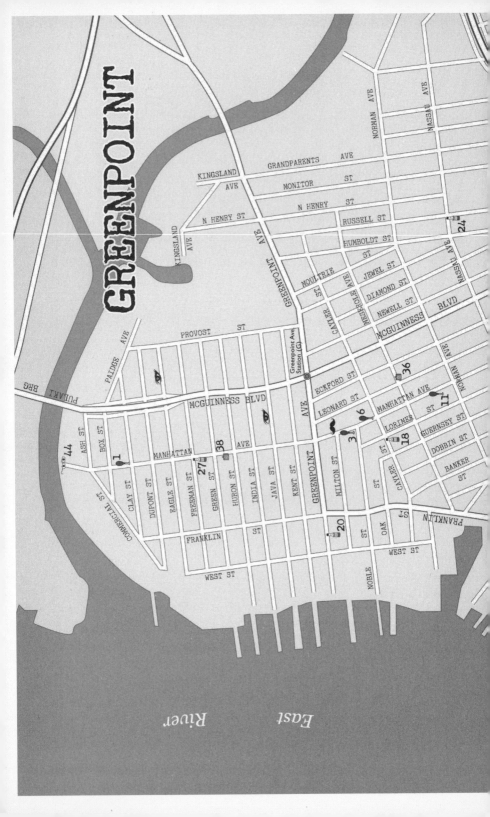

Downtown & Fort Greene

T he third largest business district in New York, Downtown Brooklyn is where lots of money changes hands, and not a whole lot else happens. During the day, there are plenty of cheap options for eating, but many of them are fast food chains, and at night there isn't much to do at all except possibly see a performance at the Brooklyn Academy of Music (BAM). Downtown Brooklyn does have a handful of excellent buildings to ogle, like the Williamsburg Savings Bank, and a few museums to explore, but the main reason most people come down here is because they get paid to do it; this is where their job is.

Fort Greene, on the other hand (there are a lot of hands going on in this introduction) is infinitely more happening. It's a truly racially integrated middle- to upper-middle-class neighborhood, where good restaurants sit on beautiful streets lined with trees and brownstones and live jazz can sometimes be heard emanating from hip bars. If America was able to figure out its backwards-ass, fucked up race and class problems, this is what all of our urban centers would be like. Just ask Spike Lee, his 40 Acres and a Mule Studios is right here.

Who the hell put a castle in Downtown Brooklyn?

When I grow up I wanna live in Fort Greene.

The borders of **Downtown Brooklyn** are roughly York St. to the north, Navy St. to the east, Atlantic Ave. to the south, and Adams St. to the West. **Fort Greene** is roughly bound by Flatbush Ave. in the west, Atlantic Ave. to the south, Washington Ave. to the east, and Flushing Ave. to the north.

Food

Black Iris

228 Dekalb Ave. @ Clermont Ave.

It's always weird when you come across food that you regularly eat after a night at the bars and realize that, not only do people eat it in normal circumstances (meaning not burning my tongue scarfing down chicken shawarma while standing in front of Bereket on Houston), there are actual sit down restaurants, with ambience, that serve the food, too. Black Iris is such a place. The food here is so good that, get this, people actually come in from Manhattan to eat here. I have friends who think you need a passport to get into Brooklyn. And while the food isn't gonna be as cheap as a 24-hour spot somewhere in the East Village, 85 percent of the menu still costs ten bucks or less. Word to some of that Mediterranean soul food.

Habana Outpost

757 Fulton St. @ S. Portland Ave.

Seeing that I'm out there constantly trudging through these city streets looking to bring a little light to your lives (or at least some cool shit), it's only fair that I occasionally run across pure awesomeness. My dear, dear friends, while I have neither the time nor desire to suss out whether the Habana Outpost is NY's first Eco-Eatery, as it claims, I can absolutely confirm that HO (apparently I haven't the time nor desire to type out whole restaurant names either) fits into the above-mentioned category of pure awesomeness. Running off solar energy, having cups and cutlery made from biodegradable cornstarch, being adorned by bright murals and having a smoothie machine powered by either you or some kid on a bicycle (Attn: child services) is only the tip of the compost pile, er, iceberg of HO's twice-mentioned pure awesomeness. There's also a big outdoor patio/cerveza garden that has a local artisan bazaar on the weekends and the joint doubles as a community event space hosting things like summer movie nights, art, and burlesque shows. *And*, they have local beers on tap for only $2.50! Since it is technically a restaurant, I should mention that the

Cuban/pan-Latin food served here is great but it isn't super cheap ($7.75 chicken burrito). That being said, the corn ($2) is so good I'd beat up the kid on the bicycle for it without thinking twice.

P.S. The Manhattan location **Café Habana** (17 Prince St. @ Elizabeth, Soho) has basically the same menu, it just doesn't have all the other stuff that makes HO purely awesome.

Justin's Island Cuisine
144 Lawrence St. btw Fulton & Willoughby Sts.

My girlfriend lived in the Virgin Islands for three years; so right before moving to New York we went to St. John for a wedding. Prior to that trip, I didn't know shit about island food. But on our last day in the islands we took a boat trip from island to island drinking. On the island of Jost Van Dyke we went to a spot called the Soggy Dollar Bar, and this is where I had my first roti. If you've never had it before, it's kinda like Indian naan bread that's crammed with a bunch of good stuff. I had a roti at Justin's that, while not being as good as the one in the islands, was pretty decent, very big and very cheap. In fact everything on the menu at this simply decorated downtown spot comes in huge portions and doesn't cost too much. And if you go during the day, you get to catch up on *Days of Our Lives*. That Bonnie Lockhart is a real bitch.

Little House on Clinton
150 Clinton Ave. @ Myrtle Ave.

Chicken and waffles is a marriage as holy as anything you can think of. Roscoe has been holding it down out in LA for years with his famous recipes, but this isn't LA, this is Brooklyn, son, and folks out here got that shit on lock, too. Just step into the Little House on Clinton and let the sweet, matronly ladies behind the counter fix you up a plate of some of that good stuff. Just don't bother with any of the other grub though; you came here for the chicken and waffles, don't forget that. Keep your eyes on the prize.

Marquet Fine Pastries III
680 Fulton St. btw S. Elliot St. & S. Portland Ave.

What's strange is that in all the research that I've done, I haven't found Marquet Fine Pastries I or II. But that's fine, I'm perfectly content with III since 90 percent of their food hovers in the $7 and below range. It's a pretty busy spot, probably because the food is yummy and cheap. But I wonder how much of their popularity is derived from the fact that their walls are plastered with the funnies. I've always felt that Garfield and croissants are a pretty good combination.

Not Ray's Pizzeria
690 Fulton St. btw S. Oxford St. & S. Portland Ave.

I'd just like to congratulate the owners of this pizza spot for their cleverness. This might be the best name for a pizzeria in all of New York. If you don't get the joke, I'll explain it to you: all around NYC there are tons of different variations of the name "Ray's Pizza" which are all unaffiliated with each other. There's Famous Ray's, Original Ray's, Original Famous Ray's … you get the picture, and so these guys had the genius to completely flip that shit and call themselves Not Ray's Pizza. I love it!

Rice
166 Dekalb Ave. @ Washington Park

Rice is a vaguely affordable Asian fusion restaurant with a view of Fort Greene Park that plays hip music, like Aretha Franklin songs you've never heard before. The old tile floor points to the place's former life as, whatever the hell it was before it was a hip Asian fusion spot. It's the type of place where hot chicks sit, sip tea, and catch up with each other for an hour, even though they just saw each other last weekend.

Seafood Fried Fish/Ocean Fresh Fish
60 Willoughby St. btw Lawrence and Bridge Sts.

I wonder why more places don't merge the idea of a fish market with the idea of a fried food place; it seems like the perfect combination. When you walk into this fishy smelling place, the left side is the fry up where everything is $3–$6 and you can get shit like flounder, snapper, and scallops. To the right is where you can get the fresh fish like our friends from the previous sentence, flounder, snapper and scallops, as well as other of their water-breathing brethren. That's all I have to say about that.

Bars

Alibi

242 Dekalb Ave. btw Clermont & Vanderbilt Aves.

Mike and I went here one night after having $12 all you can eat mussels at nearby **Chez Oskar** (211 Dekalb Ave. btw Adelphi St. & Clermont Ave.). I would've put it in this book, but it only happens on Tuesday nights, and it's not all that broke-ass any other time. Just as we were heading back to Mike's car (yes, he has a car. I've forgotten what that's like) an accident happened and blocked his car in. Since we had at least an hour to kill before a tow truck would be there, we did the only sensible thing: we went to a bar. That's when I met the Alibi, in all its divey glory. Everything here is nice and worn like a dive bar should be. A couple old guys sit at the bar watching the sole TV, while locals take some easy money off a sensitive Pratt kid over at the pool table. I sat outside on the back patio and drank a couple of beers while Mike smoked some cigarettes and we got into a conversation with a guy who told us that you used to be able to buy weed from the bodega around the corner. But those days are long gone and everything seems to have changed in Ft. Greene–except for Alibi.

Frank's Cocktail Lounge

660 Fulton St. @ Lafayette Ave.

Frank's is one of those rare old school bars that, instead of changing to suit the times or closing altogether, just continued on doing its thing and let the gentrifying neighborhood come to it. A crazy stucco ceiling hangs above the bar while glass topped tables are illuminated by candles and, on any given night, the crowd can include poorly dressed hipster kids with fashion mullets, impeccably dressed old black dudes in three-piece suits, blue collar guys who just got off work, and grown folks dressed like they're looking for some action. Frank's is a perfect reflection of what this neighborhood is, a place with one foot in the future and one foot in the past. Weekend nights see DJs, while on Sunday evenings a live jazz band plays for free. My man Frank also puts out a free food buffet, but when I asked when and how often he replied, "sometimes we put it out, sometimes we don't". I'd like to say that every neighborhood should have a bar as perfect as Frank's Cocktail Lounge, but that would mean every neighborhood would have to be as unique as Ft. Greene, and I just don't think that's possible.

Freddy's Bar & Backroom

485 Dean St. @ 6th Ave.

There's so many good things to say about this bar that I'm tempted to leave it blank and just let you go see it for yourself ... you know what, that's exactly what I'm gonna do. Just go to Freddy's and you will be stoked by how cheap and great it is. But you have to hurry up and go now because it may not be there soon. They are trying to redevelop the whole area.

P.S. I know it's technically in Prospect Heights, but I figured I'd just lump it in with Ft. Greene because I could.

Moe's

80 Lafayette Ave. @ S. Portland Ave.

You know when you walk down the street and see a kid of mixed ethnicity and think to yourself, "Wow, what a beautiful little child"? Well chances are, that kid's parents met at Moe's. That's just how this place gets down; it's like Dr. King's dream, except a hell of a lot sexier. That's actually my favorite thing about Ft. Greene, not only is it mad diverse, but everyone's all mingling with each other, too, and I can dig that because I love me some sistas. The DJ here is usually playing some decent shit and the bar's darkness, combined with the $3 Dos Equis, means everyone is gonna be on top of their game. So why don't you head out to Moe's tonight and go find someone you might wanna make beautiful babies with? I'm definitely not saying you should make babies tonight, but maybe you can get some practice in.

Shopping

Fulton St. Mall

Fulton St. btw Flatbush Ave. & Boerum Hall

The Fulton St. Mall is truly a thing of wonder. Where else in the world can you walk down the street and fulfill the sudden urge to buy a red leather belt with your name written on it in rhinestones? Where else could you find stand after stand of book vendors selling fiction specifically written for black audiences with names like *He Got Game but the Game Got Him* and *God Bless You Girl, Let Me Holla at You for a Minute*? Where else could you find a guy selling bootlegged DVDs who's holding a brand new plasma screen TV, just to prove to you that the DVDs are good quality? The answer is: nowhere. You can find almost anything you want on the Fulton St. Mall, and many things you don't. A commercial pedestrian street trafficking in the flimsier commodities of modern urban black culture, Fulton St. Mall is lined on both sides by various stores and stands selling sneakers, incense, sneakers, gold, cell phones, street wear, sneakers, baseball caps, hoodies that look like skeletons, sneakers and shoes. A few of my friends from LA described it as the "black version of Santa Monica's 3rd St. Promenade", and while that's funny, it's not exactly true; there are a lot more street performers in Santa Monica. Then again, with the gentrification steamroller moving through Brooklyn and the possibility of an H&M opening up on the Fulton St. Mall, it may unfortunately become like Santa Monica sooner than expected.

Gold Dragon Video

258 Duffield St. btw Fulton & Willoughby Sts.

I was walking by here one day when I saw a few big Tony Jaa posters in the window. I thought to myself, "How could I not go into a place that reps Tony Jaa this hard?" and so I went in and flipped my shit when I realized that Gold Dragon Video specializes in martial arts DVDs. Are you kidding me? God's DVD library isn't even this good and that fool invented DVDs! Plus, all the movies are only $10–$15. Of course this joint also sells video games and Japanimation, too, but we all know the real reason to come here–*Ong Bak* bitches!

Sights & Entertainment

Brooklyn Borough Hall

209 Joralemon St. @ Court St.

Built back when Brooklyn was its own city, Brooklyn Borough Hall is now the seat of power for the Brooklyn Borough President Marty Markowitz (at least that's who's in charge at the time I'm writing this). I don't really know what kind of decisions this guy gets to make (although I was told he's the one who put up the "Now Leaving Brooklyn: Oy Vey" sign, which makes him hilarious as far as I'm concerned), but they must be at least kinda important because why else would they let him do his thing in such a nice looking building? Keep on keepin' on, Marty! I'm sure you're doing a great job even though I don't quite know what that job is.

Fort Greene Park

Between Myrtle & DeKalb Aves. and
Washington Park & Brooklyn Hospital

Opened as Brooklyn's first park in 1847, after years of Walt Whitman bitching in the *Brooklyn Daily Eagle* about wanting to breath clean air or something, this site (designed by Fredrick Olmstead and Calvert Vaux) once held a fort and still contains a memorial to the prisoners held in British ships during the Revolutionary War. These days things are a little more quaint. There's a year round farmers market (Saturdays from 8am–5pm), an artisan fair in the summer, and tons of families picnicking and playing on nice, sunny days. Plus, you can occasionally find some guys cruising here late at night. Maybe that's the real reason Walt Whitman wanted a park so badly.

Museum of Contemporary African Diasporan Art

80 Hanson Pl. @ S. Portland Ave.

The MoCADA is a museum of contemporary art by black artists that focuses on educating all its visitors about the history, triumphs and struggles of the African Diasporan community. Besides showcasing visual art, they also have lectures and performances throughout the year. The suggested donation is $4, which is the cheapest suggestion I've ever heard. Not too shabby, hey pal?

New York City College of Technology
300 Jay St. @ Tillary St.

I originally planned on putting a "Broke-Ass Health and Beauty Tips" section in this book but considering how close I am to deadline, and how big this fucker already is, I'm not sure it's gonna make it. But this one is important, so I figured I'd sneak it in here. Most people I know don't have dental insurance because it's crazy expensive, so if you wanna get your teeth cleaned for $10 by a senior dental student (it's overseen by a dentist) call (718) 260-5074 and make an appointment. How much money did I just save you? If you were skeptical before, now you feel justified in buying this book right? So now, go tell all your friends about it so I can sell more copies. C'mon, I'd do it for you.

New York Transit Museum
Boerum Pl. & Schermerhorn St.

Moscow's transit system may have more stations, but no major metropolitan area other than New York can claim 24-hour service and thousands of miles of track. It is art. It is the veins and arteries of the city. It is an attraction in itself. Great art on the walls, history, street performers, weirdos; New York is nothing without the subway. The New York Transit Museum celebrates this and serves it all up to you in a tangible way that actually makes it cool and interesting. Of the many exhibits that occupy this museum located in an old station that hasn't been used since 1946, the best is the one where you can see the old original subway cars from back when the system first opened. This place is totally worth the $5 admission fee. Just don't try to come on Mondays, because it's closed.

Weird Dog Statue in Brooklyn Polytechnic College
Between Jay St. & Flatbush Ave. Ext. and Tillary and Willoughby Sts.

I was walking through the quad here when I saw this thing that looked like a real dog that was just standing completely still. I've

You can get anything you want on the Fulton St. Mall, and a hell of a lot of things you don't want.

known a lot of dogs and most of them aren't even still while they sleep, so it totally fucked with me enough that I had to walk up and check it out. Then I pissed on it to let all the other dogs know that this bitch was mine.

DOWNTOWN and FORT GREENE

♥ Grub-a-dub-dub

1 Black Iris

2 Habana Outpost

3 Justin's Island Cuisine

4 Little House on Clinton

5 Marquet Fine Pastries III

6 Not Ray's Pizzeria

7 Rice

8 Seafood Fried Fish/ Ocean Fresh Fish

♠ DRINKS DRINKS DRINKS

9 Alibi

10 Frank's Cocktail Lounge

11 Freddy's Bar & Backroom

12 Moe's

▪ Shopping

13 Fulton St. Mall

14 Gold Dragon Video

👓 Stuffis to See and Do

15 Brooklyn Borough Hall

16 Fort Greene Park

17 Museum of Contemporary African Diasporan Art

18 New York City College of Technology

19 New York Transit Museum

20 Weird Dog Statue In Brooklyn Polytechnic College

♥ Cute little mixed ethnic kid

🌿 Street vendors selling afro-centric books and goods

!!! Someone who just realized how awesome Brooklyn is

THE SHOT AND BEER COMBO

When I first met my buddy Mac and told him about my book, he immediately decided that I needed to have a section about all the places that had a $5 shot and beer combo deal, and all the great names those specials had. He listed off the ones he knew  off the top of his head and then emailed me a couple more. At that point I couldn't say "no" (the idea was perfect), so I put in some research time myself and added to the list. I'll be honest. I'm sure there are more bars throughout New York that have such a deal, but I figured that I'd give you a good jumping off point from which to compile your own list. I call this interactively enabling alcoholism. Anyway, what follows is this list. Not all of the specials have great names, and not all are $5, but they're pretty much all good deals. Maybe some bar will eventually have the Broke-Ass … probably not. Drink up!

P.S. Mac's advice is this: Ask for your shot on ice and you'll probably get a better pour.

Manhattan

Lower East Side

Iggy's: 132 Ludlow St. @ Rivington St.

Iggy's deals all depend on who's working. At happy hour they always have a PBR and a shot for $5, but often times, like when Pirate Mike works, they have the deal at night also.

Boss Tweeds: 115 Essex St. btw Delancey & Rivington Sts.

No fancy name here, just a can of Bud and a shot of Jack or Jim for $5.

East Village

Blue & Gold Tavern: 79 E. 7th St. btw 1st & 2nd Aves.

Blue & Gold, bastion of booze and poorly made decisions, has three great specials with equally great names: **The Dirty Hipster** is a PBR and a shot of Jager; **The Redneck** is a PBR and a shot of Jim Beam; and **The Dude** is a Blue and Gold lager with a shot of Southern Comfort Lime. Southern Comfort Lime sounds gross.

Cherry Tavern: 441 E. 6th St. btw 1st Ave. & Ave. A

The Cherry Tavern's addition to the list is **The Tijuana Special,** a can of Tecate and a shot of tequila for $5.

Double Down Saloon: 14 Ave. A btw E. 2nd & Houston Sts.

A PBR and a well shot for $6, and that extra buck doesn't even buy you a cool name.

Finnerty's Irish Pub: 221 2nd Ave. btw E. 13th & 14th Sts.

While there is no fancy name here for the special, at least you get a PBR tall boy and a shot of your choice for $6.

The Lakeside Lounge: 162 Ave. B btw 10th & 11th Sts.

A well shot and a PBR sets you back $6 at this venue for free shows.

The Library: 7 Ave. A @ Houston St.

Once again, no special name, but a Natural Light and a well shot is just $5 Thursday and Sunday nights.

Brooklyn

Williamsburg

Artland: 609 Grand St. btw Leonard & Lorimer Sts.

At Artland, a PBR and a shot of well whiskey is called **The Combo**. Welcome to drunkland.

Bushwick Country Club: 618 Grand St. @ Leonard St.

Called **The Supersize,** you get a PBR tall boy and a shot of rotgut whiskey for $6. My advice is to ask for the "pickle back" which is a shot of pickle juice to chase the whiskey. I know it sounds gross ,but it's actually *really* good. Cuts right through the whiskey.

Clem's: 264 Grand St. btw Driggs Ave. & Havemeyer St.

The always solid Clem's holds it down with **The Patriot,** a PBR and a shot of Jim Beam, and **The Federale,** a Tecate and a shot of Sauza Tequila.

duckduck: 161 Montrose Ave. btw Graham Ave. & Humboldt St.

Probably the best named special on this list, **The Schmidtface** is a can of Schmidt beer and a shot of well whiskey for $5.

Levee: 212 Berry St. @ N. 3rd St.

The Levee gives you plenty of options for getting completely trashed. **The Sportsman** is a can of Black Label and a shot of Evan Williams for $4; **The Texas Two Step** is a bottle of Lone Star and a shot of tequila for $5; and **The Frat Boy** is a bottle of Bud and a shot of Jager for $5. This last one hurts my feelings because I really like to drink Bud and Jager shots.

Boerum Hill, Cobble Hill & Carroll Gardens

Abilene Bar: 442 Court St. btw 2nd & 3rd Pls.

When asked if there was a name for the special, the guy behind the bar said, "Yeah, it's called a can of Genesee and a cheap shot". I told him he wasn't being very creative.

Floyd NY: 131 Atlantic Ave. btw Henry and Clinton Sts.

Good old Floyd presents **The Colt .45 & a Bullet,** which is a can of said beer with a shot of Jack or Wild Turkey for $6. I've had quite a few of these and let me tell you, they do the job quickly.

Boerum Hill, Cobble Hill & Carroll Gardens

These days it seems every single neighborhood has a ridiculous, realtor-invented, acronym, like Nolita (North of Little Italy), Soha (South of Harlem) and Etsa (Enough of this shit already). Bococa is the only one that actually makes sense to me because I'm far too lazy to say or type Boerum Hill, Cobble Hill, and Carroll Gardens each time I mention this area. If I wanted to use that many syllables, I'd learn to speak Azteca (I'm looking at you Huitzilopochtli*).

Until the '60s or '70s, the area comprising Bococa, as well as Gowanus and Red Hook, was known simply as South Brooklyn because it was south of the original town of Brooklyn. Then once people began to see the potential value in Brooklyn real estate, these neighborhoods were divided and called by separate names. Before the '90s the majority of Bococa's residents were Italian-American families, and to this day, many people feel that part of the reason these neighborhoods are so safe is that they're under the Mob's protection. Today

---

*My spell check knows "Huitzilopochtli" but not "Frida" or "Kahlo".

many from the old neighborhood are still around, but more so, this area has become populated with upwardly mobile young families with lots of expensive strollers.

The main drags here are Court and Smith Sts., both of which have seen such an influx of bars, boutiques, and especially restaurants, that Manhattanites have even been known to (gasp) come to Brooklyn on the weekends to dine here. While there are some solid deals to be found on these streets, the best place to look for cheap eats, drinks, and things is generally Atlantic Ave. This is especially so around the Atlantic Ave. and Court St. intersection, which has tons of Middle Eastern stores, imports, and restaurants nearby.

Roughly speaking the boundaries for these neighborhoods are as follows: **Cobble Hill** is from Atlantic Ave. in the north, the BQE in the west, Degraw St. in the south, and Smith St. to the east. **Carroll Gardens** (named after Charles Carroll, the only Catholic signer of the Declaration of Independence) is bound by the BQE in the west, the Gowanus Expressway in the south, Hoyt St. in the east and Degraw St. in the north. **Boerum Hill** is defined by Atlantic Ave. in the north, Smith St. in the west, Baltic St. in the south, and 4th Ave. in the east. Park Slope begins on the other side of 4th Ave., and the space between it and Bococa is called Gowanus. A few places from Gowanus may have crept into this chapter. "Gowanus" is a funny sounding word.

Food

Amazon Café
227 Smith St. @ Butler St.

Considering that there are Amazon Cafés in 10 states and DC, it's pretty much the opposite of an independent business. But for people like me who decide every few months that "this will be the month that I start eating better", Amazon Café is perfect because it's cheap and healthy. I've pretty much decided that if there does happen to be a God, he/she/it is really a sick and sadistic fuck. Anything that feels, tastes, smells good is bad for you. Sex? Can lead to STDs and babies. Food? All the tasty stuff will make you fat and kill you. Sniffing paint thinner? Wait, what am I talking about again?

Bedouin Tent Restaurant
405 Atlantic Ave. btw Bond & Nevins Sts.

When I was 16 and traveling through Israel, I was the beneficiary of the famous Bedouin hospitality. For thousands of years, the Bedouin people have been wandering through the desert, and because of this, it became a tradition that, if someone was to approach their camp, that person would be welcome to stay for three days (logically speaking, turning away someone in the hot desert is practically murder). While you stay in their tents, the Bedouins treat you like you are part of their family (which in my house meant that my mom would yell at you too; that meant she liked you). The interior of this place does remind me of the tents in the desert (though the tent I stayed in didn't have a back patio), and the family who runs it is sweet as can be, but I don't think I would call what they do "Bedouin hospitality"; they wouldn't let me sleep in the restaurant for three nights. I guess I understand though; you can't let every bum who's bedazzled by your food spend the night; this is New York, not the Negev.

Cubana Café
272 Smith St. btw Degraw & Sackett Sts.

This is the first place I ate when I moved to New York. It was one of the few times I conned my good friends Ben and Caroline into coming to Brooklyn, so them, Krista, our friend Lili, and I all came here to catch up. While the plates run within the $10–$12 range, the food is excellent and the servings are plentiful. It was truly a great time; the feeling of seeing old friends, the excitement of knowing I'd just moved to New York, and the deliciousness of being introduced to *elote*, was one of the best combo of emotions I've come across. But I'm sure many of you know the feeling I'm talking about.

Donut House
314 Court St. @ Degraw

Don't let the name fool you; there really isn't much of a donut empha- sis at this little neighborhood diner. In fact, the only mention of do- nuts, besides the name, is in the dessert section. But considering the neighborhood, Donut House is a great place for a cheap bite; a burger is only 5 bucks. Besides the cheap prices, I'm a fan of this place be- cause it has a lunch counter and sells those tiny boxes of cereal that I used to get at the Truck Stop Diner in El Paso, Texas.

P.S. If you do find yourself in El Paso, the Truck Stop has possibly the world's most fantastic huevos rancheros.

P.P.S I've been back to El Paso since I wrote this and the Truck Stop went out of business. You know our economy is fucked when a truck stop in El Paso goes under ... even the place where truckers get crank and hookers is being outsourced to Juarez.

El Nuevo Portal
217 Smith St btw Butler & Baltic Sts.

Every neighborhood in New York has got a cheap Spanish food res- taurant, and El Nuevo Portal is the one for Carroll Gardens. You can get lunch specials here for $5.50 and dinner specials for $6. There's not a whole lot else to say about this joint.

Hanco's Bubble Tea & Vietnamese Sandwiches
85 Bergen St. @ Smith St.

Why did I not find this place until after I moved out of this neighbor- hood? You can get any sandwich for $4.70 and a bowl of vermicelli noodles (my favorite) goes for $5.50. Plus it smells and tastes almost as good as some of the stuff on the West Coast (look don't get all huffy with me; because of its proximity, the West Coast just has more Vietnamese, meaning better Vietnamese food.) There's a handful of tables where you can sit and enjoy your favorite dishes from the Indochina Peninsula, and if you're alone and didn't bring any reading material, there's lots of magazines, like *Maxim*, for you to read. Nothing compliments Vietnamese food like half-clad girls with their nipples airbrushed out of the photo (I once met a guy while in line for an Isaac Hayes concert whose job it was to airbrush out nipples. I cursed him vehemently).

Jill's Vegan Organic Café
231 Court St. @ Warren St.

Vegan, healthy and expensive, so it only gets one sentence.

Joe's Restaurant
349 Court St. @ Union St.

Joe's is the type of fine dining establishment that sells lotto tickets and charters buses to Atlantic City. I wouldn't be surprised if they were numbers runners, too and had a craps game in the back (they don't, I checked). The food here is so-so, but it's mad cheap; most things are under $6. It's the clientele that make this place great though. They are probably all locals who've been coming here since way before this neighborhood became a stroller ghetto. Any joint that still reps its neighborhood after all the changes this one has seen is a-ok with me.

Joe's Superette
349 Smith St. btw 2nd & Carroll Sts.

Worn looking and with a signed photo of Big Pussy from *The Sopranos* hanging above the deli counter, Joe's Superette is a remnant from the old days when Carroll Gardens was a working-class Italian neighborhood and *fugetaboutit* hadn't been screen printed onto T-shirts yet. The clientele here mainly consists of pensioners inquiring about how so and so's mother is doing, and other locals from the neighborhood who have managed to stay put. But one thing is certain: everyone who comes in here comes for the same thing: the owner's balls. Get your mind out of the gutter! I'm talking about his famous fried prosciutto balls, rice-and-meat balls, and rice-and-cheese balls. How famous you ask? Famous enough to make a whole long article in the *New York Times*. These little fritters of heaven are also super cheap; they're only 50 cents each. Plus they seem to expand in your stomach, so you only have to eat a few of them to ditch your hunger. Paul's first meal of the day was six of these little guys, and he wasn't hungry for hours afterwards. I just hope that they sell enough balls to put the missing letters back up on the store's marquee, because that shit looks ragged.

Joya
215 Court St. @ Warren St.

Wanna see how the other half lives, but not pay what those suckers do? Check out Joya. Low lighting, long brick walls decorated with art, a weekend DJ, and an open kitchen give it the feel of some hip downtown spot, but the prices of this popular Thai place are lower than what you'd pay at some Midtown steam plate lunch buffet. It's absurd that everything here is under $8; my feeble brain just can't figure it out. It's like my mind is playing "Who's on First?" with itself. It's going, "Joya's got hella ambiance—but it's cheap—but it's got hella ambiance—but it's cheap—but it's got hella ambiance … aaaagh!!!"

Lucali
575 Henry St. btw Carroll & Summit Sts.

I've eaten at almost all the famous places in the New York pizza game: Grimaldi's, Di Fara, Patsy's, Totonno's, etc. All of which have been honing their pizza-making skills for decades or, in some cases, more than a century. The youngest of the bunch, Di Fara Pizza, has been doing it for almost 50 years. So I was blown away when some friends and I came to Lucali and had some of the best pizza of our lives. I mean that seriously. This place has only been around for a couple of years, and it is already in the same class as all these giants of pizza. Sounds great right? The only thing is that Lucali is a little bit of a splurge; a cheese pizza is $19 and they don't do slices. *But* it is BYOB, so you can bring your own bottle of wine, or be a dirt bag like me and bring a 40 ounce. Because of the low lighting and the ambiance, it's a great place for a date, and if the date sucks, there is plenty of eye candy. All the servers and hostesses here are ridiculously cute,

This is Paul's favorite mural in NY. Seriously.

sweet 19-year-old girls from the neighborhood, and the guy behind the counter is some type of pizza dough kneading Italian Adonis. The girls I was here with kept getting up to wait in line for the bathroom, just so they could stare at him again.

Nicky's Vietnamese Sandwiches

311 Atlantic Ave. btw Hoyt & Smith Sts.

A favorite of Boerum Hill's young, broke, and beautiful class, Nicky's Vietnamese Sandwiches is exactly what the name suggests it is. But it also sells pho, too! A person with a tooth for Vietnamese food can't solely survive on delicious $5 sandwiches, he or she needs some variety for his or her palate. Mmmm … pho.

Bars

Abilene
442 Court St. btw 2nd & 3rd Pls.

As with most bars in random, far flung places in New York, I came
here with my dear associate and colleague Paul. He's a good sport
and puts up with the monotony of visiting bar after bar very well
(he's afflicted with the Thirst like myself). He's also quite observant,
despite his need for corrective lenses, and was the first to point out
that Abilene is not a destination bar by any stretch of the imagination.
But it is a good place to come to if you live in the neighborhood and
feel like playing a board game or partaking in one of their two happy
hours: 5–8pm and 12–1am. At these times, one can procure a pint of
beer or a well drink for $3. Otherwise one's thirst can be pacified (it's
never quenched is it?) with $3 bottles of Bud and $2.50 cans of Genesee Cream Ale. Plus if feeling daring, one may tack on a shot to the
aforementioned Genesee to bring the total to $5. These are the neces-
sary weapons we must use to battle the Thirst.

Boat
175 Smith @ Wyckoff

Despite the name, there really isn't a lot of nautically themed stuff in
this bar except a couple pirate flags, a model boat and a framed picture
of some type of seafaring vessel. I guess I'll have to go to Red Lobster if
I want buoys and netting for ambience. But Red Lobster doesn't have
$3 Miller High Life, a pinball machine or comfy couches ... or does it?
I haven't been in ages, so I don't know, but I do remember that when
I was a kid my grandparents always took me and I would eat the fuck
out of some popcorn shrimp. Dammit, now I kinda wanna make this
about Red Lobster, but I know I shouldn't. One time my girl and I went
to Boat and the female bartender only charged me $4 for a well drink
but charged Krista $5. She was really annoyed and I explained to her
that this shit happens to guys all the time, but that she doesn't notice it
because she's usually on the receiving end of the preferential treatment.
I wonder which one of us will get extra popcorn shrimp at Red Lobster?

Brazen Head

228 Atlantic Ave. @ Court St.

Founded in Dublin in 1198, the Brazen Head is the oldest pub in all of Ireland. The Brooklyn bar of the same name is not nearly as old, but what it lacks in age, it makes up for in free food. On Mondays start your week with free wings; on Wednesday tackle the mid-week blues with free cheese; and work off your Sunday hangover with free bagels. And all that grub can be washed down with $2 PBRs.

Brooklyn Tavern

515 Atlantic Ave. @ 3rd Ave.

Paul and I were walking by here after a long day of research and upon noticing it was a bar, we remembered that we liked bars and decided to go in. It was total serendipity. When we talked to the bartender, we were informed that Bud Light on tap was $2.50. We promptly bought a couple of those and headed towards what looked like a back patio, but it actually turned out to be a huge backyard reminiscent of a house party. And since it was someone's going away party, people were grilling up free hot dogs and s'mores (s'mores make me sticky) and giving them to us. I wouldn't call it fate that we happened upon cheap drinks and free food, no sir, I'd call it awesome. While there's not always a going away party here giving out free food, there is always a grill and you are welcome to bring whatever you want to cook up. Brilliant I say, absolutely brilliant.

Brooklyn Inn

138 Bergen St. @ Hoyt St.

If the Brooklyn Inn were a person, it'd be one of those really fucking cool old guys full of witty comments and wild stories, who wears bow-ties, argyle sweaters and fedoras every day and hang out on park benches waiting to ask you if you know who Emma Goldman was. You know the guys I'm talking about, I'm sure Sean Connery has played one before. Other bars must seriously be jealous of how much better this place looks than them. While the Brooklyn Inn has been through a few incarnations, pretty much everything looks exactly like it did back when the original drinking establishment opened here in 1875. There are huge mirrors that sit behind the imposing, carved dark wood bar, there is a stained glass something or other that might be cabinetry, and there's ornate woodwork throughout the interior, all of which are original. The only thing I'm a little skeptical about is the jukebox; I don't know how popular Traffic was during U.S. Grant's administration. The last time I was here, there were two guys in tuxedos, a handful of cute girls, and a biker in a sleeveless motorcycle jacket who was covered in tattoos. While the crowd isn't always this diverse, especially on weekends, it speaks volumes about this place. Anything as beautiful and unique as the Brooklyn Inn must have friends and admirers of all sorts.

Floyd NY

131 Atlantic Ave. btw Henry and Clinton Sts.

Dotted with various vintage church pews, love seats, chairs, tables, and turn-of-the-century photo portraits of somebody's Bubbie and Zadie, Floyd NY looks like the lovechild of the Salvation Army and an East Village dive bar. And you know what else they have? Motherfucking bocce ball! Where do genius bar owners come from and why can't that place produce more of them? Why would I go to some dipshit place that sells Versace-flavored cosmos for $15 when I could come to Floyd and get a Colt .45 and a bullet (a can of Colt .45 with a shot of Jack or Wild Turkey) for $6? Fuck that! Floyd is the type of place where you can totally meet a hottie who reads Leonard Cohen's poetry, follows professional boxing, can kick the shit out of you at bocce ball, and will take you back to their place around the corner and not make it awkward the next time you see them at the bar. Did I mention I like this place?

Gowanus Yacht Club

323 Smith St. @ President St.

The promise of yachts is a little disappointing. In fact the closest thing to yachts around here are the F and G trains that run beneath this outdoor drinkery. But what it lacks in seafaring vessels, the Gowanus Yacht Club makes up for in cheap beer. Whether your taste is micro or macro, they've got you covered ... well not literally, there's no roof here, but you know what I mean. Because of the aforementioned no roofness, this place is only seasonal, as one would imagine. Who needs roofs when you have cheap booze anyways?

Leo's Corner

481 Court St. @ Nelson St.

I think Leo's Corner is just as surprised that it exists as everybody else is. Why else would they price their drinks so cheaply? All draft beers, other than Guinness, are $2 and all well drinks are $4, all the time. That's fucking awesome! But the awesomeness pretty much stops there. The inside of the place looks like a display room for an interior designer who only decorates the houses of nuevo riche rappers who appear on MTV's *Cribs*. Cheesy doesn't begin to describe it. And the crowd here is fairly frat boyish, which is amazing considering that there aren't any colleges nearby. That said, I've endured a lot worse for cheap drinks.

Montero's Bar & Grill

73 Atlantic Ave. @ Hicks St.

There are lots of dive bars in this book that, for all intents and purposes, are only called such because the drinks are fairly cheap and the clientele looks intentionally scruffy. Montero's does not fall into this category. Montero's is the type of dive bar where old drunks, with noses busted from years of falling down and street fighting, sit and trade stories of the open road or the open sea or the old days. I don't mean this in a romantic way, either; these are the guys who you often hope don't sit next to you on the train. But me, I can appreciate a good yarn every once in awhile, just as much as I can appreciate the $2 PBRs and Rolling Rocks sold here and the many decades worth of memories that seem to fill every inch of the walls. This stretch of Atlantic used to be packed with sailors and longshoremen back in the days when Brooklyn's docks were busy and America hadn't yet outsourced all its labor to cheaper Third World countries. That's obviously changed, as has the rest of New York, and it seems the only thing that hasn't changed since Montero's opened its doors in the 1940s is Montero's itself.

Trout
269 Pacific St. @ Smith St.

During summertime, drinking outdoors is almost a hobby for anybody worth a shit in New York. It's too hot to do anything else outdoors, so why not have some beer and meet some new people? Trout facilitates this by selling PBR for $3 and having drink specials that are determined by spinning of a wheel of fortune. This might be the best use of such a wheel ever since Cicero (the dead Roman) not Merv Griffin (the dead Californian) first thought of the concept. The décor is of picnic tables, old metal Phillies cigar signs, and dingy boats hanging from the rafters, while the bathrooms are lined with ads for old cars and cigarette brands you've never heard of. But the two best pieces of decoration are the framed photo of Curtis Mayfield shaking hands with someone in front of a *Super Fly* banner and the 1916 class photo from Askin College of Embalming that hangs in one of the bathrooms. Apparently Trout serves moderately priced food, too, but I've never eaten it because I'd rather spend my money on whatever special the wheel has dealt me that night.

Shopping

Bookcourt
163 Court St. btw Dean & Pacific Sts.

A solid and sizeable independent bookstore, Bookcourt has a wonderful selection of books and puts on great author events throughout the year. And if you're one of the people who've moved to Cobble Hill so you can breed and push around strollers that cost more than my computer, well then I think you may have picked up the wrong book. But if you're one of these people's poorer friends and want to get them a great book for the little one who rides in that stroller Cadillac, Bookcourt has a big selection of children's literature.

Brooklyn Indie Market
Corner of Smith and Union Sts.

If you want some gear that none of your friends is gonna have, check out the Brooklyn Indie Mart. Every Saturday and Sunday afternoon, local independent designers and artists set up shop here in Carroll Gardens and slang their shit. Supporting indie designers is sexy, so do it!

Community Bookstore
212 Court St. @ Warren St.

This place is so piled with books that part of the Dead Sea Scrolls could be buried in here and no one would know about it. While the prices here are cheap as it is, the owner often discounts the books even further, making it foolish not to buy from them. They also sometimes put out a free book box, and I once got a Bukowski anthology from it. My problem is that I move around so much I always end up having to get rid of all the great books I pick up. Those fuckers are heavy.

Winn Discount
299 Court St. btw Degraw & Douglass Sts.

The only store you'll ever need. You could furnish a luxury bomb shelter here. Whatever that means.

Sights & Entertainment

Gowanus Canal

the thing full of water that runs through
this part of Brooklyn

Gross and sludgy, the water in this canal (which was once one of the
Brooklyn shipping industry's main arteries), is not something you'd
ever want to imbibe, or even let touch your skin. But for some reason
that doesn't stop the Gowanus Dredgers Canoe Club, who paddle
around this old canal and seem to enjoy doing it, too. If this sounds
like your kind of thing, you should visit them at *www.waterfrontmu-
seum.org/dredgers*. I'm personally more interested in its history as a
dumping ground for Mafia bodies and its future as the hot new shit. If
you hadn't heard of the Gowanus Canal up until now, you are sure to
hear more as the city began redeveloping the area surrounding it. My
hopes are that they turn it all into community recreational park land,
but if history is any indicator, the city will probably sell out to greedy
developers and turn this area into ugly fucking high-rise condos and
end up calling the place SoGo or something like that. Let's hope not.

Hank's Saloon

46 3rd Ave. @ Atlantic Ave.

The reason Paul and I came to this bar, named after the late, great
Hank Williams, was that we'd heard a rumor they gave out free hot
dogs and burgers. While we were crestfallen to learn that the free
grubbery no longer existed, our spirits soared after we got drunk off
$3 PBRs. We also managed to learn a lot about Hank's that night. We
learned that the location had been a bar for more than 100 years, but
that Hank's had only resided here for the past eight of them. We also
learned that there is a dilapidated apartment upstairs that has been
abandoned since the '50s and can only be accessed by a hidden staircase inside the bar. When asked, the barkeep said it was creepy as
hell up there. And best of all, we learned that there is free live music
(mostly country, bluegrass, new grass etc.) almost every night of the

This photo pretty much sums up my life.

week, including Monday night's Country Karaoke. Considering that it's a live band for karaoke, how many fucking songs do you think they must know?

Manhole at Atlantic Ave. & Court St

Paul and I were walking by this intersection one day when he pointed to a manhole and told me that underneath us was an abandoned LIRR tunnel that had only recently been rediscovered, and that the only way to access it was through that manhole. I of course told him that I thought he was a dirty fucking liar and that I wouldn't tolerate this kind of shit anymore. Used to my sudden outbreaks of belittling name calling, he calmly responded by telling me to look it up and "decide who's a dirty fucking liar then, asshole". Which I did, and he was right. According to *www.forgotten-ny.com* (which is one of the best websites in the world for anyone who loves New York history), the tunnel was built in 1844 and used for 14 years for passenger transit. In the 1860s it was sealed up and largely forgotten about until 1979 when a man named Bob Diamond heard a rumor about it on a radio program. Then with the help of the NYCDEP and Brooklyn Union Gas, Diamond was allowed to go down the manhole and explore it for himself. If you're interested in learning more about this and seeing photos, check out, *www.forgotten-ny.com/subways/tunnel/tunnel.html*. You were right this time Paul, but I'll catch you one of these days.

They say happiness is a warm gun. I say it's a cold beer. Photo by Maleeha Khan

BOERUM HILL, COBBLE HILL and CARROLL GARDENS

Grub-a-dub-dub
1 Amazon Cafe
2 Bedouin Tent Restaurant
3 Cubana Café
4 Donut House
5 El Nuevo Portal
6 Hanco's Bubble Tea & Vietnamese Sandwiches
7 Joe's Restaurant
8 Joe's Superette
9 Joya
10 Lucali
11 Nicky's Vietnamese Sandwiches

DRINKS DRINKS DRINKS
12 Abilene
13 Boat
14 Brooklyn Inn
15 Brooklyn Tavern
16 Floyd NY
17 Gowanus Yacht Club
18 Leo's Corner
19 Montero's Bar & Grill
20 Trout

Shopping
21 Bookcourt
22 Brooklyn Indie Market
23 Community Bookstore
24 Winn Discount

Stuffis to See and Do
25 Gowanus Canal
26 Hank's Saloon
27 Manhole at Atlantic Ave. & Court St.

Free Food Bitches!!
28 Brazen Head

Herbivore Friendly
29 Jill's Vegan Organic Café

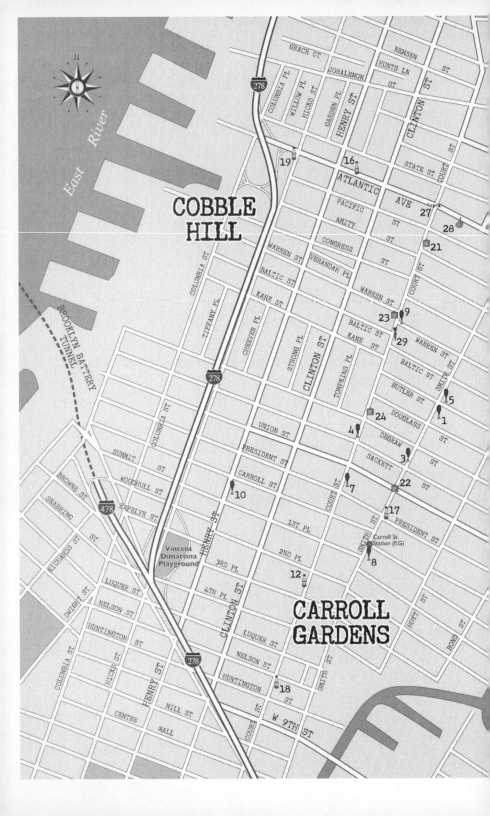

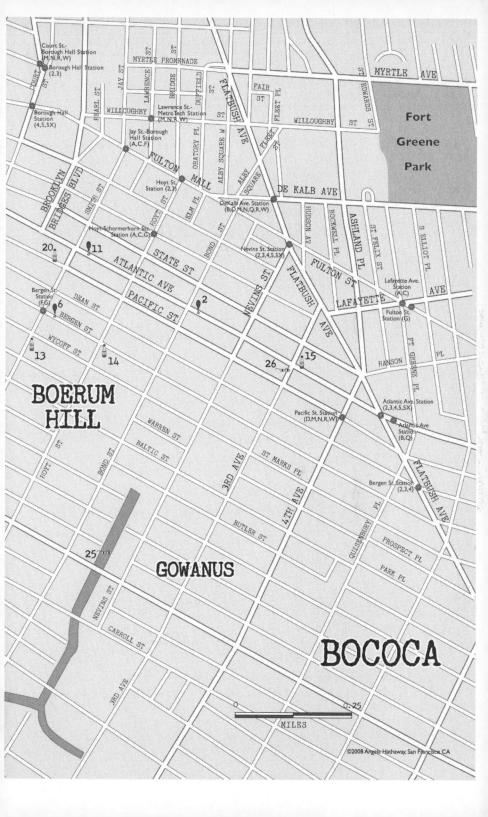

Park Slope

When I first moved to New York, I lived in Carroll Gardens. I had called my Grandma Ethyl, who is originally from Brooklyn but now lives near Baltimore, to tell her that I was living in Brooklyn. When I said I lived in Carroll Gardens, she said she hadn't heard of it (it was called South Brooklyn back then) so I told her it was near Park Slope, to which she replied, "Very fancy!". Considering that she was born in the 1920s, she was right.

For most of its existence, Park Slope has been considered one of the loveliest parts of New York City. During the late 19th century, many wealthy Brooklynites built huge mansions along Prospect Park West, while people of more modest means moved into gorgeous brownstones in the same vicinity. All of these people wanted to be near Prospect Park, which had been opened in 1867.

While the neighborhood enjoyed prosperity until the middle of the 20th century, Park Slope became a working class area for much of the 1960s, '70s, and '80s. It wasn't until the 1990s that it once again began to see a resurgence of wealthier families. These days Park Slope tends to be a bit of a stroller ghetto full of upwardly mobile couples and their spawn. It's also home to a large number of lesbians, which is why it is jokingly referred to in the LGBT community as

My block is about 1/805th as pretty as this one.

Dyke Slope. The proper name, Park Slope, is derived from the fact that this area slopes uphill toward the park. Very creative.

Park Slope's borders are roughly Flatbush Ave. to the north, Prospect Park to the east, Greenwood Cemetery to the south, and 4th Ave. to the west. Gowanus begins on the other side of 4th Ave. and a couple of things technically there might have made it into this section. Who really gives a fuck?

Food

7th Ave. Donuts

324 7th Ave. btw 8th & 9th Sts.

The prices here are cheap even by Kansas City standards, not that I've ever been to KC (other than the airport), but I figure it's gotta be a cheap place. A jumbo cheeseburger only costs $3, a BLT is $3.75, and from 6–11am, $3.25 gets you two eggs, juice, coffee, potatoes, and toast. That's what the fuck I'm talking about; 7th Ave. Donuts is the stuff dreams are made of. It's more than 30 years old, open 24 hours, has a long lunch counter, lots of booths, and thick waitresses with bedroom eyes.

Blue Sky Bakery

53 5th Ave. @ Bergen St.

I'd like to be the first one to say "fuck the great New York cupcake debate". I'm jumping ship, and to be honest, I never really cared anyways. I was just in it for the sugar rush. I've decided that muffins are the new hotness (remember you heard it here first) and that Blue Sky is the baddest bitch in Brooklyn when it comes to the muffin game. Hell, it might be the best shit in the whole city. Who the hell thought up a pumpkin apple walnut muffin? That's on some Copernicus shit, straight up changing the way cats are looking at the universe. Whoever the hell you are, you owe me some new underwear.

City Sub

450 Bergen St. btw 5th Ave. and Flatbush Ave.

I'd like to think that the people who work here were all test tube babies born and reared for the sole purpose of making perfect sandwiches. Because that's what's done here. These people must sleep on egg crates in the cellar and wake up at 4am everyday for bread slicing calisthenics. These are not sandwich artists, these are craftsmen (and women) who care less about giving you your sandwich quickly than they do about making it the best fucking thing you'll eat that day. Now if they could only do the same thing with the assholes who work at the DMV, the world would be a better place.

Gorilla Coffee
97 5ᵗʰ Ave. @ Park Pl.

People love this shit. So much so, that other places in the neighborhood carry their coffee. I'm told that it's good, but I don't drink coffee (one of the few vices I don't have), so you'll have to judge it for yourself. They have a great logo. It's a picture of a gorilla. I like gorillas. *Gorillas in the Mist* made me sad.

Maria's Mexican Bistro
669 Union St. @ 4ᵗʰ Ave.

Well Maria, I'll be the first to admit that I misjudged you. You really do know how to shake some pots and pans; you make up some pretty tasty food. It's a bit more expensive than I'm usually willing to pay for cuisine from NAFTA's southernmost member, but it's damn good. I've got you figured out though, you sweet and seductive temptress; your wiles and charms are no match for my Broke-Ass sixth sense. I know all about your $5.95 lunch special where I get to choose an appetizer, an entrée and a soda. Yes, yes, I know all about how good your main dishes are; people won't stop running their mouths about them. But listen love, I'm trying to save up for a Cadillac, and $12 entrees just aren't in my financial plan ... whatchu mean "you don't have no financial plan and why you want a Cadillac for anyways?" It's a Caddy baby, what the fuck kinda question is that? Come to think of it, I'm not sure this thing between us is gonna work out. Sure I love your *elote* more than God loves to smite people, but is that enough? How bout we talk it over when I come in next week for lunch?

Mr. Wonton
73 7ᵗʰ Ave. @ Berkeley Pl.

Mr. Wonton is not a person, it is an average Chinese place where almost all things cost less than $10 and the lunch special is $5.50. It also has big windows for looking out of. I was so disappointed that he wasn't real because I had tons of questions to ask him like: who the hell General Tso is and why Chinese people are always yelling at me?

Purity Diner

289 7th Ave. @ 8th St.

One of the waiters here is like 70 years old and still working tables. Every time I see this, and I do see it in New York diners sometimes, it scares the shit out of me and I say to myself, "Oh fuck, oh fuck, oh fuck, oh fuck … please don't let that be me in the future. Oh fuck, oh fuck, oh fuck…." For anyone who has ever waited tables, it's the most frightening thing in the world. Purity Diner opened in 1929; how long has this dude been working here? Maybe he's just some super rich guy who loves waiting tables and does this to keep his mind sharp during retirement. I sure fucking hope so. As for the food here, it's pretty good and decently priced, too, but the real winner is the two eggs with cheese and bacon on a roll for $3. The only catch is that you have to get it to go.

'Snice

315 5th Ave. @ 3rd St.

(see p. 126 *West Village)

Song

295 5th Ave. btw 1st & 2nd Sts.

Wait, didn't I just see this place in Cobble Hill but instead of being called Song, it was called Joya? Let's see, weekend DJ? Check. Super modern and chic interior with an open kitchen, brick walls, and low lighting? Check. Everything on the menu under $8? Check. What the fuck is going on here? Do these places know each other exist? Where are all these Tribeca looking restaurants with Philly prices coming from? I want answers dammit!

The V-Spot Café

156 5th Ave. btw Degraw & Douglass Sts.

Sounding like some place one of my lesbian friends would tell me to touch my girlfriend, the V-Spot is actually a 100 percent vegan restaurant, which means they're not to be trusted with important matters. While the average entrée here costs $15, all the wraps, soups, sandwiches, burgers etc., are under $10. There's also a small collection of books to peruse while you eat, which all seem to be about progressive ideas. Is there such a thing as a right wing vegan? All I know is that vegan stuff tastes funny.

Bars

4ᵗʰ Ave. Pub

76 4ᵗʰ Ave. @ Bergen St.

Last time I was in here, there was a collection of religious Jews hanging out at the bar, and while this is Brooklyn, it's still not the most common sight. I wondered to myself what they were doing here. Were they doing research for some guidebook like I was? Am I gonna be competing with *Bupkis-Ass Sholomo's Guide to Meeting Drunk Shiksehs in New York City*? Or were they here for the same reason as everyone else—the extensive beer list? Who knows? All I care about is that 4ᵗʰ Ave. Pub gives out free popcorn and that you can get an awesome 25-ounce Heffeweizen for $7 which is actually a pretty good deal when you consider that a 12-ounce bottle of Bud is $4. Maybe that's why everyone loves this bar so much.

Cattyshack

249 4ᵗʰ Ave. @ Carroll St.

It's actually pretty amazing how few lesbian bars there are in New York. There are hundreds of bars for gay men (see: the entire West Side of Manhattan) and a few dozen that are mixed gay and lesbian, but really Cattyshack is one of the few strictly lesbian bars in New York City, and certainly the only one with any remote claim to the title of Broke-Ass. Considering it's rarity, I'm happy to announce that they totally came correct with this motherfucker. The Cattyshack is two stories, with two dance floors, go-go dancers, a pool table, and a wicked rooftop patio. Word! Plus, they also do a thing on Thursdays and Sundays where $20 gets you all-you-can-drink domestic beer and all-you-eat BBQ. Makes you wanna go right now, huh? Me too, especially considering that I've never actually been and had to pry all this information out of friends of mine. So what if I'm a little intimidated; have you seen what Paul and I look like? Do you really think they'd let us in?

Jackie's 5th Amendment

406 5th Ave. @ 7th St.

Five people were in the bar when Paul and I walked in around midnight. One of them was a bartender in her late 50s/early 60s who was missing a few teeth, while the other four were shitfaced, chubby, middle-aged and dancing to disco music emanating from the jukebox. Neither of us had had enough drinks yet to handle this caliber of shit, so we saddled up to the bar and ordered a round of Budweisers. Apparently Jackie's was about to close for the night, but a lifetime of serving drinks had given our sweet bartender the talent to spot those of us who had the Thirst, and she let us buy a couple rounds and answered some of my questions in her thick Brooklyn accent. It seems that Jackie owned the bar for a long time before she passed away a few years ago, and before that it was a bar with ties to the mob (hence the name). It was also a speakeasy back in the 1930s. Our patron saint of prolonging last call also told us that the best deal in the house was the bucket of six 7-ounce beers for $9 and that the peak hours here are during the day. We thanked her for her hospitality and headed towards the door where I saw a flyer advertising a local stickball game as "The Olympic Sport of Brooklyn". Sometimes drinking with old drunks is more interesting than drinking with young ones.

Lighthouse Tavern

243 5th Ave. @ Carroll St.

Nautically themed with a back patio to boot, this sports bar caters to Red Sox fans who like to feel exotic by drinking $3 Imperial beer from Costa Rica. Truthfully, the most interesting thing about this place is the backroom with the couches and board games. I give this place a resounding *meh*. Plus, I hate the fucking Patriots.

Lucky 13 Saloon

273 13th St. @ 5th Ave.

Beavis and Butthead are alive and well and living in Brooklyn. They go to the Lucky 13 Saloon on a nightly basis and rock out with the other metalheads, goths and punks, who patronize this bar. If you list Pantera, Ministry, the Misfits, Mastadon or Black Flag as your favorite band, you should probably be here every night, too, especially on Thursdays for Scaryoke, which is karaoke done to music by bands that sound like those I just listed. Plus they often have hot girls with tattoos and brightly died hair dancing on polls on the bar. Ever since junior high, I've had a thing for girls with dyed bright hair, and one of the highlights of my life was singing Danzig at karaoke, so I like this place a lot. If you don't know who Beavis and Butthead are and don't like $2 beers, this probably isn't the bar for you.

O'Connor's
39 5th Ave. btw Bergen & Dean Sts.

The world needs O'Connor's more than O'Connor's needs the world. I say this because O'Connor's lets us believe that there are still some things worth romanticizing. How else would you describe a bar that opened in 1931 (prohibition wasn't repealed until 1933) and which, as of a few proprietors ago, was owned by a Brooklyn native named Dutch Joe? The last time I hung out here, the bartender was a guy my age who seemed like he unintentionally dressed like James Dean and looked like he could've been a bartender in any decade from the '50s on. The only songs he played were early soul music and he was cool in the traditional sense of the word, never smiling but not unapproachable. O'Connor's feels like a Jim Jarmusch movie, both strange and wonderful. While the place gets crackin' on the weekends, I prefer to spend my time with the old timers who come here during the week and talk about all the great New York City bars that have come and gone. The drinks are cheap, so it's easy to sit here and talk all night.

Pacific Standard
82 4th Ave. @ St. Marks Pl.

Well, it looks like you won't be seeing any pictures of this bar because dumb ass me forgot to take my camera out the night I researched it, so I'll just have to use lots of adjectives. What's not to like about Pacific Standard? They carry mostly West Coast microbrews, are decorated with California and Washington flags, have a neat stained glass window and even fucking It's-It ice cream sandwiches!! Wait, I don't think you know what those are unless you've lived in the Bay. Too bad for you. Pacific Standard also has a large backroom with a skylight that makes it seem like an arboretum filled with books, couches, and drunk people instead of … um, arbors. The cheap beers here are $3 Shaefer and Miller High Life, but you can get a great microbrew for $5. Because of the size of this space, the owners also throw cool events like the poetry and fiction reading series (how about shit talking guidebook reading series?). Here's a word of advice: if you do decide to make this one of your regular spots, make sure to sign up for a frequent-drinker card. It gets you special privileges. Unfortunately immunity from being 86'd isn't one of them.

Smith's Bar

440 5th Ave. @ 9th St.

Wanna see a whole bunch of modern day Bukowskis who don't have all that genius baggage? Come to Smith's Bar. It's full of old drunk fucks who drank away their good years and figure that drinking away their bad years won't make a goddamn difference at this point either. You might call this place sad, but I call it the place that sells $1.50 mugs of Bud.

Union Hall

702 Union St. @ 5th Ave.

Looking like a private club for old rich white guys who smoke cigars and make wagers that end up ruining the local economies of small developing nations, Union Hall is surprisingly cheap. With the plush couches, dark wood, a big fireplace, floor to ceiling bookcases, amazing wallpaper and paintings of old guys in fez hats, it really looks like one of those places that would have a sign outside saying, "No Blacks or Jews Allowed". Thankfully it's not because otherwise, neither me nor most of my friends would get to enjoy the $3 PBRs, Negro Modelos, and Rolling Rocks. Even the bathroom here is nice–it smells all fruity and lotion-y like a hot chick's bedroom, which is convenient because there are plenty of them here. Downstairs is a small venue and a display of taxidermy animals (how many places have taxidermy in this book? I've lost count), while upstairs has bocce ball. It's apparently owned by the same guys who own Floyd. They're starting to be my own personal heroes.

Shopping

Bierkraft

191 Fifth Avenue @ Berkeley Pl.

When I asked my friend Aaron about places for the book, he wrote so eloquently about Bierkraft that I figured I'd just give it to you in his words:

> *Open seven Days a Week. Take a Tuesday night off and stop by this Park Slope gem for a bier tasting of outrageous sorts. Ask for Ben Granger, he's an owner and a god. He may look like a normal dude. But just ask him about beer, cheese, or mushrooms, and you'll never want to leave his side. It's a great shop, not totally pricey but a growler (an old school jug) or some local brew will treat you right for a few nights, and looks a hell of a lot cooler than a sixer.*

Brooklyn Superhero Supply Co.

372 5th Ave @ 5th St.

Visiting the Brooklyn Superhero Supply Co. suddenly cheapened my entire childhood experience. Before that moment, I had thought that tying my blankey around my neck when I was a five-year-old and pretending I was Superman was cute and imaginative; now I just think I was a little retarded. I mean how can my blankey and some pajama bottoms with footies compare to real capes, goggles, and masks? They even have a cape-testing area where you stand over a fan and it makes your cape billow up behind you, and a Devillainizer machine that asks you a bunch of questions and then tells you what kind of villain you are (I was a fucking realtor!). The best part about this place is that all the money made here goes to supporting 826 New York, which is a nonprofit started by author Dave Eggers that helps kids with their creative writing skills. And

Brooklyn Superhero Supply Co: Cheapening my childhood since 2004.

you wanna know how to get to 826 New York? There's a secret passageway at the back of this store!

P.S. 321 Flea Market

7th Ave @ 1st St.

Well there's not much one can really say about a flea market. You can get lots of cool shit here and you can get lots of crap here. Everything is negotiable, so make sure to bargain with them.

Unnameable Books

456 Bergen St. btw 5th Ave. & Flatbush Ave.

This great independent bookstore used to be called Adam's Books until a bitch-ass textbook company called the Adams Book Company filed a cease and desist order over the name. Really? That is some childish shit! Do you know how many bars are called the White Horse Tavern or the Blarney Stone? You don't see any of them filing lawsuits against each other. Adams Book Company should be ashamed of themselves. Textbooks are a scam to begin with. I remember in college not being able to sell back a two-year-old Spanish textbook because the company was putting out a new edition. It's not like they discovered more fucking Spanish. How many ways can you explain that Maria has a new backpack? Fuck the Adams Book Company and long live Unnameable Books! Make sure to support them in their effort to bring affordable used books, poetry and zines to the masses.

P.S. They'll probably try to sue me now, too.

Sights & Entertainment

Montauk Club

25 8th Ave. @ Lincoln Pl.

Places like the Montauk Club don't let people like me inside of them, but there's nothing stopping me from standing outside and gawking at the magnificent architecture. Oh yes, and I gawk loudly, too, just to spite them ... in fact they thought I was having a seizure. Maybe if we all come here together sometime and gawk loudly in unison, they will let us in and give us a tour.* I had actually taken a photo of this gorgeous private club built in the 1890s, but it kinda sucked, so I didn't include it in this book. Which means that you'll just have to go see it for yourself.

Prospect Park West

The street that runs along the west side of Prospect Park

One of the best free things you can do in Brooklyn, besides going to Prospect Park, is taking a stroll down the street that runs next to it. Many of Brooklyn's late–19th century millionaires built impressive mansions on Prospect Park West so they could be near the park. While the chances of you getting to see the inside of one of these beauties is far less likely than you getting to see the inside of a jail cell, walking down the street and marveling at the buildings is completely free.

Southpaw

125 5th Ave. btw Sterling Pl. & Douglass St.

Williamsburg is a bitch to get to, Manhattan is 25 minutes away, and you're in Park Slope desperately wanting to see live music. For fuck's sake, aren't you glad Southpaw is around? It's no slouch either. Southpaw is actually one of the better venues in NYC, because it has a large capacity, good sound and gets great acts. Among those who've

---

Publisher's note: We are not responsible for any actions you take after heeding Stuart's advice.

I love any building that looks like it belongs in a comic book.

played here are Ted Leo, KRS-One, Cat Power, and TV on the Radio. So now that you have nothing to complain about, what are you gonna do with the rest of your night? How about buying me a drink?

PARK SLOPE

♦ Grub-a-dub-dub
1   7th Ave. Donuts
2   City Sub
3   Blue Sky Bakery
4   Gorilla Coffee
5   Maria's Mexican Bistro
6   Mr. Wonton
7   Purity Diner
8   Song

▮ DRINKS DRINKS DRINKS
9   4th Ave. Pub
10 Cattyshack
11 Jackie's 5th Amendment
12 Lighthouse Tavern
13 Lucky 13 Saloon
14 O'Connor's
15 Pacific Standard
16 Smith's Bar
17 Union Hall

▩ Shopping
18 Bierkraft
19 Brooklyn Superhero Supply Co.
20 P.S. 321 Flea Market
21 Unnameable Books

⚓ Stuffis to See and Do
22 Montauk Club
23 Prospect Park West
24 Southpaw

♦ Herbivore Friendly
25 Earth Tonez Café
26 'Snice
27 The V-Spot Café

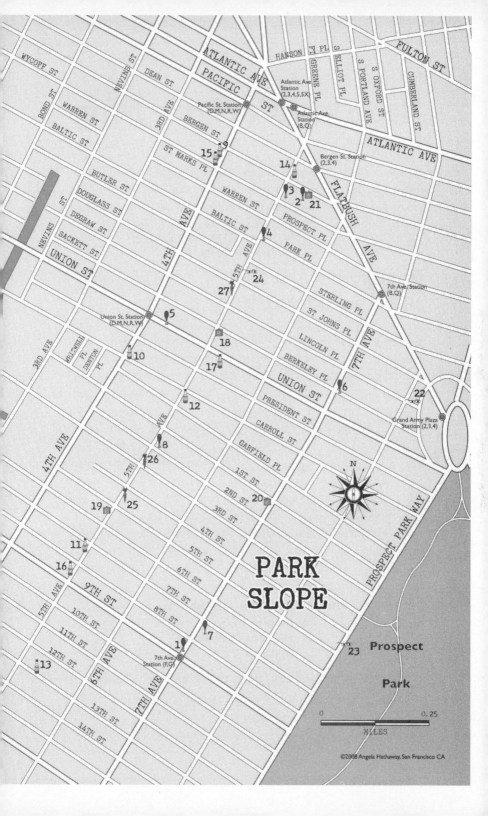

Brooklyn off the Map

There are so many neighborhoods in Brooklyn that it would have taken me a lifetime to research them all for this book, so sorry if your particular neighborhood wasn't represented. That being said, the following are some really terrific things this borough has to offer that are actually some of the best places in the whole book.

Prospect Park and the Near Vicinity

Prospect Park: The big mass of foliage and grass in the middle of Brooklyn. The main entrance is at Grand Army Plaza.

Smaller and hipper than it's Manhattan sibling, Prospect Park, which opened in 1867, was designed by the same people who created Central Park, Fredrick Law Olmstead and Calvert Vaux. Good things happen in Prospect Park, and why shouldn't they? It's a fucking 585-acre urban paradise where puppies and babies frolic in the grass, birds sing in the trees, and grown folks barbecue and drink brown bagged tall boys. There are few better places in the world to deal with your Sunday morning palsy than on a blanket in Prospect Park on a nice day with some good friends, some good weed, and some good tunes. But for those of you who, for some strange reason, prefer to do something active with your weekend instead of lying in the grass with your slacker friends recovering from a hangover, here are some other great things to do in Prospect Park:

• Go to the Prospect Park Zoo. It's not quite the Bronx Zoo, but hey, they got animals and shit and it's only six bucks to get in.

• Check out the nation's only urban Audubon center, which has something to do with interactive exploration of nature or something like that.

This is why Prospect Park is awesome.

• Play some baseball or soccer or frisbee or tennis … or don't.

• Hike around in the trees since this the closest you'll get to forest in Brooklyn.

• Go fishing. According to my friend Ben, they haven't done it in a few years, but they used to stock the lake here. In fact, it has the highest concentration of largemouth bass in New York State. You're supposed to have a state fishing license but nobody ever checks. It's real good fishing considering you're smack in the middle of the largest city in the U.S., and it's a fun, free, way to kill an afternoon. Plus if you're lucky, maybe there will be a big family reunion BBQ or something, and you can make some friends and get some free food.

• Lie around on a blanket in the sun, nursing your hangover and chilling with friends. Oh, I already said that.

• See free concerts all summer long at the band shell by world famous artists like Isaac Hayes, Phillip Glass and Medeski, Martin and Wood. Check out the Celebrate Brooklyn concert series at *www.briconline. org* to get info on the summer lineups.

• If you honestly can't figure out anything else to do here, well then you're just shit out of luck.

Brooklyn Botanic Gardens: 100 Washington Ave. @ Montgomery St.

52 acres of loveliness greet you when you arrive at this world-renowned botanic garden. Now, I'm not much of a plantologist (I barely even eat vegetables), so I'm not gonna sit here and talk about a bunch of guff I know nothing about. Instead I'm gonna give you one solid suggestion: come here when the cherry blossom trees are in bloom; it's stunning. Don't know when that is? No worries, me neither, and we don't have to. You can just go to their website www.bbg.org, and they give you a month-by-month breakdown of which flowers are blooming when. Genius, right?

Brooklyn Museum of Art: 200 Eastern Parkway @ Washington Ave.

The second largest museum in New York and one of the top museums in the world, the Brooklyn Museum of Art has a ginormous collection ranging from a very well-respected treasure trove of Egyptian artifacts to pieces by artists living in Brooklyn today. I saw one of my all-time favorite pieces of art here at the Brooklyn Museum. It's a painting by Kehinde Wiley called *Napoleon Leading the Army over the Alps,* which takes the posture of a famous 1801 painting of Napoleon on a horse, and puts a 21st century black man in camo and Tims in the Frenchman's place. It's fucking brilliant. While the admission to the museum is always a suggested donation (pay what you wish), the absolute best time to come here is on the first Saturday of the month when the whole place turns into a free party from 5–11pm with live music, performances and drinks for sale.

New York Puppet Library: Inside the Soldiers and Sailors Arch in Grand Army Plaza

What if I told you that were you to enter the Soldiers and Sailors Arch in Grand Army Plaza, you would be transported to a land of life-size ponies, birds, monsters, monkeys, dragons and more? You'd probably say, "Here? In Brooklyn? What kind of drugs are you on? Talkin' bout some *Labyrinth* ass shit and tryin' to get my ass up in some magical arch at Prospect Park. Hell no, I'm not goin'. You've done lost your goddamn mind." I know, I can hardly believe it myself, but it's real and it's fucking sweet. Just walk up the staircase and feast your eyes upon scores and scores of giant puppets that are there, not just to be stared at, but to be actually *borrowed* should you ever need a puppet. That's why it's a puppet library and not a puppet museum. I mean really, a puppet museum? Come on, who's ever heard of that? That's just absurd.

P.S. Since I wrote this I heard a rumor that they may have moved the puppet library to Brooklyn College.

Brooklyn Heights and the Near Vicinity

Brooklyn Heights Promenade: Runs from Montague St. to Middagh St. and the nearest parallel street is Columbia Heights.

Just out of pissing distance from the lovely Brooklyn Bridge and just above (totally in pissing distance) of the remarkably less attractive BQE, sits the Brooklyn Heights Promenade. This public park has a staggering view of the East River, Lower Manhattan, the Empire State building, possibly the Chrysler Building and definitely the Statue of Liberty. There is also a view of Brooklyn Bridge Park, or at least where they plan on building it. The Promenade itself looks like the type of place where secret meetings or money handoffs happen in movies. I guess, if I was doing a money handoff, I'd like it to be somewhere with a nice view as well.

Empire Fulton State Park & Brooklyn Bridge Park: Directly under the Brooklyn Bridge

Right under the Brooklyn Bridge are Empire Fulton State Park (EFSP) and Brooklyn Bridge Park (BBP), and as far as I know, the only thing separating them is the Bridge itself. On the north side is EFSP, which is run by the state and is possibly the best place in the city to get good photos of the Brooklyn Bridge. It's a really pretty little park on the water that has the preserved ruins of a couple hundred-year-old coffee and tobacco warehouse on its grounds. The BBP on the other hand is really not much to look at ... yet. Currently, it's a little bit of grassland surrounding unused warehouse space, which is going to be a huge waterfront park, whenever they finish the fucker. The BBP is going to be run by the city. I'm just elated they're not letting developers turn all this land into goddamn condos.

Grimaldi's Pizza: 19 Old Fulton St. btw Water & Front Sts.

Grimaldi's is one of only a handful of places still allowed to use a coal oven which were outlawed in the '70s to save the environment. But you can't fucking remove a 200-year-old oven. It's a national fucking landmark! Just ask all the tourists. Pizza: 1. Environment: 0.*

Midwood

Di Fara Pizzeria: 1424 Ave. J @ E. 15th St.

This is it, you've finally found it. You've been waiting the whole book to find out where the best pizza in New York is and you were just about to give up, weren't you? Well here it is, way the fuck out here in Midwood, and holy shit is this pizza gorgeous. Domenico De Marco has been hand-making each pizza, personally, at this far-flung location for over 40 years, and they are remarkable. People come from all over the city to sometimes wait in line for an hour, just to have some of this magic. And you know what the secret ingredient is? Neither do I (you thought I was gonna say love, huh?), but I'm afraid that if this old guy kicks the bucket as soon as he looks like he's going to, he'll take the damn secret to his grave. The man doesn't let anyone else touch the pizza, for fucks sake. Let's just hope that in his will, he leaves the recipe to the people of New York.

Red Hook

Red Hook Ball Fields: Clinton St. & Bay St.

The Red Hook Ball Fields is the perfect cure for the missing-Latin-America blues. Honestly, it's like a dream team of food vendors, all hailing from various parts of Latin America, who get together to gangbang your taste buds with one of the best culinary experiences of your life. Papusas from El Salvador, arepas from Colombia, tacos from Mexico, elote from Cuba, ceviche from Peru, and whatever the hell it is that they eat in Guatemala, can all be found here. And it's all so fucking cheap, too! Come on any weekend day in the summer and fall to fill your belly with this amazing food, and get the free entertainment of watching ten-year-old kids play soccer.

Coney Island

To be honest, I don't know what state Coney Island will be in by the time you get your hands on this book, so I wanna make a suggestion: go there as soon as you can, so you can see it while it still exists. It may not be the one of a kind place that it is now for very much longer.

Sent from the desk of Paul T. Alkaly, Correspondent at large

Ever since the trains first reached Coney Island, it has always been the playground of the working class. It's a world famous ocean side carnival, replete with rides, games, food stands (you can't eat everything, but you can try), and one of the last remaining circus sideshows in the US. It's really one of the best things in all of New York City and a vital part of its history. Recently though, the city has been accepting bids to redevelop Coney Island and turn it into what amounts to basically a mall with big chains like Niketown, highrise hotels, and you guessed it, motherfucking condos. There would still be about nine acres of carnival left but that's pretty meager considering that at its peak the Coney Island amusements spanned 70 acres. It would be the most disgusting thing possible, a seaside Las Vegas without the gambling. Capitalism has no mercy; aren't rich people content with the Hamptons?

So as I said, get out there and see Coney Island while it still exists. Eat a Nathan's hot dog from the original location, ride the Cyclone, play a game and win your sweetie a prize, go through a haunted house, see the sideshow, get stuck by a hypodermic needle in the sand–have a Coney Island experience while you can. Also, make sure to check out *www.coneyisland.com*, the website for Coney Island USA, a nonprofit dedicated to preserving as much of this wonderland as possible. They are the ones responsible for the Coney Island Museum, the Coney Island Circus Sideshow (and sideshow school), Burlesque at the Beach, and the Mermaid Parade, a gonzo summer Mardi Gras festival celebrating Coney Island's past.

P.S. The most unique of any of Coney Island's attractions, Lilliputia, existed from 1904 to 1911 and was a "Midget City". The 300 Little People who inhabited this 80 x 175 foot, half-scale cardboard city, had been culled from circuses throughout the US, and were encouraged to take part in sexually promiscuous activities to entertain the attraction's visitors. This led to 80 percent of babies born in Lilliputia to be born out of wedlock. In addition to orgies, onlookers watched the inhabitants take part in everyday activities like running a midget parliament and going to the Midget Theater. They even had their own midget fire department. Unfortunately, the fire department must not have been very good because the whole city burned down in 1911. Lilliputia sounds infinitely better than reality TV.

Queens

Oh Queens, I wish I'd had enough time and space to include you in this book. There is so much to love about you, my vixen, but it's just that sometimes you seem a world away. I love that you're the most ethnically diverse county in the world, and that I can get off the train in **Jackson Heights** and have it feel like I just stepped into Calcutta … kinda. And then three blocks over I almost feel like I've wandered into the country of Colombia. I love that **Astoria** is still an ethnically Greek neighborhood, yet it has a few blocks that are almost entirely Egyptian, and includes the amazing **Kebab Café** (2512 Steinway St. @ 25th Ave.). Plus, there's Astoria's famed **Bohemian Hall and Beer Garden** (2919 24th Ave @ 29th St.) which is a Queens institution and has been serving up Czech beer and culture for more than 100 years. You also have New York's best Thai food restaurant, **Sripraphai** (6413 39th Ave. @ 64th St.) in your neighborhood of **Woodside**. I'd ask if you could be any more perfect, but I know you'd respond, "yes" and lead me to **Corona,** where I'd get a world class Italian Ice at **The Lemon Ice King of Corona** (5202 108th St. @ 52nd Ave.).

Not only are you tasty my dear, but you're hip and cultured as well. **Long Island City** is quickly becoming such a cool place to be because of it's art scene, loft spaces and bars, but also because of the fantastic contemporary art museum **PS1** (2225 Jackson Ave. @ 46th Ave.). And that's not it's only museum either; it also has the Queens branch of the **Museum of Modern Art** (45-20 33rd St. @ Queens Blvd.). Plus, **Flushing** has a museum of its own. The **Queens Museum of Art** (51st Ave btw Grand Central Pkwy & 111th St.) not only has a great collection, but is also home to the 9,335 square foot Panorama of the City of New York, a miniature model that includes every single building constructed before 1992 in all five boroughs.

Yes Queens, you certainly have a lot to offer a lad like me, but the one thing that bugs me about you is that you're just like every girl I've ever dated; you confuse the fuck out of me. Why do you have to keep sending me mixed signals by doing shit like having 43rd Ave. cross 43rd St. while 39th Pl. is just around the corner? That's just retarded.

The (soon to be famous) List of Free Food

Ah yes. The moment you've all been waiting for. You can't bullshit me. We both know the real reason you bought (or stole) this book. I could have filled the rest of the pages with the most insightful social criticism yet written in the 21st century (yeah right, this is bathroom reading) and you would still have picked it up because of the (soon to be famous) List of Free Food. When you tell your friends about this book, you'll probably be like, "Yeah, that motherfucker Stuart is kinda a douche bag, but at least he gave me all these places to eat free food." I hope you enjoy filling your little bellies with all these goodies, and if so, buy me a drink if we ever meet. Also, don't forget to tip on the mandatory drink that you have to purchase at these fine (and not so fine) establishments. Without further ado, here we go:

Financial District

Ryan Maguire's Ale House: 28 Cliff St. btw John & Fulton Sts.

Bless you Ryan Maguire, you sweet Irish bastard, for giving out free food during happy hour from 5–7pm, Monday–Friday. Wings and pasta my not be traditional Irish food, but then again, I'm not Irish.

Civic Center, Chinatown & Little Italy

The Spring Lounge: 48 Spring St. @ Mulberry St.

According to my notes they have free bagels on Sundays and free hot dogs on Wednesdays. My notes never lie ... most of the time. See p. 41

Soho & Tribeca

Cupping Room Café: 359 W. Broadway btw Grand & Broome Sts.

What the fuck is a cupping room? Apparently it's a place that gives out free wings at the bar and ½ off drinks from 4:30–7:30pm everyday.

Lower East Side

Boss Tweed's: 115 Essex St. btw Rivington & Delancey Sts.

Instead of trying to buy your votes, this Boss Tweed is just trying to buy your love and affection (and business) by giving out free wings and pizza from 5–7pm, Monday–Friday.

Iggy's: 132 Ludlow St. @ Rivington St.

Tuesday is free hot dog night at Iggy's and if I'm not mistaken, they also give them out during happy hour throughout the week. Depending on who's working, there are generally free snacks on the bar like popcorn, peanuts and chips. See p. 80

East Village

11th St. Bar: 510 E. 11th St. @ Ave. A

While I advise coming here during the week for some free live music, which often includes a traditional Irish music session, I endorse visiting on Fridays from 4–7pm even more wholeheartedly. This is when they give out free wings.

Aroma Kitchen & Wine Bar: 36 E. 4th St. btw Lafayette St. & Bowery

At Aroma, *aperitivo* means from 4:30–7:30pm, $15 you gets a flight of three wines and an antipasto platter. Is this considered free food? I guess it's all in the way you look at it. *Aperitivo* sounds awfully sexy doesn't it?

Cha An: 230 E. 9th St. btw 2nd & 3rd Aves.

Monday–Thursday, buy some sake, wine or beer and the fine people of Cha An will send out three small appetizers. Hooray for them (and us)!

Cooper 35: 35 Cooper Square @ 3rd Ave.

Buy a drink and get free edamame every night but Friday and Saturday. I've been told that edamame is one of the healthiest things you can eat, but I don't believe it. Nothing that tastes good is good for you. See p. 103

Crocodile Lounge: 325 E. 14th St. btw 1st & 2nd Aves.

A free personal pizza with every drink, all the time, is just about the best you can ask for in life. See p. 104

Croxley Ales: 28 Ave. B btw E 2nd & 3rd Sts.

Goddamn the wings here are good, and they're free on Friday from 5–7pm. See p. 104

Cucina di Pesce: 87 E. 4th St. @ 2nd Ave.

Free mussels in marinara all night long with purchase of a $6 beer. But all beer costs the same from Bud to Stella, so you can't go wrong.

D.B.A: 41 1st Ave. btw 2nd & 3rd Sts.

Help yourself to some free cheese plates on Monday from 5–9pm and free bagels and lox on Sunday from 1–4pm.

Nevada Smith's: 74 3rd Ave. btw E. 11th & 12th Sts.

The good thing about sports bars is that they generally serve food, and if you're lucky, they sometimes serve free food. Stop in here to watch some Premiership football (soccer to us Yanks), and get some free wings and sandwiches at happy hour on Fridays.

Standings: 43 E. 7th St. @ 2nd Ave.

Free cheesy pizza every Friday night is better than no cheesy pizza on Friday night. I learned that somewhere.

The Thirsty Scholar: 155 2nd Ave. btw 9th & 10th Sts.

A free buffet is put out every weekday at 5pm. The food varies according to whatever the gods of free food feel like bestowing upon us regular people. Every time I go, it's something different and every time I like it because its free.

West Village & Greenwich Village

Bar 13: 35 E. 13th St. @ University Pl.

I don't go to dance clubs unless there is free shit for me. I'm much more of a drinker than a dancer. But on Thursdays from 5–7pm, I'm much more of a free food eater. Come here for a buffet of hot and cold stuff like pasta, chicken, salad, meatballs and more.

Dell'Anima: 38 8th Ave. @ Jane St.

Friday–Sunday, starting at 4pm, this fancy shmancey place gives out olives, asparagus, salads and other noshes. Drinks, though, aren't too cheap, so eat a lot of food.

El Cantinero: 86 University Pl. btw E. 11th & 12th Sts.

El Cantinero docs a free buffet during happy hour with Mexican treats like chimichangas and chicken wings (are either of those even really Mexican?)

Spain Restaurant: 113 W. 13th St. btw 6th & 7th Aves.

A groovy little Spanish restaurant (duh), this joint doles out free meatballs, chips and other appetizers at the bar.

Union Square & The Flatiron District

Tarallucci e Vino: 15 E. 18th St. btw Broadway & 5th Ave.
Stop into this Italian sounding place from 5–10pm to catch some quiche, olives and sandwiches.

Chelsea

Rocking Horse: 182 8th Ave. btw 19th & 20th Sts.
It's just chips and salsa at this point but a real broke-ass knows that there is no "just" when it comes to free food.

Gramercy Park & Murray Hill

Hook and Ladder Pub: 611 2nd Ave btw 33rd & 34th Sts.
During football season, Hook and Ladder puts out free pizza and wings at halftime. See p. 191

McCormacks Pub: 365 3rd Ave. btw E. 26th & 27th Sts.

Another Irish pub doing free wings on Fridays for HH (that's happy hour, not Humbert Humbert).

Rodeo Bar: 375 3rd Ave. @ 27th St.

In addition to the vats of free peanuts they let you throw on the floor, Rodeo Bar also puts out a free buffet of shit like wings and nachos every weekday from 4–7pm. See p. 196

Rolf's: 281 3rd Ave. @ 22nd St.

Free little sandwiches at Rolf's everyday from 5–6pm. Is that what German people eat with their beer? I thought it was sausages.

Tracy J's Watering Hole: 106 E. 19th St. btw Park Ave. South & Irving Pl.

This spot has been holding it down as a free food joint for years. So, on behalf of the poor people of New York City, I'd like to officially thank Tracy J's for all the pizza, fries, and wings. I love you, man … or woman (Tracy is a unisex name, after all).

Midtown East

Ashton's Bar and Grill: 208 E. 50th St. @ 3rd Ave.

A free buffet with different food every night of the week. Watch out for the old drunk at the bar–he's a weeper. See p. 208

Channel 4: 58 W. 48th St. btw 5th and 6th Aves.

Free food, tall leggy blondes, and a lot of guys who make more money than I do. It's happy hour at Channel 4! See p. 209

Keen's Steak House: 72 W 36th St. btw 5th & 6th Aves.

Oooh, this one's fancy! I wish I could afford to eat the steak here, but I guess I'm satisfied with the free bar appetizers like tuna salad on Monday, wings on Tuesday, ribs on Wednesday, meatballs on Thursday, and crispy shrimp on Friday. Plus, they have hard boiled eggs at the bar at all times. All this could be yours for the price of a $6 beer from 5:30–7pm.

Pig n Whistle: 922 3rd Ave. btw E. 55th & 56th Sts.

Pop by after work Monday–Friday from 5:30–7:30 for a free buffet of wings, and pizza, mozz sticks, chicken fingers, and black and white pudding. Well, not really B&W pudding, I just wish it was. That shit is delicious.

T.G. Whitney's: 244 E. 53rd St. btw 2nd & 3rd Aves.

Peep the wings, veggies and dip that they give out here on Thursday and Friday from 5–7pm. It's free, and you know what else it is? FREE!

Hells Kitchen & The Theatre District

Ben Benson's: 123 W. 52nd St. btw 6th & 7th Aves.

Fried chicken and paprika fries, bitches! The food comes out around 6pm on weekdays and the price of a beer is $6.50. Sounds worth it to me.

Kennedy's: 327 W. 57th St. btw 8th & 9th Aves.

Wings, roasted potatoes and cheese seem to always greet me when I get here for happy hour, but that's because I time it to make sure I arrive on weekdays from 4:30–7pm. Food tastes so much better when it's free.

Langan's: 150 W. 47th St. btw 6th & 7th Aves.

Langan's gives you a solid three hours from 5–8pm to stuff your gourd with free chips and salsa and the goodies from their hot buffet. The selection varies, but it's always typical bar food like mozz sticks, wings, chicken fingers, and jalapeño poppers. It's like ordering the sampler platter at Denny's, but getting it for free.

Pig n Whistle: 165 W. 47th St. btw 6th & 7th Aves.

Free wings and chicken fingers during happy hour make me happy. I have a feeling they do the same for you.

Port 41: 355 W. 41st St. @ 9th Ave.

Free hotdogs and popcorn. I've heard rumors of free wings on Fridays, but nobody there seems to know shit. See p. 234

Rudy's: 627 9th Ave. btw 44th & 45th Sts.

I love you Rudy. I may just name my first born after you. May he be a strong, masculine son named Free Hot Dogs. See p. 235

Zanzibar: 401 W. 45th St. @ 9th Ave.

They hand out free hors d'oeuvres from 5–8pm that differ every day. Drinks are also $2 off.

Upper East Side

Iggy's: 1452 2nd Ave @ E. 76th St.

How many free chicken wings do you think are given out throughout NYC on a given weeknight from 5–7pm? Enough to make me wish I was in the chicken-raising business. Not really.

Vudu Lounge: 1487 1st Ave. btw 77th & 78th Sts

Come on Vudu. What are you, a 15-year-old girl who spells crazy "krazy" and see you later "cu l8ater"? Get it together and get rid of your stupid dress code while you're at it. But please keep the free Spanish food on Thursdays and the free pasta and salads on Fridays. Thanks pal.

Upper West Side

Peter's: 182 Columbus Ave. btw W. 68th & 69th Sts.

My man Peter hooks up the free food for happy hour. It varies each day, but you can usually find good shit like fresh veggies, pasta, and chicken strips. When I was a kid I was a really picky eater and basically lived on chicken strips. My friends' parents used to hate having me over for dinner because I never ate anything. They should have served chicken strips.

Williamsburg & Greenpoint

Alligator Lounge: 600 Metropolitan Ave. @ Lorimer St.

When you get a free pizza with every drink you buy, it's easy to get frivolous with that shit. It kinda makes you feel like the king of Pizza-land and say things like, "Only peasants eat the crust." See p. 343

The Charleston: 174 Bedford Ave. @ N. 7th St.

Remember what I just said about the free pizza at Alligator Lounge? It applies here, too, you crust-eating peasant.

Sweet-Ups: 277 Graham Ave. @ Graham St.

Mondays at 8pm, some sweet and generous soul gives out burgers, hot dogs, and veggies dogs/burgers. Occasionally there's special stuff like fresh sea bass and sausages. They had a whole bunch of free gourmet sandwiches on the night of my birthday, which was a far better present than the one the skies gave me; my very first experience with freezing rain. That shit sucks.

Metropolitan: 559 Lorimer St. btw Metropolitan Ave. & Devoe St.

Can I make a weenie roast joke about a gay bar and it be funny? Not at two in the morning after a ten-hour day writing, I can't. Free BBQ and wieners on Sundays from 5pm until food runs out. Not in winter though I think. See p. 347

Trash: 256 Grand St. @ S. 1ˢᵗ St.

Free tater-tots are genius, so is the little machine they use to heat them up. I want one. See p. 349

Boerum Hill, Cobble Hill & Carroll Gardens

Brazen Head: 228 Atlantic Ave. @ Court St.

Free wings on Mondays, cheese on Wednesdays, and bagels on Sundays. Not too shabby eh, pal? See p. 387

Vegetarian and Vegan Restaurants

Here's a list of various exclusively veggie/vegan spots around New York City. I haven't actually eaten at all of them, so they're not all reviewed elsewhere in the book. Also, not all of them are super cheap, but I figured that I make enough references to eating copious amounts of chicken wings and shit like that, that I might as well do something for those out there not properly using their incisors. Besides, what can I say, I love you motherfuckers.

Financial District

Little Lad's Basket: 120 Broadway (concourse level) btw Pine & Cedar Sts.

A vegan lunch buffet for $3.99? The hell you say. Blech I say.

Civic Center, Chinatown & Little Italy

House of Vegetarian: 68 Mott St. btw Bayard & Canal Sts.

Chinese food with no meat, and I don't even think they use pork fat!

Vegetarian Dim Sum House: 24 Pell St. btw Mott & Bowery Sts.

Fake meat is actually pretty good. There, I said it. See p. 38

Wild Ginger: 380 Broome St. btw Mott & Mulberry Sts.

With a menu that is 98 percent vegan, you can guarantee you are gonna have some stinky-ass farts later on.

Lower East Side

Teany: 90 Rivington St. btw Ludlow & Orchard Sts.

Opened by Moby and his (now ex) girlfriend, this is a tiny, utterly hip vegan restaurant that focuses on tea.

Tiengarden: 170 Allen St. btw Stanton & Rivington Sts.

Holding it down for almost 15 years, this Chinese vegan restaurant is a favorite for people who like, um, Chinese vegan food.

East Village

B & H Dairy & Vegetarian Restaurant: 127 2ⁿᵈ Ave. @ St. Mark's Pl.

Perfect for anyone who is kosher, veggie or both. L'chaim! See p. 95

Café Viva Natural Pizza: 179 2ⁿᵈ Ave. btw E. 11ᵗʰ & 12ᵗʰ Sts.

Vegan pizza? Has the world gone mad?

Hummus Place: 109 St. Marks Pl. btw 1ˢᵗ Ave. & Ave. A

Making a Middle Eastern place vegetarian is easy–just get rid of the spit with the slow cooking meat.

Kate's Joint: 58 Ave B @ E. 4ᵗʰ St.

Fake meat/fake cheese Philly cheesesteaks and $2 PBRs make hipsters swoon over this hip veggie place. See p. 97

Lan Café: 342 E. 6ᵗʰ St. btw 1ˢᵗ & 2ⁿᵈ Aves.

Mmmmm ... Vietnamese food.

Pukk: 71 1ˢᵗ Ave. btw 4ᵗʰ & 5ᵗʰ Aves.

Mmmmm ... Thai food.

Punjabi: 114 E. 1ˢᵗ St. @ Houston

Mmmmm ... Indian food and cab drivers. See p. 99

West Village & Greenwich Village

Gobo: 401 6ᵗʰ Ave. @ W. 8ᵗʰ St.

Expensive. I once ordered a steak here. The waiter balked. When was the last time you made someone balk?

Hummus Place: 99 MacDougal St. btw Bleecker St. & Minetta Ln.

Again, making a Middle Eastern place vegetarian is easy, just get rid of the spit with the slow cooking meat.

Maoz: 59 E. 8th St. @ Mercer St.

Israeli falafel goodness. Writing about food always makes me hungry.

NY Dosas: Food cart on Washington Square South

Some of the best street food in all of NYC; and it's veggie, too!

Papaya Dog: 333 6th Ave. @ W. 4th St.

Nah, I'm just fucking with you. There's nothing veggie here.

Quantum Leap: 226 Thompson St. btw W. 3rd & Bleecker Sts.

I fucking loved this TV show! I don't think Sam was a vegetarian though.

Red Bamboo Vegetarian Soul Café: 140 W. 4th St. btw 6th Ave. and MacDougal St.

The lunch specials here are where it's at, dollar wise. Veggie vegan soul food–fake meat at its finest.

'Snice: 45 8th Ave. @ Jane St.

Good looking people and hearty vegetarian delights. Take that, ugly meat eaters. See p. 126

Temple in the Village: 74 W. 3rd St. btw LaGuardia Pl. & Thompson St.

Vegetarian food for $6.95 a pound. I stopped treating my body as a temple years ago.

Taim: 222 Waverly Pl. @ Perry St.

Falafels *and* smoothies? You had me at "fa".

Chelsea

Blossom Vegan Restaurant: 187 9th Ave. btw W. 21st & 22nd Sts.

Highfalutin (actual word in the dictionary) vegan place. Have you ever smelled a vegan's farts? They are hateful.

Union Square & The Flatiron District

Maoz Vegetarian: 38 Union Square East btw E. 16th & 17th Sts.

Israeli falafel goodness. See p. 172

Gramercy Park & Murray Hill

Chennai Garden: 129 E. 27th St. btw Park & Lexington Aves.

When I moved to New York, there was pretty much only one place that did dosa in SF. I thought maybe it was our little secret. Then I realized it is everywhere in New York. Even here at Chennai Garden. I fucking love dosa.

Franchia Teahouse & Restaurant: 12 Park Ave. btw E. 34th & 35th Sts.

What is it with vegans and their moderately priced tea houses? This joint serves Asian fusion. Fuck, I'd really like to be out eating at a restaurant right now instead of stuck behind this computer. My eyes hurt.

Saravana Bhavan Dosa Hut: 102 Lexington btw 27th & 28th Sts.

Say this three times fast with food in your mouth ... wow you actually did it. I'm really impressed. I will never doubt your capabilities again.

Tiffin Wallah: 127 E. 28th St. @ Lexington Ave.

Yummy, yummy, yummy. I've got averaged priced Indian/Pakistani vegetarian food in my tummy. No I don't, that was some strawberry yogurt from my refrigerator.

Midtown East

Zen Burger: 465 Lexington Ave. btw E. 45th & 46th Sts.

Vegetarian fast food. I've been known to eat a veggie burger every once in awhile, but don't tell anyone. It'll ruin my street cred.

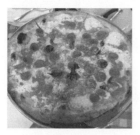

Upper West Side

Café Viva: 2578 Broadway @ W. 97th St.

I'm still blown away from the concept of vegan pizza, and I talked about it all the way back at the East Village section.

Hummus Place: 305 Amsterdam Ave. btw W. 74th & 75th Sts.

Making a Middle Eastern place vegetarian is easy, just get rid of the spit with the slow cooking meat.

Upper East Side

Gobo: 1426 3rd Ave. btw 80th & 81st Sts.

Veggie/vegan and expensive. Don't say I didn't warn you.

Morningside Heights & West Harlem

Strictly Roots: 2058 Adam Clayton Powell, Jr. Blvd. @ W. 123rd St.

Vegan soul food with a Rasta vibe? What the fuck is this, Berkeley?

Williamsburg & Greenpoint

Bliss Café: 191 Bedford Ave. btw N. 6th & 7th Sts.

Any place that consistently has this many cute hipsters in it is bliss. Good choice of a name I must say.

Foodswings: 295 Grand St. btw Havemeyer & Roebling Sts.

Vegan fast food. Fake meat and real tattoos. See p. 337

The Lucky Cat: 245 Grand St. btw Roebling St. & Driggs Ave.

Even though it sounds like it should be a lesbian bar, it's not. It's actually a cool performance and art café with a veggie and vegan menu. Apparently lesbians don't have the monopoly on businesses with the word "cat" in the name.

Wild Ginger: 212 Bedford Ave. btw N. 5th & 6th Sts.

Mostly vegan and mostly hipster. Welcome to Williamsburg, bitches!

Boerum Hill, Cobble Hill & Carroll Gardens

Jill's Vegan Organic Café: 231 Court St. @ Warren St.

Can you guess what kind of food they serve at this café? See p. 383

Park Slope

Earth Tonez Café: 349 5th Ave. btw 4th & 5th Sts.

100 percent meatless and almost as successful at being nice to the environment. All their take-out stuff is biodegradable.

'Snice: 315 5th Ave. @ 3rd St.

You know how making comments in that Borat voice actually didn't get old for a long time? Well it has now, so I won't. See p. 126

The V-Spot Café: 156 5th Ave. btw Degraw & Douglass Sts.

This place is vegan and the last thing I have to write about on this list. Yay!!

Best Street Food

I love street meat. One of the single best perks of being a broke-ass in New York is that you can still eat amazing food and not pay tons of money to do it. My favorite part of going to county fairs or street festivals has always been eating the fair food, but in New York, it's like every day is a carnival (in more ways than one). And while this city's food carts are known for their hot dogs and pretzels, the variety of cuisines sold on the streets here is staggering. You can find anything from Korean food to burgers to Middle Eastern food to tacos, and a lot of it is super good. Of course everyone has their favorite food cart and maybe even a running joke with one of the employees (this one guy keeps asking me when my stupid fucking book is coming out), but I've put together a little list of what is considered by my acquaintances, associates and dirt bag friends, to be the best street food in New York City. Many of them have been participants in the Vendy Awards, a yearly cook off to see which food cart really has the best food. If you want to stay up on all things happening in the world of street vendors, make sure to check out *www.streetvendor.org*.

Financial District

Dominic's Italian Sausage: Whitehall & Bridge Sts.

Holy fuck! Where did this cat Dominic come from? These sausage sandwiches are almost too good. If you're standing at this intersection, look for the large red and white truck, and you'll find my man. You may also find a long line if you come here too close to lunch time.

Veronica's Kitchen: Front St. btw Pine and Wall Sts.

I dream about Veronica's jerk chicken. She must be putting some voodoo spell on that shit because I wake up at night screaming "VE-RONICA!!" and I think my girlfriend is starting to get jealous. I'd sell my soul to get some of that good stuff right now, if I still had one to sell. I haven't had one since I traded it for some Rolling Stones tickets in 8th grade.

Soho & Tribeca

Calexico: Wooster & Prince Sts.

Probably one of the closest things you'll find to California-style Mexican food in New York. Keep on keeping on, my Southern California brethren. See p. 55

East Village

From Atlantis With Love: E. 2nd St. & Bowery

You know, I'm not sure if this guy is still around or not, and it's not like he's got a listed phone number for his food cart so I can call him. I used to see him all the time when I first moved to NY, but I haven't seen him in ages. Regardless, you'll know who he is if you do see him. He's the Native American cat with the psychedelic food cart replete with fake flowers, dangly shit, and tons of fresh veggies. As for what he serves? Well, pretty much anything you want, just ask him. He's got more ingredients stuffed away in there than a drug mule has up his butt.

Mud Truck: 4th Ave & E 8th St.

Gourmet coffee from a truck. I don't drink the stuff but Krista seems to love the shit. They also screen print their own line of really cool t-shirts that look like rock posters. The shirts really aren't cheap, but they are sweet looking.

West Village & Greenwich Village

Dessert Truck: 8th St. & University Pl.

Jesus, I wish I had thought of this. I bet these guys get more pussy than Jay-Z and Colin Farrell combined.

N.Y. Dosas: Washington Square South & Thompson St.

My main man Thiru Kumar slangs the bomb-ass, cheap, veggie dosas from his cart on the south part of Washington Square Park. He also has a moustache that could shame any hipster into using a razor. I'd like to see Thiru and Sam Elliot in a 'stache-off. The man already won the 2007 Vendy Award.

Mud Truck: 7th Ave. & W 4th St.

I could cut and paste the one from the East Village, but I don't want to, so just look there.

Union Square & Flatiron District

World's Best Sandwich Truck: E. 20th St. & Broadway

I'm always the sucker that gets reeled in by any "world's best" advertising. I'm like, "Holy shit, I gotta try this if it's the world's best". This is of course how I came to be acquainted with this here sandwich truck. And you know what? It's damn good, it's cheap as hell, *and* you can phone your order in ahead of time! I'd definitely vote it World's most efficient sandwich truck.

Midtown East

53rd & 6th Halal: W. 53rd St. & 6th Ave.

Dude. Seriously. This is so good and so famous that they've been written about in *The NY Times* on multiple occasions and have a dedicated fan website, *www.53rdand6th.com.* They got their shit on like a gangster lean. Most food stands in this area come and set up to get the lunch rush, but 53rd & 6th is all like, "Nah man. We do this shit on my time, and I'm a night owl." They open at 7:30pm and close at 4am, and I've seriously seen lines down the block for this shit. My advice is this: get the platter and get extra white sauce. You'll thank me for it.

Biriyani Cart: 46th St. & 6th Ave.

I could eat here every day. It's just so damn good and cheap. You can get two rolls that are like Indian burritos for $4. Are you kidding me? That's like half the price of a pack of cigarettes, not that I smoke, but it's a decent comparison because this shit is addictive. They also have a ton of different platters to choose from if rolls aren't your thing, including Asian food. Fuck that, I want my rolls!

Hallo Berlin: 54th St. & 5th Ave.

German "Soul" food ☺. You can't hate on that, or the fact that it won the Vendy Award in 2005. My favorite part is that the sausages are named after cars (the Volkswagen being the cheapest and the Maybach being the most expensive) and the combo meals are named after different political leaders and their forms of government. For example, the Joseph Stalin (dictator) gives you no choice on what meat and toppings you get, while the Winston Churchill (democracy) lets you choose any two wursts and their toppings.

Kwik Meal: W. 45th St. & 6th Ave.

Mmm … street meat.

Hells Kitchen & The Theatre District

Bulgogi and Kimchi Street Cart: 49th St. btw 6th & 7th Aves.

I fucking hate kimchi. The smell makes me want to vomit. But people seem to love this cart. I actually really like Korean food, especially the bulgogi, as long as there isn't any kimchi involved. The best part about this cart is that it's the only Korean food cart I've seen around.

Daisy May's BBQ USA: W 50th St. & 7th Ave.

Not the cheapest street cart, but definitely delicious. You can get a stellar pulled pork sandwich for like $8. Show me some BBQ sauce, and I will show you a man who will make a mess of his clothing … me.

Upper West Side

Super Tacos: W 96th St. & Broadway

It took me months to find really good Mexican food in New York City. I had thought that all hope was lost until I found Super Tacos. I was so excited about it that it was all I talked about for days afterwards. See p. 250

Off the Map

Arepa Lady: Roosevelt Ave. btw 78th & 79th Sts. (Jackson Heights, Queens)

In San Francisco we have a very special woman named Virginia Ramos, known to the world as The Tamale Lady. She's more than just a cult phenomenon, she's a folk hero who doles out sage advice along with her amazing tamales. So I was stoked to find out that New York had someone kind of similar, Maria Piedad Cano, the Arepa Lady. She is probably the most well regarded street food cook in all of NYC; so much so that she has been written about in *The New York Times,* and her fans made a MySpace page to detail what nights she planned on working. While she doesn't give out advice like my dear Tamale Lady, rumor has it that she used to be a lawyer in her native country of Colombia. She also sells some of the best street food you will ever have. Stop by her cart from 10pm–5am any Friday or Saturday night to have one of her amazing arepas. Just don't try during the winter, because that's when she's on vacation.

Red Hook Ball Fields: Clinton St. & Bay St. (Red Hook, Brooklyn)

The Red Hook Ball Fields is the perfect cure for the missing Latin America blues. Honestly, it's like a dream team of food vendors, all hailing from various parts of Latin America, who get together to gang-bang your taste buds with one of the best culinary experiences of your life. Papusas from El Salvador, arepas from Colombia, tacos from Mexico, elote from Cuba, ceviche from Peru, and whatever the hell it is that they eat in Guatemala, can all be found here. And it's all so fucking cheap, too! Come on any weekend day in the summer and fall to fill your belly with this amazing food, and get the free entertainment of watching ten-year-old kids play soccer.

Sammy's Halal: 73rd St. & Broadway (Jackson Heights, Queens)

Jackson Heights might just be the best place on earth. There is just so much cheap, good food that I always weep a little bit whenever I have to leave. Sammy's makes it easier by being right by the train station, so I can get some of this amazing food to take home. It also helps that Sammy uses some kind of magic spell as one of the ingredients in all of his dishes. I mean, how else can you explain why his food tastes so damn perfect?

Awesome and Helpful Websites

I don't know what kind of clever things you want me to say here, people. Quite simply, these are just a bunch of websites that, if used correctly, will greatly enhance your life in New York. Consider it like *Chicken Soup for the Soul*, except that these sites will probably ruin your eyesight, help you destroy your liver, and might even assist in scoring you a case of gonorrhea.

artcards.cc: Art openings are a broke-ass's wet dream. Free wine, free munchies and the opportunity to meet lots of sexy people who are either there for the same reasons you are or are rich. If they are rich, well then maybe you can turn on a little bit of that charm and find yourself a sugar daddy/mama. Oh yeah, I guess some people are there for the art, too. Anyway, artcards makes your life easier by listing all the art openings for each night of the week, and gives suggestions as to which ones will be best. Theoretically, through this site, you should be able to eat and drink for free most nights of the week. You love me. Unfortunately the site doesn't list which places are best for finding your future benefactor.

allny.com/thrift.html: Want to know where every single thrift store in New York is? Go to this website and they will tell you. The list is enormous and I would spend the rest of my life transcribing it, so I just didn't bother. I'm sure you understand.

bigapplegreeter.org: Yeah I know, you live here and don't need some strange motherfucker leading you around and telling you shit about this city (wait, why did you buy this book?), but seriously, this is a really great resource and a fun thing to do. Big Apple Greeter attaches you to a local who then shows you around his or her neighborhood and tells you all about its history. Sweet right? What's even sweeter is that it's free. Go to the website to learn more about it. Also, if you wanna practice your Hindi, you can get your tour in 22 different languages.

cenyc.org: Not only is this the website for the nonprofit Council on the Environment of New York City, it also lists all the locations and hours of all the farmers markets in NYC, so I don't have to do it. Thanks cenyc.org!

P.S. I guess they call them green markets on this website. Weirdos.

cheapassfood.com: As comrades in the Broke-Ass Revolution, the fine people of cheap ass food, are fighting the good fight by telling you about all the great budget eats throughout the city of New York. Listen people, these folks totally get it; they are part of our struggle. The site is constantly updated with restaurants and recipes to help you survive in this costly city, and they seem to have a conscience, too (which is more than I can say for myself). There is always a featured charity on the home page of their website. Plus, they're really good at taking photos of themselves stuffing their faces with food, which makes them my kind of people.

clubfreetime.com: Despite this website's visually jarring yellow and red color scheme, it's actually really helpful (unless of course you're prone to fits of epilepsy). Besides detailing all of the city's free activities like concerts, lectures and movies in the parks, clubfreetime one ups the competition by informing you of the free walking tours that happen throughout the year. It's a fun thing to do if you're trying to stay off the sauce for a little while.

craigslist.org: Whether you are looking for a job, an apartment, the cute redhead you saw on the L train, a used bike or simply some no-strings-attached oral sex, craigslist has it all. This giant online bulletin board makes living in New York *so* much easier. In fact, I've found all of my apartments on here. Whatever, I know you already know all about the wondrous world of craigslist, but I just had to tell you the best thing I ever saw posted. It was in the "missed connec-tions" section for San Francisco and said, "Last night at King Diner I was the man who puked all over the place. You were the woman who helped me clean it up. I think I love you and want to see you again. That may be fairly easy because I'm pretty sure you are a prostitute. If you want to find me, I'll be the guy at 5th & Market playing chess with the brown bagged King Cobra 40." I'm not joking.

flavorpill.com: A smidgen more highbrow than some of the other sites listed in this book (I'm looking at you hotchickswithdouchebags. com), flavorpill.com hips you to what's going on in the worlds of art, books, music and fashion. Some of the events are not cheap, but the ones that are are worth checking out. This site also has a mailing list that you can sign up for, which I can't think of a single good reason for you not to do. Unless you're too *cool* for mailing lists.

forgotten-ny.com: I fucking love this site. It brings all my nerdiness to the forefront and makes me foam at the mouth from pure joy, like I've got a bad case of Sid Vicious. If you are at all interested in the history of New York, you will love this site, too. Kevin Walsh has taken his affection for all things gone or vanishing from this glorious city and created a website dedicated to preserving their histories for posterity. Whether you're curious about some old mansion in Bushwick, have a fetish for faded signs painted on brick walls, or wonder where your street name came from, this site will keep you rapt for ages. And if this sounds heavenly to you, there are Forgotten NY tours four to five times a year. Check the website for details.

freelancersunion.org: For those of you who just can't do the regular 9 to 5 thing, getting health, disability, and life insurance can be a really expensive hassle. The Freelancer's Union is exactly what the name implies–a union representing America's independent workforce. Even their slogan is righteous: "Working for the radical notion of fairness". If you're a freelancer, you should definitely look into the programs they offer. While they still aren't crazy cheap, they are a lot less expensive than trying to do this shit on your own.

freenyc.net: If you're looking for some fun free shit to do in New York, than you've found the right website. Free NYC dishes out the goods on all the free events that happen year round. So yeah, basically you should bookmark them right now. It'll be good for you.

freewilliamsburg.com: Unless you're some Upper East Side heiress who thinks that Brooklyn is only for peasants and rappers, you've probably figured out by now that most of what's happening culturally in New York is taking place in Brooklyn (sorry Manhattan, you blew it). That's where Free Williamsburg comes in. They've been on the scene hipping people to Brooklyn's happenings for years now, and should always be referenced when trying to figure out what's crackilackin' on that side of the bridge.

going.com: Often, the best way to find out about the coolest happenings is by word of mouth. Going.com has taken this premise and made it electronic by creating a website devoted to people sharing info about awesome events. It's like MySpace, except that instead of creeping out people by putting up photos of you flexing your muscles in front of your car, you find out about the ill shit going on every night. Plus, for all you stalkers out there, it lets you know who plans on going also. Wait, you already know about going.com don't you? Nevermind.

herebeoldthings.com: I don't really have the time or space to list every flea market in NYC, but luckily someone else does. Just go to this site and you can find up to date listings of all the flea markets, auction houses, and antique fairs in the city.

hopstop.com: Do you live in Harlem? Want to go see some band in a part of Brooklyn you've never been to? While I can't guarantee the band isn't gonna suck (come on, most of them do) I can tell you that hopstop is probably the best tool around for telling you how to get there. It's like Mapquest or Google Maps except for public transportation. Just enter a starting address and destination, and Hopstop will tell you the best combination of walking, trains and/or buses that will get you there. Sure you can go to mta.info, but anyone who's ever used it can tell you that the site is less accessible than *Ulysses*. Hopstop is the perfect way for figuring out how the hell to get to wherever it is that you're going.

hotchickswithdouchebags.com: Just in case you haven't figured out what a douchebag is yet, or you're afraid you might be one yourself, check this website. You'll know the answer to your dilemma in about six seconds.

hx.com: Short for Homo Xtra, hx.com is *the* site to find out what's going on each night in the land of the gays. Pretty much every good party, happy hour, and festival is listed, and many of them are really cheap, like the Boxers and Briefs party where you get a free drink if you take off your pants.

menupages.com: So we've all been in situations before where someone invites you out to dinner and says, "Oh yeah, no problem, this place is totally cheap," and then you get there and realize that the plates are like $16 each. Considering you only have $16 for the rest of the week, you end up ordering a cup of soup and eating all the bread that you can get. Well, with Menu Pages, you never have to deal with that again. This website lists the menus of almost 7,000 NYC restaurants, so you can see exactly what the prices are for each dish before you get suckered into sipping soup for supper.

midtownlunch.com: Midtown can be an ocean of mediocrity when it comes to food options. If you're a tenacious little cunt, then maybe you've found some of the more stellar places to eat, but if you're lazy, then you probably haven't. Thankfully, there's Midtown Lunch. If you work or live in midtown, then this site is a must know for you. Homeboy does all the exploratory work for you, making it so that you just have to check his blog to get the tips on the best places to fill your gullet. Granted, not all of them are gonna be cheapo, but you just don't have to go to those places, now do you?

mta.info: A pretty shitty website if you wanna know how to get from one place to another. I fucking hate the drop down menus on here because they barely work. Just go to hopstop.com instead.

nyc.myopenbar.com: Are you fucking kidding me? I can't think of a better thing in the world for broke-asses than myopenbar.com. I almost feel like these guys are my long lost brothers. Basically this site gives weekly updates on where to get free and/or really cheap drinks in NY, SF, LA, Chicago, Honolulu and Miami. The content is really well written and funny, too. And for those of you too lazy to check the website, you can sign up for their mailing list and get the goods emailed to you once a week. These guys should get a Nobel Peace Prize. If you don't check this shit out, there's nothing else I can do for you; you're reading the wrong book.

nyc-architecture.com: While this really is just a guy named Tom Fletcher's random website about New York City's buildings, it's pretty awesome. What it lacks in designy-ness, it makes up for in detailed notes about each building and tons of photographs as well. Peep all the photos of the old Penn Station. Can you believe they tore that shit down and replaced it with the mouse maze it is today? If you don't know who Robert Moses is, you should Google him and then spit on your computer screen when his photo comes up.

nymag.com: *New York* magazine knows everything about this city. It's like it thinks it's God or something. Every single time I found some hole in the wall place that I thought no one else knew about, I'd Google it and almost invariably *NY* magazine had already written about it online. I felt like I was in that "Simpsons already did it" *South Park* episode. Familiarize yourself with this site; it's awesome.

nycvisit.com: This is the official site for New York's tourism Bureau. It is unbelievably helpful for those of you who, like myself, are far too lazy to actually go and find a visitor center because it has all the standard info for all the basic things one might do and see in New York. It's perfect for when you have out of town guests who aren't interested in watching you smoke blunts and play Grand Theft Auto all day.

subwaycrush.com: If you took away Craigslist's apartments, used furniture, and no-strings-attached sex, and just kept the missed connection section, you'd have subway crush. Basically, if you are riding transit in NY, SF, Chicago, Boston or London, and make eyes with some hottie but are too pussy to talk to them, you can post about your encounter here, and masturbate at the thought of what might happen if they respond.

yelp.com: Think you can do this shit better than me? Go ahead and give it a try. Yelp is a site where you can log on, write your own reviews about almost anything from dermatologists to Ethiopian food, and share it with other people. You can also read everyone else's reviews and decide whether or not you actually want to spend your hard earned cash on that one-armed stripper with the eye patch. It's a fantastic site run by fantastic people and it's a whole lot of fun. I do have to admit that there are a few whiners on there, but whiners are everywhere, probably including your roommate. My only bit of advice is this: You can be honest in your reviews without being mean. Sometimes that's the funniest shit in the world.

Thanks

First and foremost, I've gotta give a shout-out to my brother Ross because I'm a fucking asshole and forgot to put him in the "Thanks" for the SF book. Sorry kid, you know I love you. Next, I'd like to thank the good folks at Falls Media for their patience and for putting out this book so I wouldn't have to do all this shit by myself. I'd also like to thank all the contributors who helped to make this book the essence of pure awesomeness that it is: Thanks to Kenny Liu, my savior and sanity, who, whether working on the book or not, makes this whole Broke-Ass Stuart experiment possible. Thanks to Angie Hathaway for her always cool and stylish maps, and for dealing with all my last minute corrections. Thanks to Paul T. Alkaly for being my own personal Sacagawea and for contributing some of the funniest material in this book. Thanks to Nicki Ishmael and Victoria Smith for contributing their photographic genius and making me look like a sexy beast. Also, thanks Nicki for the amazing cover shot. Thanks to Mike Force for all the design work and the great comic. I predict big things for you, my friend.

Thanks to Krista, my amazing and beautiful girlfriend, for being my partner, and for moving to New York with me, and for putting up with my bullshit. I know I'm not the easiest person to date. Thanks to my parents for being supportive and not being disappointed that I didn't want to grow up to be a doctor, lawyer or an accountant. Thanks to my brother (again). Thanks to my grandparents for thinking I'm cool no matter what my current endeavors are. Thanks to all my aunts, uncles and cousins for helping me spread my message. Thanks to all the people who were kind enough to show me their favorite places, even though they knew I'd share them with the world: Josh Bernstein, Ben Wise, Simon Keegan, Aaron Oster, Vanessa Van Dongen, Nick Burns, Robert Reid, Zora O'Neal, Mac, Producer Laura, Reggie Cameron, and all the strangers who were nice enough to give me suggestions.

Thanks to all my awesome New York friends who were always supportive of my endeavors and often came along with me to shitty bars in shitty locations, all in the name of research and getting drunk: Ben Leduc-Mills and Caroline McGovern, Naomi Edelson and CJ

Evans, Arik Nagel and Rebecca, Lili Toutounas, Alexis Miller, Nick Perrotta, Mike Hruska, Maleeha Khan, Jon Kule, Set Oya, Tobias Womack, Mateo Goldman, David Cohen, Mac, Jason Langdon, Becky Ohlson, Molly, Brendon, Joel Englestein, Josh Spector, Kelli Rudick, Michelle Gross, Stacey Falkoff, Meredith Stiglitz, everyone from Smile Sushi.

Thanks to all the people who were cool enough to let Krista and me into their lives and homes as subletters: Anna Graizbord, Piper, Zoe, Detroit, and all the random ass people from the Carroll Gardens House. Thanks to my proof readers: John Armenta, Katie Hauser, Roya Rose Platsis, Shira Brown and Jacqueline McCarley. Thanks to my lawyers Michael Silver and Ric Cohen.

Thanks to Glennon Travis for letting us shoot in the Chelsea Hotel. Thanks to Anthony Bourdain for giving me a new goal. Thanks to Tapatio salsa for making everything taste better. Thanks to Katz's Deli for making the best sandwich in the world. Thanks to all my research buddies and people who gave me ideas for the book who I may have forgotten to thank.

Thanks to all of you who've bought this book and are on the front lines of the Broke-Ass Revolution. I wrote it for you. And, most of all, I would like to thank anyone who ever bought any of the books or shirts I've done in the past. Your support means the world to me.

I love all of you! Thank you (just thought I'd throw one more in there for good luck).

Contributors

Featured Writer: When Paul Todd Alkaly was a little boy living in Los Angeles he dreamed of visiting far flung and exotic places that he read about in National Geographic. Since then he has become quite the armchair traveler and has done extensive reading on Argentina, Morocco and India. Paul is also handy with giving directions and although he has never been to Rome he can give you accurate directions from the Coliseum to the Trevi Fountain in any time period. Hopefully his dreams of world travel will come true someday and those African tribal babes he gazed at as a child will become a reality. For now, Paul has cut out a niche for himself in the Greenpoint section of Brooklyn. *paultodd@mac.com*

Maps: Angie Hathaway is an insanely spunky, geography-obsessed cartographer. Amongst her numerous hobbies, such as yarn-hoarding and designing clothing, she also enjoys enriching people's lives with custom maps infused with a splash of humor. A lot of people have no idea where they are or where they're going, so if you are looking to find yourself, this is the girl to contact. *angielovesmaps@gmail.com*

Cover Photo & other photos: Nicki Ishmael is a witty, charming, energetic photographer with a passion for people, cameras and lighting. Her dramatic and intriguing work focuses on candid portraiture and good old rock n roll. She currently resides in Brooklyn, New York. *www.NickiIshmael.com.*

Cover photo as well as other photos: Victoria Smith is a queen, a rebel, a renegade, a lover of life and wannabe-er of good will. Her photos are some of the best in the world and you should employ her as much as possible so she may continue to light up her own life, as well as the saps around her. Seriously though, this shit don't stink. *www.VictoriaSmithPhoto.com, mamavic22@yahoo.com*

Comic & Interior Design: Mike Force lives in Brooklyn. He is currently developing a cartoon show called *Hawk Town* about a slumlord in suburbia. See clips at: *mikeforce.org*

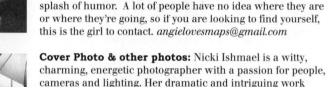

Cover Design: Kenny Liu has a lot of vices. One of which is design...he's one of the happiest boys I've ever met. *Structives.com*